THE MANUFACTURE OF AUSTRALIAN HISTORY

The Manufacture of Australian History

Rob Pascoe

MELBOURNE
OXFORD UNIVERSITY PRESS
Oxford Wellington New York

Oxford University Press

OXFORD LONDON GLASGOW
NEW YORK TORONTO MELBOURNE
WELLINGTON NAIROBI DAR ES SALAAM CAPE TOWN
KUALA LUMPUR SINGAPORE JAKARTA HONG KONG TOKYO
DELHI BOMBAY CALCUTTA MADRAS KARACHI

© *Rob Pascoe 1979*

First published 1979

NATIONAL LIBRARY OF AUSTRALIA CATALOGUING IN
PUBLICATION DATA

Pascoe, Frederick Robert, 1953-
The manufacture of Australian history

Index
Bibliography
ISBN 0 19 550569 7
ISBN 0 19 550579 4 Paperback

1. Australia—Historiography. I. Title
994'.00722

Jacket design by Ward O'Neill

TYPESET AND PRINTED BY HEDGES AND BELL PTY LTD, MELBOURNE
PUBLISHED BY OXFORD UNIVERSITY PRESS, 7 BOWEN CRESCENT, MELBOURNE

For Suzie

Contents

Acknowledgements

The author gratefully acknowledges and thanks all those who consented to be interviewed for the purpose of this study; his colleagues at Murdoch University and the University of Western Australia, especially Marian Aveling, Geoffrey Bolton, Stuart Macintyre and Tom Stannage; the ideas and criticisms unselfishly provided by Bob Connell, Greg Dening, Bill Gammage, Humphrey McQueen, John Poynter and Keith Sinclair; and the typing excellently performed by Julie Austin, Meredith Beevers, Fay Davey, Jill Finneran, Geraldine Grahame, Melanie Harris, Anne Hesford, Leonie Pimm, Lesley Chute and Annette Whiting.

F.R.P.
St Catherine's College
10 July 1978

1 The ground rules of criticism

1 The ground rules of criticism

Two centuries of European settlement in Australia have produced many versions of what it has all been about. This study sets out to examine and to categorize some of these historical interpretations of Australia's past. Images of the past portrayed by film-makers, novelists and journalists may have had a greater impact on popular consciousness, but a nation's conception of itself is fashioned not only by the myths, traditions and stereotypes of popular culture but by its historians' selective interpretations of past events. An awareness of the way historians have 'manufactured' our past and a knowledge of the different models of Australian history which they have advanced or downplayed is therefore vital to our understanding of the Australian national ethos.

This study examines the published output of some fifty prominent historians, whose careers stretch back from the present day to the First World War. It concentrates solely on the output of the leading professional historians, analysing the inner logic of their interpretations of the past and exploring their ideological implications and underpinnings. Passing reference is made to the intellectual, social and political traditions which helped fashion the outlook and style of each of these historians but the main emphasis is placed on what they have actually produced.

In the course of researching this study it soon became clear that many of these historians shared certain features of style, emphasis and outlook, and also adhered, sometimes unwittingly, to one particular view of history rather than another. In some cases these common features of style were sufficiently pronounced to enable one to postulate the existence of a distinct school of historians; in other cases these shared features, principles or programmes were not sufficiently developed, nor the historians sufficiently united in purpose, to postulate the existence of a school, even though their work could be meaningfully categorized together as exemplifying distinct tendencies in Australian history-writing. Certain schools readily identify themselves through their ideological stands. The radical historians, for example, have openly declared their standpoint and, in certain cases, have openly declared themselves as schools. In the late 1960s a group of young historians emerged who called themselves the New Left: prominent among these were Humphrey McQueen, R. W. Connell and T. H. Irving. These historians regarded themselves as 'New' in relation to a tradition of left-wing historiography which went back as far as Brian Fitzpatrick and even V. G. Childe. They attacked the history-writing of an older group of marxist historians, who had styled themselves 'radical nationalists' in the 1950s but who became more widely known as the 'Old' Left following the younger radicals' attacks on them. A comparable iconoclasm can also be discerned in the work of a third group of Australian historians who have recently begun to explore women's history: Anne Summers and Miriam Dixson have taken as their starting-point the contention that most historians to date have been concerned almost exclusively with male history, and set out to present a conception of the past which takes account of the 'other half'. Their account of Australian history is strikingly different from other historians', for their conception of Australian society as a patriarchal system leads them to regard as historically noteworthy certain aspects of the past which earlier historians had deemed insignificant.

These three schools have not only reacted against each other but can also themselves be seen as reactions against the liberal tradition of Australian history-writing. Just as the Old Left and the New Left historians disagree over fundamental principles and have different research interests, there is an obvious discontinuity in the liberal tradition. Both Sir Keith Hancock and Hugh Stretton, to cite two exemplars of liberal historiography, profess an attachment to reformist rather than revolutionary methods of social change. But there the similarity ends. Hancock denies the efficacy of employing laws of history in explaining social change; Stretton is 'sociological' insofar as he uses invariant principles of cause-and-effect to explain the past and predict the future. Hancock, as later discussion will show, belongs to a school of 'liberal patriots'; Stretton's work has been classified with that of the 'sociological historians'.

Two main criteria have been used for classifying historians into schools or tendencies. Firstly, the ideological tenor stated or implied by their history-writing and, secondly, the mode of social theorizing characteristically employed. (See the diagram on the opposite page.)

	LIBERAL	RADICAL
CONTEXTUALIST	LIBERAL PATRIOTS	OLD LEFT
MECHANIST	SOCIOLOGICAL HISTORIANS	NEW LEFT

	ANARCHISTIC	CONSERVATIVE
FORMIST	MANNING CLARK	EMPIRICIST CONSERVATIVES
ORGANICIST	FEMINISTS	SYNCRETIC CONSERVATIVES

To elaborate the second criterion: to say that Hancock rejects the search for laws of history is to begin to define his characteristic mode of social theorizing. Hancock rejects the notion that reality can be explained by constructing rules of social structure and change which will apply across time and space and instead professes that events, persons and ideas can best be understood by locating them within their actual period and place. Stephen C. Pepper, an American philosopher, would describe the mode of social theorizing implicit in Hancock's history as contextualist; by 'contextualism' he means that some intellectuals understand the task of explaining social processes as showing the definite connections between particular phenomena and their general context; since these connections are definite rather than abstract there can be no necessary and invariant laws of history which always hold true, and there is no direction in which history is ultimately tending. In his book, *World Hypotheses,* Pepper contends that contextualism is one of four different ways of thinking generally.[1] His typology of four 'world hypotheses'— contextualism, formism, mechanism and organicism—has proved a useful criterion for classification, for it elucidates how historians theorize about social processes. Historians whose characteristic mode of social theorizing is the postulation of universal laws of cause and effect are, according to Pepper's typology, mechanists: Stretton and the other 'sociological historians', and Connell, a representative of the New Left, both share this approach. Contextualism, emphasizing the context in which events occur, underpins not only the scholarship of Hancock and the 'liberal patriots' but that of the Old Left. An organicist mode of social theorizing, which conceives of history as the narrative of an all-encompassing theme which absorbs and consolidates new historical phenomena, is shared by the feminist historians and another group, whom I have termed the 'syncretic conservatives'. Perhaps the ideological stance implicit in feminist historiography is best described as 'anarchistic', for their history presents a pattern of male domination which can only be challenged by the separatist activities of small groups. But anarchism is not the only possible ideological implication of organicist historiography, for a school of conservative historians also employs this mode of social theorizing. This group, the 'syncretic conservatives', includes historians such as F. K. Crowley, A. G. L. Shaw and N. B. Nairn, who postulate a theme of uninterrupted harmony within Australian history and seek to integrate the events of the past into that broad rubric, producing an essentially conservative account.

Formist interpretations of the Australian past are also divided in ideological implication between the anarchistic and the conservative. Formism, according to Pepper, is the concentration on the unique and the particular. Unlike other historians, formists attach significance not to common properties but precisely to that which makes unique an event or idea, an individual or a value system. Some formist historiography takes the form of narratives which are restricted only to particular phenomena. The history of A. T. Yarwood, L. L. Robson and B. K. de Garis shares this tendency, which also carries with it a conservative implication, and their history-writing is analysed together with that of other empiricists. Manning Clark's history, on the other hand, although essentially formist, is better described as anarchistic rather than anything else, for although it conveys a sense of pessimism about the Australian past it does not contain any clear programmatic principles of either a liberal or a radical nature.

Manning Clark's undoubted achievements in Australian history-writing have inspired some emulators, but no well-formed school of historians. Schools of history are therefore not immobile or static, but are the salient features of general historiographical trends. The leading historians become recognized as such partly because their work charts out possible directions for others to follow. The historians whose work is discussed in this study are some of the obvious representatives of the eight schools or tendencies I have discerned in Australian history-writing. Their intellectual careers, to state the obvious, are not necessarily fixed within the confines of any one category, whether it be one of their own definition or one in which they have been placed for analytical purposes.

This classification should yield a richer understanding of Australian historiography. Previous commentators have either refrained from systematically dissecting the various streams of history-writing or have posited dichotomous camps of historians, such as the 'Whigs' and the 'anti-Whigs', 'bourgeois' and 'radical' history and even 'the rough' and 'the smooth'.[2] None of these pairs of labels does justice to the complexity of Australian historiography and, more importantly, tends to reduce the difficult task of critically evaluating history-writing to a conflict between opposing camps. However to categorize historians according to their view of how social processes are to be explained and their ideological position greatly clarifies this task, because such a classification provides two clear ground rules of criticism. In the first place, the criticism of factual accuracy, which can often prove banal, is thereby placed in a specific context. It is fair to judge a historian's account by the degree to which it accords with what may be known of the past either directly or through the interpretations of others; but it is insufficient to criticize this account solely on the grounds that it does not recognize all possible facts and interpretations. Criticism must be sympathetic to the purpose and design of each school or tendency in Australian history-writing: the critic must first appreciate the typifying features of each approach before assessing the degree to which each historian accomplishes his specific project. This first principle of criticism is the main theme of the next four chapters, which are organized around the four 'world hypotheses' of Pepper's typology. The order of the chapters is roughly chronological: the contextualists ('liberal patriots', Old Left) are followed by the formists (Manning Clark, the 'empiricist conservatives'), the organicists ('syncretic conservatives', feminists) and the mechanists ('sociological historians', New Left). A second principle of criticism flows from the first. In the course of assessing how well individual historians explain the Australian past it becomes clear that some approaches are on average more successful than others. The concluding chapter attempts to discover why this should be so, and thus points towards a method of evaluating the many versions of what two centuries of European settlement in Australia have been all about.

2 From the general to the particular

2 From the general to the particular

In this chapter the primary concern will be to establish the defining features of the two contextualist schools, the liberal patriots and the Old Left. How did these historians produce an account of the past which, despite the ideological difference between them, unified their stated purposes? Given that the Old Left announced that their history would be distinct from the orthodoxies of the patriots, how was it possible that they shared so much in their respective interpretations of the past?

This chapter will analyse in turn the scholarship of important contextualists: the liberal patriots, especially Bean, Portus, Hancock and Crawford; the most significant Sydney historian of the era, J. M. Ward; Brian Fitzpatrick, and the subsequent Old Left historians—Russel Ward, R. A. Gollan, Ian Turner and Geoffrey Serle.

The Liberal Patriots

By the 1920s there was a diverse range of models for the writing of Australian history both within the infant universities and outside. There had been an astonishing interest in the history of the colonies and the newly federated Commonwealth: this curiosity was met by numerous authors of varying backgrounds, employing fairly distinct modes of inquiry. Some were antiquarian chroniclers who tactfully steered clear of controversial topics, such as the state public librarian of Western Australia, J. S. Battye (1871-1954), whose *Western Australia: A History from its Discovery to the Inauguration of the Commonwealth* enjoyed only limited success. Another public servant, T. A. Coghlan (1856-1926), published his mammoth *Labour and Industry in Australia: From the First Settlement in 1788 to the Establishment of the Commonwealth in 1901* in 1918, but this also faded from sight, belatedly resurrected in a 1969 reprint. Coghlan's enterprise was remarkably 'modern', but did not inspire any immediate emulators. Nor did *How Labour Governs: A Study of Workers' Representation in Australia,* a perceptive analysis of the internal history of the labour movement up to 1921. Its author, V. G. Childe (1892-1957), had been involved in the anti-conscription campaign and was, at one time, private secretary to Labour premier John Storey, but left Australia to pursue a career in archaeology overseas.

Alongside these histories was developing a paradigm of patriotic and liberal historiography which, during the inter-war period, would attract a large enough group of historians to warrant them being regarded as constituting a school. Most of these historians were academics, but not all, and there were indeed 'professional' historians during the first decades of the century who did not subscribe to this conception of history, which later became orthodox. Foremost amongst these was E. O. G. Shann (1884-1935), who graduated from Melbourne University in 1903, and later taught in the department of social studies at the new (1910) University of Queensland for two years, before taking up the inaugural chair of history and economics at the University of Western Australia in 1913. In a prophetic pamphlet, *The Boom of 1890—and Now,* Shann likened the economic condition of the late 1920s to those of the late 1880s; in subsequent years he published his forthright and outspoken interpretation of the national story in *Bond or Free? Occasional Economic Essays* and *An Economic History of Australia.* Shann's argument was that the State had exercised too paternalistic a role, that 'private enterprise' was thereby stifled and that a fully market economy would be a more effective regulator of wages and prices. A non-conformist academic of a slightly earlier period was the Englishman, Edward Jenks (1861-1939), who occupied the chair of law at Melbourne from 1889 to 1892 and produced *The History of the Australian Colonies.* This textbook offered a 'kings-and-queens' approach to Australian history by emphasizing the role of the colonial governors; despite its original successful reprintings this approach proved to be out of step with the historical scholarship which emerged during the early years of the new century. A third academic deviant of the period wrote a competing textbook, a *History of Australia: With Chapters on Australian Literature and the Early History of New Zealand.* A. W. Jose (1863-1934) found a political 'purpose' to national history: the idea of 'progress'. But it was not necessarily this emphasis which marked off Jose's conception from what was emerging as the hegemonic view of Australian history. The nature of his deviance can perhaps be grasped by observing the differences between his contribution and that of others to the official history of Australian involvement in the First World War. Jose was commissioned to write volume IX, *The Royal Australian Navy, 1914-18*; the result was a competent if monotonous account of the to-ing and fro-ing of the Australian ships, based almost exclusively on official sources and bereft of the character-sketches and anecdotal vignettes which characterized those volumes written by the general editor of the series, C. E. W. Bean.

C. E. W. Bean (1879-1968) brought to the writing of the six volumes of *The Official History of Australia in the War of 1914-18* which he allotted to himself, a warmth of understanding for the common fighting man; a strong sense of the relation between individual skirmishes and the overall course of the campaigns; a journalist's ability to describe a particular scene or action vividly and succinctly; and most importantly the gift of synthesis, with which he tied together the minutiae of historical detail into a coherent paean of patriotism. This patriotism—which surfaced in Bean's writings from his description of the 'national characteristics' he discerned in Australian men—can be traced back a decade before the commencement of the war history to his journalistic exploration of the Australian outback. In 1909, as a young reporter for the *Sydney Morning Herald*, he was sent by his editor to write a series of articles on the wool industry in New South Wales. The young man was at first dismayed by this assignment, but started thinking about it as he walked up Pitt Street: 'Before he caught his tram in King Street the first article had shaped itself in his mind'.[1] Bean's theme was city-bred: the outback 'is a region where bad men are very bad, and good men are magnificent, but where all men are interesting'.[2] Life back of Bourke, then, is writ large: in the 'Real Australia' everything is hyperbole. The articles found publication in 1910 as *On The Wool Track*; this was revised in 1925 to include references to the First World War, then the 1945 edition was footnoted to point out 'some of the more recent changes' which had taken place in the meantime.[3] By then the process of codification was complete: in the introduction to the 1945 edition, Bean justifies his study of the shearers by arguing that

> . . . men from this life and industry, together with similar folk from New Zealand, formed a considerable fraction of the 'Anzac' forces in the First World War; and—as probably also in the Second World War—the traditions of this back country weighed far more heavily than the mere number of its representatives among the influences that moulded the Australian and New Zealand soldier.[4]

On the Wool Track is essentially a study of those 'peculiarly' Australian character traits which earlier writers such as Lawson and

Furphy had 'discovered' among the men of the bush, but which Bean now wedded to a social theory with new ideological implications. For example, Australian union leaders are chided by Bean for denying or limiting the 'natural resourcefulness' of the bush worker. This makes the union leaders 'like the great capitalist-organizers of America'.[5] Conversely, the station boss is no exploiter of those under him:

> Slow of speech, great of limb, courteous, understander of men, lover of animals—conservative though he might be, aristocrat though he undoubtedly was in fact, whatever he was in name—his day's work out with the kookaburras had made him probably the finest of all Australians, and the simplest. He asked for no better requiem than that of his old friends when it came to the setting of his sun.[6]

But, despite these rather iconoclastic remarks, the Bean who wrote *On the Wool Track* is no uncomplicated ideologue of 'private enterprise', for he admits some possible advantages should the wool industry be nationalized, a view which perhaps suggests some link with the nineteenth-century radicals.[7] However his main interest in the Australian personality is his search for some higher significance in what he sees as the stereotypical qualities of the men he meets in the wool industry. This higher significance or 'meaning' is still not apparent to him, even after his next book, *The Dreadnought of the Darling,* which is another example of outback reportage. By the time of his naval study, *Flagships Three*, Bean's approach has moved very close to that of Kipling;[8] but any tendency to translate the Australian experience into an exaltation of the British Empire disappears as soon as Bean begins to report and document the First A.I.F. Notebook in hand, the gaunt figure of Bean could be seen wherever Australian soldiers were in action.[9] The jigsaw then fell into place: the character traits which made the Australian soldier so invincible (his easygoing bravery, his inventive self-reliance, his indomitable pluck in the face of heavy odds, and so on) could be traced back to his bush origins. This mode of theorizing has two chief conceptual elements to it. One is its ability to cope with both the universal and the particular: environmental determinism allows the historian to explain the detail of narrative by reference to a wider 'context', and yet does not commit him to invariant and universal 'laws of history'. The other is its sophistication in driving home a 'moral' to the reader: the selection of certain character traits rather than others appears to be 'objective' (and there is no doubting Bean's sincerity), but leads inexorably to an unmistakable message of patriotism.

Yet 'moral' and 'fact' are scrupulously kept separate by Bean and the newly emerging school of patriots. And it was with these historians that the future lay: by the Second World War their approach would be orthodoxy. Shann, Childe, and others who admitted 'bias' 'before the facts were in' were doomed not.to enjoy the same influence as Wood, Scott, Bean, Melbourne, Roberts, Portus and others. G. A. Wood (1865-1928) was a graduate of Manchester University who took up the Challis professorship of history at Sydney University in 1891, but did not publish until *The Discovery of Australia* (1922) owing to his heavy teaching burden. Attempting to work out his liberal principles in the antipodes—most significantly over his opposition to the Boer War—Wood found that 'free speech' was not tolerated in the colonies, and incurred the displeasure of the university senate.[10] It may have been such collisions with intolerance that shaped the approach of later liberal patriots, notably in their careful division of 'fact' and 'value'. At the University of Melbourne, Sir Ernest Scott (1867-1939) certainly 'did not encourage [bringing] to history a point of view'.[11] Scott began as a Hansard reporter, but wrote three history books in his spare time and was appointed professor of history in 1914. The six monographs he produced before his retirement in 1936 bear eloquent testimony to his capacity for work, but their emphasis on chronicling the stories of exploration suggests his lack of critical distance from the historical document. But this was not an antiquarian propensity: his 'moral' position was always clear. For example, in his account of social conditions during the First World War, Scott approved of the necessity to impose strict wartime precautions yet criticized the excessive lengths to which these could be carried.[12] Scott also initiated the first full-length course in Australian history in 1927: Wood had usually taught the subject as a segment of imperial history. By 1931 Scott and his students 'occupied the most important four out of six chairs of history in Australia: Scott at Melbourne, Roberts at Sydney, Hancock at Adelaide and Alexander at Perth'.[13] A. C. V. Melbourne (1888-1943) and S. H. Roberts (1901—) were, as academic historians, less important in the process of evangelism which characterized the patriots. Roberts 'presided over one of the dullest history schools in Australia',[14] and Melbourne's influence was slight. Both men nonetheless wrote within the same tradition and conception of history. Melbourne's *Early Constitutional Development in Australia,* for instance, traces back the constitutional reforms of the nineteenth century to their social origins—rather than viewing the social formation first—and thereby is able to imply a Whig interpretation of Australian history: the gradual 'democratization' of the political forms.[15]

Arguably the most influential of all the patriots, however, was G. V.

Portus (1883-1954), professor of history at Adelaide from 1935 to 1954. Portus produced an elementary school textbook for the teaching of Australian history which was to enjoy a very wide readership: *Australia Since 1606* had been through two editions and sixteen reprints by 1963. Part of its charm for schoolchildren was probably the exquisite scent of books produced in that period: countless children were enchanted by the smell to be got from putting their noses between the pages. Another attraction for children was the unprofessional quality of the hand-drawn illustrations dotted throughout the book, which Portus included because he thought 'that boys and girls are more intrigued by home-made sketches than by the finished products of professional artists'.[16] But the third and most important reason for the immediacy of the book for children was Portus' genial and lilting manner of writing: to read *Australia Since 1606* is to engage in a pleasant conversation with a friendly parson or father figure. These are the opening lines of the text:

> When Queen Elizabeth was walking about England and stepping on Sir Walter Raleigh's coat through the puddles, no white man knew anything about Australia. If you ask why, perhaps the best answer is: Some say this and some say that, but we say that the time had not yet come for Australia to be discovered.[17]

Without resorting to the use of dates, Portus is able to situate the young readers precisely in the period of the late sixteenth century, by reference to the popular image of Elizabeth I stepping on Raleigh's coat, a device which permits him to begin from something the young reader can confidently be expected to know already. Dates only gradually begin to be used in the text over the next twenty pages or so. Finally, Portus leads into an excursus on the astronomical predictions of the transit of Venus—and simultaneously drives home an unforgettable message about chronology:

> In 1679 Halley, another English astronomer, said: 'There will be a transit of Venus again in 1761 and another in 1769, but I shall be dead by then. So, for goodness' sake, let all English astronomers be watching for those transits' . . . For remember, if this chance was missed, the transits would not come again until 1874 and 1882. They really did happen in 1874 and 1882, as the astronomers said they would. The next are due on 8th June 2004, and 6th June 2012. Some of you might see these when you are very old, but I am certain I shall not.[18]

Taking the book as a whole, there is a preponderant emphasis on the nineteenth century, which takes up fifteen of the twenty-six chapters in the second edition of 1948.

In almost every other way, *Australia Since 1606* is a faithful mirror of the view of Australian history which has remained dominant until very recently: it is the tale of a sturdy egalitarian people, moulded by pioneering experiences in the harsh new environment. Their defensiveness, their fears of external threat, even their stratification into classes is admitted, but what lingers in the reader's mind is the more optimistic vision of diggers, selectors and workers struggling on against almost indomitable obstacles. A chapter entitled 'The land we live in' sets out the 'geographical facts' about the continent, with two purposes in mind. The first is to illustrate the environmental influence on Australian history—the prelude to the chief theme of the book—and the second is to celebrate a love for the soil:

> We love our motherland very much, and it would be strange if we did not. But is a poor sort of love which continually misrepresents the object of its love. We gain nothing by not seeing our Mother Australia as she really is . . . Behind the blue and the gold and the green are those leagues of sand and sun and scrub. To admit this does not mean that we love our motherland any the less. The love of a poor boy for his poor mother is just as beautiful and sustaining as the love of a rich boy for his rich mother. Nor would we think it a very admirable thing for the poor boy to keep on insisting that his mother was rich because he imagined that the world would think more highly of her as a rich woman. No good ever comes from spreading false ideas, either about our mothers or about our motherlands.[19]

This is powerful imagery indeed, striking into the subconscious of the young reader, yet it fits smoothly into the text: Portus has the happy knack of weaving fact, interpretation and moral titbit together. From the opening lines (quoted above) to the last page, Portus readily admits the subjectivity of history ('Some say this . . . some say that'), but is able to foreclose many an argument by deft persuasion.

This overarching motif reaches a climax in the closing pages of the final chapter, which deals with the Second World War and its aftermath:

> It may be that we think of our State too much and of the Commonwealth too little. Or it may be that our parents are employers of labour, and we think of their interests and regard the Labour Party as just plain wicked. Or it may be the other way about. But whatever you grow up to be employers or wage workers, city people or country

people, Queenslanders, Victorians, or Tasmanians, you will still be
Australians, living in the community that is called the Australian
community. Only if we remember that we must put the good of the
whole community before the interests of any section of the community
shall we solve the problems which face us. The great thing to aim at is
unity in peace as we had it in war.[20]

The resort to this doubtful idea of a 'common good' may seem odd in
view of Portus' implicit acknowledgement of the unequal distribution
of power within Australian society, but it fits easily with his notion of
Australia as a cosily integrated society, a theme he is at pains to
develop. Throughout the book, political and religious strife are played
down in favour of environmental factors and economic development,
these two themes being held in harness together. The theme of constitutional development, for example, which was the subject of A. C.
V. Melbourne's contemporaneous monograph, is dealt with in one
chapter by Portus, 'This business of self-government'. Portus obviously has an eye for what will interest young schoolchildren, and
political struggle presumably fails to meet his criterion. This occasionally leads to a trivialization of the political process: 'Different men
have different ideas about governments, just as they have about
cricket, and food, and neckties'.[21] The labour movement is mainly
discussed in one place, a few pages of chapter XXII, and provides the
key example of the way in which Portus conveys the idea of a har-
monious consensus within Australian society. Unionization, payments
for members of parliaments, the arbitration system and the activity
of the A.L.P. in office receive Portus' approval, while strikes and
lockouts are said to be 'very wasteful'.[22] The theory of parties of
resistance and initiative concludes this section.

Other cherished notions of the era appear throughout *Australia
Since 1606*, such as the laconic bravery of the Anzacs during the First
World War; and, as usual, Portus adds a new touch to the account
in order to bring it alive for the young schoolchildren: 'A new kind
of Australian began to appear in our streets—bronzed and khaki-
clad—whose nailed boots rang on the pavements as he walked'.[23] The
Anzacs (including women in the Second World War[24]) are the heroes
of twentieth-century Australia, but Portus has a Great Men theme
running through the previous century which takes up most of the
book. Explorers such as Sturt, and governors such as Phillip and even
G. A. Robinson, are held up as men worthy of praise; no individual
woman, not even Caroline Chisholm, is mentioned anywhere in
Australia Since 1606. Another stock theme of the era in which Portus
was writing, that of exploration and settlement—part of the environ-

mental emphasis broadly conceived—is given new point under the memorable chapter heading 'The veil is torn away'.

Portus was not the first to write an Australian history for young schoolchildren, but *Australia Since 1606* 'ranks with Wood's *Voyage of the Endeavour*', according to R. M. Crawford, who regarded the latter as 'one of the best children's histories ever written'.[25] In essence, then, Portus fused the style of one patriot (Wood) with the ideas of another (Scott), and produced a popularization of Australian history which would remain on secondary school curricula for quite some time. Despite the enormous influence which a popularization of an intellectual tradition such as a school-text may enjoy, however, the intellectual validity of any complex, sophisticated set of ideas requires at least one precise formulation, some definitive statement. In the case of the patriotic conception of Australian history, this succinct spokesman proved to be Sir Keith Hancock.

In his preface to *The Story of Australia,* A. G. L. Shaw writes: 'My debt to Sir Keith Hancock's *Australia,* first published nearly a quarter of a century ago, will be clearly apparent to those who studied this brilliant essay'. During the next three hundred pages, Shaw refers to Hancock by name no less than six times.[26] Likewise, in his preface to *Australia: A Social and Political History*, published in the same year, Gordon Greenwood describes *Australia* as an 'admirable interpretive essay', and quotes Hancock in chapter 5 without footnote.[27] Even the marxist historian, R. A. Gollan, consults Hancock on questions of class consciousness. Russel Ward refers to Hancock twice, though on the second occasion he quibbles with the argument of one of his lesser-known essays.[28] These citations may be no more than a touching of the forelock in recognition of Hancock's stature in the historical profession, for all these historians differ from Hancock in one way or another in terms of their view of history, but it is difficult to disagree with R. W. Connell's judgement of 1968:

> *Australia* prefigured the main themes of almost every interpretation of Australia and Australian history that has been written since. Some twenty books and uncountable articles have been written, by historians, journalists, and social scientists of every persuasion, to present the image and interpretation of Australia. Far from showing variety, the great bulk of this literature forms a single tradition of social comment and criticism, with a limited set of basic ideas. Most of them can be found in Hancock's one book.[29]

Given the seminal importance of this book in the intellectual history of Australia, what are its major themes, and whence do they derive? Commentators as diverse as H. M. Green, R. W. Connell, Geoffrey

Bolton, Manning Clark and Anne Summers have written critiques of *Australia*, and have detected six closely interrelated themes within it: the importance of the state as milch cow; an implicit acceptance of masculine experiences as the authentically Australian experience; a rural bias, deriving from a concern with the transplantation of European civilization in a weird environment; the essentially egalitarian if not classless nature of the social structure; a commitment to nationalism; and the hypothesis that the Labor Party is a party of initiative.[30]

Australia has to be understood in terms of at least three levels. The first of these is at the level of the argument itself, how the elements of the implicit social theory are wedded together in a highly readable style. This argument, in turn, has to be related to what went before: Hancock's book viewed in this way is a crystallization of the ideas of his intellectual predecessors. The third level, and the logical starting point of this analysis, is an account of Hancock's career and intellectual development (though his middle-period career as a commonwealth historian cannot find room here).

Hancock has described his life with elegant loquacity, and in such detail that it is difficult to know where to begin. The autobiography he wrote in the early 1950s, *Country and Calling,* is his own explanation of one mighty theme of his life—the divided loyalties of birthplace and profession. Born in Melbourne, in 1898, William Keith Hancock spent his childhood mostly in rural Bairnsdale and suburban Brighton. He was educated at Melbourne Grammar School, and went on to the University of Melbourne during the First World War. His elder brothers served in the A.I.F., but Hancock's mother refused to allow him to join his brothers in the 'baptism by fire' at the Front. One brother, Jim, was reported missing at the Somme and Mrs Hancock wept and fretted continually. Hancock also suffered: 'I felt the strain too and used for many years afterwards to have a horrible dream in which Jim came back to us mutilated and mad'.[31] It is obviously very difficult to gauge whether (and in what ways) Hancock was affected by not serving in the First A.I.F. He could only live their experience vicariously, relying on the official ideologues such as C. E. W. Bean: an interesting testimony to Bean's influence on his thinking is that the very title of his memoirs, *Country and Calling*, is a phrase plucked from the last sentence of the 1945 introduction to Bean's *On the Wool Track:*

> If ever the wool industry of Australia were to be not merely supplemented, but supplanted, by other industries there would go with it some of the most vital types which a few years after our visits, went to

make up the men of Anzac; of which types, *and their country, and their calling* the following chapters tell. [Author's emphasis.]32

From the University of Melbourne he went to the University of Western Australia, and from thence to Oxford, before going on to Italy in the mid 1920s to study land-use. As he later explained, he 'was the blundering disciple of a brilliant but viewy Italian, Benedetto Croce'.33 Returning from Tuscany in 1926, Hancock gave a paper to the Australasian Association for the Advancement of Science in Perth that August, and spoke in glowing terms of a particular form of social organization he had encountered there:

> The Tuscan *mezzadria* is a most striking example of the vitality of a social institution persisting through the centuries in complete indifference [to] radical changes in government . . . Its central principle is that landowner and tenant should cooperate in the task of exploiting the land, and should share its produce.34

The owner provides the land, fully equipped for farming; the tenant and his family provide the labour; the yearly expenses of cultivation are divided equally between landowner and tenant; and, most importantly, annual profits are also divided equally. As it turns out, however, there is another contemporary estimate of the *mezzadria*, provided by the Italian marxist Antonio Gramsci:

> This is the most hideous and unhealthy means of capital accumulation, because it is founded on the iniquitous usurial exploitation of a peasantry kept on the verge of malnutrition, and because it is inordinately expensive, since the small saving of capital is offset by the incredible expenditure which is often necessary to maintain a high standard of living for such a great mass of absolute parasites.35

Gramsci's interpretation suggests that although Hancock's view was not the only one possible, he seized upon it as a suitable model for Australia (by implication). Whatever his source, Hancock seems to have been indulging in wishful thinking on questions of class structure during this period, for when he sat down to write his great work two years later, the problem could be summarily dismissed: 'There *is* no class except in the economic sense', according to *Australia*.36 It is also significant that Hancock went to Italy to study land-use, showing the same rural bias which would recur in *Australia*. Describing this book forty-five years later, Hancock said: 'It was quite personal: I confessed I was in love with the soil'. Similarly, in discussing his motives for writing *Discovering Monaro,* Hancock explained:

> I wanted to get used to keep on walking, in country that I'm very fond of . . . I wanted an excuse to catch fish, and when I retired I wanted some continuous task . . . And then of course I have been interested in land-use for about half a century and first wrote about it in Tuscany.[37]

The environmental theme in *Australia,* then, is limited to the Bush, with little or no reference to the urban environment, despite the electrification of suburban railways in Melbourne and other signs that the Australian cities were developing rapidly—including Adelaide, where he had gone as professor of history in 1926.

This emphasis on the outback as the critical environmental theme is, of course, partly a reflection of the influence of Bean; and Hancock himself acknowledges the debt he owes to earlier Australian intellectuals, such as Eggleston, Shann and Scott. There are obvious continuities in the social theorizing of this group, and Hancock can be seen merely as an articulator and systematizer of pre-existing ideas about Australian society that were widespread amongst the intellectuals of the period. But Hancock was not as critical of the State as Shann had been, nor did he take up the critique of the A.L.P. which V. G. Childe had presented in *How Labour Governs.* Thirdly, he was not as myopic as A. C. V. Melbourne had been in emphasizing constitutional changes, as suggested by his review of *Early Constitutional Development* in 1936:

> Even for the Australian student interested primarily in his own country the most important of modern constitutional documents is the Durham Report. Because the central issues were decided elsewhere, it is not necessary for the majority of Australian students to study at great length the detail of constitutional development in Australia. They may, therefore, keep free a fairly large proportion of their time for those economic and geographic aspects which briefly constitute the individuality of Australian history.[38]

So, if Hancock's *Australia* is in some ways a crystallization of major intellectual trends of the period then, it is clearly also a new edition: it accepts some earlier interpretations, rejects or modifies others, binding them into a coherent overall pattern.

In his preface to the 1961 edition of *Australia,* Hancock offered a broader explanation of how he came to write the book:

I wrote this book in 1929, when most Australians still believed themselves to be riding the crest of a boom. I wrote it during a period of my life which was evenly divided, in more senses than one, between Australia and Europe. It is to these circumstances that the book owes its flavour of period and place.[39]

Some commentators have seized on the first sentence of this preface in order to account for the derivation of one or more of the themes of *Australia*. For example, in her chapter on the 1920s in *A New History of Australia,* Heather Radi writes:

> While the boom lasted there was the prospect of tangible gain for all ranks in society. Perhaps this helped sustain the myth of an egalitarian society. 'Society in Australia is not yet fixed and formalized. Men do not find it difficult to change their houses or town or class. There *is* no class except in the economic sense', W. K. Hancock could write at the end of the decade.[40]

There is delicious irony in Radi's remarks, because most of her fellow contributors to the *New History* are still working partly within Hancock's problematic. And Hancock has recently spelt out more clearly what he meant by the remark:

> At the crest of the boom [Australia was] a wasteful society, a society which was not thinking in a disciplined way, a society which didn't care for the arts . . . a society for the vulgar rich, the greedy . . . I would have written a different book if it had been in the depression; perhaps that was a good vantage point . . .[41]

Is *Australia* simply a product of these bouyant years, as Hancock suggests and Radi seems to imply?[42] The crucial point on this question is how the book was received: no other work of Australian history has been treated with as much reverence or respect. If *Australia* were merely a symptom of boom years, it is difficult to account for its continued reprinting, and the numerous references it receives in the footnotes of more recent works. Until recently, it was regarded as above criticism, as a lode of truisms about the Australian experience, not simply as a product of the 1920s. If a clever turn of phrase could be found in *Australia* which suited one's purpose, it was plucked out to grace the argument, much as a preacher alludes to the Scriptures. Only by considering all three aspects of the book's derivation—Hancock's personal biography, his intellectual predecessors and the nature of the argument itself—is it possible to strip away the mythology which surrounds the book, to see how these three aspects come together in a remarkably well-written and cogent world view. Then it becomes clear that Hancock did not critically examine his own bourgeois origins, mistook his own perception of Australians as an independent judgement, and thereby accepted the great dare of universalizing from his own experience, such as his summary of the 'prevailing ideology' of Australians as 'the sentiment of justice, the claim of right, the conception of equality, and the appeal to Government as the instrument of self-realization'.[43] These are profoundly bourgeois concepts, and Hancock grafted them on to all Australians. He should have been suspicious of the critical worth of his judgement when the Philistines did not savage the book,[44] for that clamour of praise suggests just how keenly his social theorizing simultaneously explained and did not explain the dynamics of Australian society. Hancock had few ideological adversaries against whom to judge how 'independent' was his analysis of Australian conditions.

Since 1930 Hancock has gradually detached himself to some extent from the book, and the self-recriminations have become stronger. In 1953 and 1954, while writing his autobiography, Hancock was already expressing some reservations about *Australia.* He wrote at this time that he was 'a little shocked at the unsophistication of my approach to many complicated Australian problems', but in general he seemed pleased with his 1930 effort:

> . . . at the beginning of the book and towards the close there were some chapters whose quality depended, not upon specialist knowledge and techniques but upon an Australian's capacity to see his own country both sympathetically and critically, both at close view and in the perspective of history. I still believe that those chapters contributed something to Australian self-awareness.[45]

In his preface to the 1961 edition he suggested a few corrections, but did not incorporate them into the text, postulating that 'critical readers of my book will discover many similar examples of the historian's fallibility when he tries to chart the course ahead.' Commenting in an interview in 1974 on his motives for writing *Discovering Monaro,* Hancock cited one of them as an act of penance for his country:

> It was a return to my own country and I wanted to make amends for a book which I didn't very much like, the *Australia* book. I don't like it very much because in it I wrote about a lot of things I knew only in a superficial way . . .

Later, he remarked that it 'was a very bright book, a young man's cheeky book'. Asked if it were 'second hand' he replied:

> I don't think it's as bad as all that, but I think a lot of—some of the ideas were, perhaps, I won't say original, but weren't authentic to the author . . . I would say there's quite a lot of plagiarism in that book . . . I was picking up bits and pieces from all sorts of places . . .[45]

As he grew older, then, Hancock became less satisfied with the 'young man's cheeky book'.

The internal logic of the young Hancock's cheeky book is quite sophisticated: it represents an ambitious attempt to view the Australian political economy as an historic process. The active components of his analysis range broadly, from highly general concepts such as the British Empire and abstractions such as 'the achievement of civilization' to intermediate or middleground phenomena ('public opinion', the Australian governmental system, the 'race' of Australianized Britons) and particular people and ideas. Hancock's *Australia,* indeed, is an archetypal contextualist history; its strength lies precisely in its author's ability to move up and down different levels of generality. Most histories allude to different levels of analysis or description, but broadly speaking only contextualists emphasize the interplay between these levels. With a great deal of intellectual gymnastics Hancock is able to synthesize the general, the intermediate and the particular, but he does not do this by theorizing. There are no invariant theses in this book about 'the nature of capitalism', for example; instead, any sub-argument in *Australia* about capitalism is more concerned with its actual manifestations, rather than its relationship to such abstract constructs as social structure. This is one limitation to contextualist theorizing, for it tends to infer that only those relationships between different levels of generality which are empirically demonstrable can be held to be 'true'.

This reluctance to assign general theoretical properties to analytic categories pervades the entire argument, beginning with the two most important general phenomena Hancock refers to: the Australian environment and the British Empire. He is not interested in contesting propositions about the supposed relation between imperialism and war, for example. Rather he seeks to argue that, 'in reality', the Empire has benign motives:

> The British Empire has everything to lose by war. It has liabilities in every quarter of the globe . . . It acts as an interpreter between Europe

and Asia, between Europe and America, between Asia and the South
Seas. In Canada and South Africa it has achieved what the League of
Nations is seeking to achieve in Europe—the reconciliation of
races.[46]

In this passage Hancock is not attempting to justify every empire that
has or might exist, for this would require either a large-scale
theoretical reply to the critics of imperialism or a case-by-case
empirical defence. On the contrary, his statement is concerned only
with an actual empire.

At the highest level of generality Australia is the fusion of this
Empire with a certain environment. 'Environment', as Hancock
defines it in 1930, is a mixture of various attributes: the geopolitical
relation of the continent to other countries, the physical environment
(especially the climate and natural resources) and the patterns of
human occupation of the landmass. The 'environment', indeed, is the
most active single component of his analysis, and is a greater determinant than the evolving economic structure. At one point in his
narrative Hancock entertains doubts about this, pausing in mid-
thought: 'Does this mean that the distinctive ethics of Australian
democracy are dependent, after all, upon its distinctive economics?[47]
Subsequent chapters show some of the connections between the
economic structure and the sphere of political ideas, but in chapters
8, 9, 12 and 13 Hancock pulls his analysis back to the underlying
environmental aspects.

At a lower level, then, the logic of economic growth (and continued prosperity) is a significant variable. The capitalist nature of
the economy is, however, taken for granted in understanding cause-
and-effect relationships, though the existence of 'private interests'
is often acknowledged—at the middle-ground of analysis—and at a
higher level the structure of world capitalism is seen to generate
'economic disciplines'. This is a convenient device (albeit unconscious), for it enables Hancock to place much more emphasis on the
constitutional form, the role of the State and the emergence of
'welfare state' policies. There is no aggressive bourgeoisie, though
(mysteriously) there is occasional mention of 'class struggle'. The
failure of the movement to 'unlock the land' in the previous century
is one instance of this, but

> The underlying reasons for this [failure] . . . must be sought, not in the
> villainy of the squatters nor in the stupidity of the legislators, but in
> the ineluctable fact that large sheep-runs paid better than small
> farms.[48]

Two other middle-ground concepts are critical to Hancock's understanding: something he calls 'public opinion',· and 'the stock' or the 'race' known as 'Independent Australian Britons'. The latter underpins an important moral judgement he makes on the convicts: although these criminals were of British origin, this does not cast aspersions on the British race, for the children of the convicts 'were in every way more virtuous, more *adequate*, than their parents . . . In the new soil, the health and vigour of the stock reasserted itself'.[49]

As one moves away from these more general phenomena, the number of variables continues to increase but fewer of these are active determinants of social change. The political parties—seen as parties of initiative and of response—are critical to this aspect of the analysis. Hancock is very good at discerning the operations within the polity, the process by which attitudes ('public opinion', 'private interests' and so on) feed into the political structures and are transformed into political ideas and policies. But, as already suggested, he is relatively weaker at observing the symbiotic relationship between business and government: the primary and secondary industries, operating within environmental constraints, are part of his concept of 'economic growth and prosperity', but they exert little influence on the policy-making process. In fact, the reverse is more characteristic, for the political parties and the 'representative government' of which they are part are defined as relatively autonomous units.

Finally, the objects of Hancock's concentration are invariably determined by the other levels of analysis and usually do not exhibit much 'reality' outside his framework. There is an example of this on the second page of the text which also neatly shows the extraordinary synthetic power of Hancock's analysis: 'Wool made Australia a solvent nation, and, in the end, a free one. The authentic founder of Australia's independence is John Macarthur'.[50] These two sentences succinctly pull together a broad category ('solvent nation'), a more specific one ('wool') and an individual (Macarthur), as well as a couple of ideological concepts for good measure. But it would be simplistic to argue that Hancock's social theorizing is merely *synthetic*, for it is also *dispersive*. It is clear from his correspondence with Nettie Palmer in 1929, while he was writing *Australia*, that the individuals he chose to include were marginal to his original conception. In a letter dated June 1929 he expressed his regret that only eight men were specifically mentioned in the chapters drafted by that time. 'Most of what we [Australians] have done seems to have been done collectively', he mused.[51] It was only later that Hancock redrafted his manuscript to incorporate other biographical vignettes, suggesting his concern to emphasize the Great Men of History at the expense of understanding social types.

There are a number of examples of particular social groups which are logically marginal to his framework. Hancock has at least three ways of dealing with these. The simplest method is to dismiss them altogether; hence his incredible statement that there are 'no paupers in Australia'.[52] A second method is to introduce them into the narrative only on those occasions when there is an actual relationship between what they are doing and the activities or ideas of others. For example, in his section on the convicts (already mentioned), Hancock finds it necessary in support of his argument to mention a 'rabble' (presumably members of the colonial proletariat), but their existence is subsequently forgotten: the logic of 'the stock reasserting itself' excises them from the historical record except for a brief reappearance of these gaudily clothed and hirsute gentlemen during the goldrushes of the 1850s. But a third method is the most common: this involves the use of sweeping moral judgements which are delivered by the narrator on the basis of historical 'facts'. For example, Hancock argues at the end of his first chapter that the Aborigines and 'the very soil' have 'suffered' as a direct consequence of the European invasion: 'The advent of the white man . . . has violently disturbed the delicate balance of nature . . . Australia has suffered too much from the greed or ignorance of her invaders'.[53] This is a theme which does not recur throughout the entire book: the severity of this moral judgement is presumably all that is required, for Hancock makes absolutely no attempt to integrate this (astonishingly acute) statement into the rest of his argument. Why should this be so? It is a direct result of contextualist logic, for if an historian is concerned primarily to establish actual rather than postulated connections between the various elements of his analysis there is a real danger that he will demarcate rigorously between 'fact'· and 'value'. As suggested earlier, this demarcation is a marked feature of liberal patriotic historiography in Australia. (Crawford, it will be argued, later explicitly formulated how this should be done; and Stretton, even later still, contrived a methodology which circumvented the problem.[54])

The critical fallacy in Hancock's social theorizing, therefore, is his attempt to suspend moral judgements until all the facts are known. This is not only an epistemological impossibility, it also complicates his perception of the role of ideas and values. Whenever Hancock refers to the 'prevailing ideology' of Australians as comprised of a nationalism circumscribed by the reality of the Empire, a radicalism of the nineteenth-century variety and a commitment to social democracy, he is also clearly talking about his *own* personal values. He was well aware of this problem at the time, as the opening sentence of the preface to the first edition demonstrates: 'My chief difficulty in writing this book has been to combine intellectual detachment with my emotional attachment to Australia'.[55] The Australia he loved was not only the Bush but also what he understood as the 'prevailing ideology'. Hancock understood better than most in 1929 how these 'ideas' related to 'facts', but exaggerated the autonomy of 'values'. Indeed, his own espousal of these values was compromised temporarily by the exigencies of the economic depression, in a manner which is less striking in *Australia* than in a school textbook he produced at the height of the crisis.

If Sir Keith Hancock distances himself from *Australia,* he is also less than pleased with this textbook he wrote four years later, which 'stinks of bias'.[56] *Two Centuries of Change: An Elementary History for Young Australians* was commissioned by the South Australian branch of the League of Nations Society and first published in 1934. New editions were subsequently published in 1939 and 1947. All three editions consisted of two parts, the history of 'Britain and her neighbours' and six chapters in part II on 'Australia'. The Anglo-Australian connection was one of the chief themes of the book: 'If it had not been for British liberty, we should not have been here in Australia', Hancock tells schoolchildren on the last page of the text.[57] Interestingly, only one part of the Australian story was promoted to a place alongside other episodes in the history of British liberty, and this (of course) was the Anzac landing at Gallipoli, suitably illustrated.[58] But the central theme was that of liberty, which Hancock defined in the following terms:

> Freedom . . . begins with the power to do things we choose to do, instead of things we are compelled by fear to do. But if we choose to do stupid and wrong things, we gradually destroy our freedom. If we choose to do wise and good things, our freedom keeps on growing.[59]

This is a forcefully liberal notion of freedom; the entire text, sadly, is an uncritical piece of propaganda lacking the measured argument so characteristic of *Australia*. At one point Hancock even comes close to denying what Crawford would later establish as the moral conception of history: 'We cannot condemn our past without condemning ourselves, for the past lives in our present'.[60] What appears to have occurred is that the liberal implication of Hancock's social theorizing has hardened into a dogmatic orthodoxy. From this point on, he seems to be contained within the ideological confines of liberalism.

At the end of 1933, Hancock resigned his professorship at Adelaide University after seven years there, and migrated to Birmingham, taking overseas an already firmly fixed view of reality through which his subsequent experiences would be filtered. His fundamentally liberal world view has not changed since. In 1940 he mused:

> There was a time when monastic map-makers, brooding over biblical texts, discovered that the world was shaped in the pattern of a T and an O. It must be so. Why sail the oceans to see it? Nevertheless, simple-minded sailors who had useful work to do in the world set sail from Mediterranean harbours and chartered the capes and gulfs and bays of the European and African coasts. Their maps were called *portolani.* They are respected today as an important chapter in the history of geographical knowledge. The monkish maps are remembered merely as an entertaining curiosity in the history of freakish speculation.[61]

This denial of the utility of 'theory' is, of course, directed primarily against marxism. The marxist approach is just as promptly dismissed elsewhere in Hancock's writings, for example, in *Country and Calling:*

> In this fanatical and sophisticated century radicals do not have moist eyes when they read the parable of the prodigal son—most of them, probably, never have read it and never will. No more have they heard of John Stuart Mill. A well-educated young minister nowadays must force a passage for his argument through the rocks of marxian assertion and the eddies of Freudian finesse.[62]

Clever use of alliteration and emotional appeal are no substitute for debating the theory of history honestly, but Hancock refuses outright: 'The historian, unlike the theorist, is bound by his calling faithfully to accept the complexity and contingency of human experience'.[63] This is not satisfactory at all, as Hancock himself is partly aware: there is an implicit theory underpinning his own historical work as much as that of the marxist historian, as he admits on the very next page:

> . . . it was a false impulse that drove me to Risorgimento studies [in the 1920s] with questions that were prompted by the Fascist march on Rome. For how can the historian avoid falsification of the past if he confronts it with questions which could never have occurred to the men who lived in it?[64]

In other words, Hancock concedes that he too asks 'non-historical' questions of the past, and fails to provide the reader of *Country and Calling* with a methodology for not doing this (precisely because there is no such method, even for the antiquarian). The argument in his

1968 lecture series similarly skirts the marxist view of history. When asked in 1974 to comment on his declared 'bourgeois liberal' world view, he interrupted the question:

> *Yesterday you described yourself as a 'bourgeois liberal through and through'* —
>
> The world is full of slogans, and there are people who don't want to discuss them, who just want to break something up . . . It is a bit of a mirage to find universal generalizations which are comparable to those of Isaac Newton.[65]

In fact, the closest Hancock gets to a formulation of a theory of history is in his 'Note on Mary Kingsley', published in a collection of essays entitled *Politics in Pitcairn*, where he describes the qualities of the best historian as 'attachment, justice and span'.[66] These, on close inspection, are no real solution to his 'chief difficulty': the 'attachment' of the historian who wants to do 'justice' to a particular body of evidence is still complicating his selection of data (despite 'span') and the interpretation he draws from that material.

The notion of 'span' has continued to be important for Hancock, and this partly explains the breadth of his intellectual interests. Yet history, he believes, is still an autonomous branch of learning, and other disciplines must be clearly defined in relation to it. Parts of *Discovering Monaro*, for example, demarcate the disciplines adjacent to environmental history, such as ecology, botany and sociology; but although he does proffer possible research topics in these related fields of study Hancock coyly leaves such problems to members of these disciplines. This might be seen as a desire to 'enrage the specialists'—a favourite Hancockian jibe at the empiricists—colliding with a resistance to overt theorizing so stubborn that it marks him off from other pioneering Australian academics. Perhaps his success in a young competitive culture put Hancock in an awkward moral dilemma: how can you, in all conscience, 'mock' a system which has worked in your favour?

Hancock has personally put into practice—the patriots see themselves as men of conscience—the Fabian socialist or Whig liberal view that the intellectual can and should intervene, but by the mid-1970s he was becoming marginally disillusioned with this creed. In 1972 he organized the co-operative Botany Bay project, an attempt to persuade the rulers of New South Wales that an environmental mess needed clearing up. If Hancock was not dismayed by the obstructionism of the Willis government on this issue, or his lack of success in the Black Mountain, A.C.T., campaign,[67] perhaps Fraser's electoral victory in 1975 was the ultimate blow. Alternatively, it

may have been Idi Amin's dictatorship in Uganda which contributed
to his pessimism, for Hancock had actively sought a benign government for that country twenty years earlier.[68] As if this was not
enough, Hancock heard in mid-1976 that the *mezzadria* of his beloved
Tuscany had given way to freehold tenure and wage-labour.[69] It
was a man much less optimistic about the efficacy of the moral conception of history who in late 1975 made this veiled reference to the
tumultuous events of November that year:

> Historians may puncture the myths, but their critical scholarship
> makes little if any impression upon the contending ideologists and
> activists, who cling to the idea of an 'ancestral constitution' because
> they find it serviceable in their struggles for power.[70]

After Hancock published *Australia* there was something of a hiatus
in the writing of Australian history. Very few works appeared from
1930 to 1937. One of these was A. C. V. Melbourne's definitive study
of the 'constitutional development' of New South Wales, which was
published in 1934. Hancock and Portus both produced their school-
texts during this period, but the former left for England in 1933.
As one historian put it: 'Shann died in 1935, Scott was old and nearing
retirement and few of the younger historians appeared interested in
working in the Australian field'.[71] By 1938, however, there were
signs of renewed interest and activity. R. M. Crawford, who had
grown up in Sydney, travelled south in 1937 to take up the chair of
history at Melbourne University, the first of a dynasty of liberal
patriots who were to reflect Hancock's influence and evangelize his
world-view. Meanwhile, the novelist Brian Penton published *Land-
takers*, and (also outside the universities) H. V. Evatt completed
Rum Rebellion and a biography of W. A. Holman, while Brian Fitzpatrick's splendid talent for polemic began to bear fruit.

It has been argued by some commentators that it was Brian Fitzpatrick who most fundamentally influenced the manufacture of Australian history during the years immediately before the Second World
War to the late 1950s.[72] Were this influence to be measured by productive capacity or originality of scholarship, then this would surely
be the case. But R. M. Crawford stands out as the real master of
Australian history during this period. It was Crawford whose idea of
history filtered through Melbourne University's school, directly
through his teaching of undergraduates and indirectly through his
secondary school-texts. He also established the first scholarly journal
devoted to the study of history in Australia, in 1940, with *Historical*

Studies.[73] Writing in 1969 G. C. Bolton summarized what are traditionally seen as the results of Crawford's professorship:

> He showed that home-bred Australians might hope to achieve
> excellence in periods and countries outside their own, concentrating
> especially on the Italian Renaissance and the English Civil War. He
> kindled an interest, hitherto somewhat lacking, in intellectual and
> social history. And he inculcated in many of his students a concern for
> issues of social conscience.[74]

Two years later the editorial committee of *Historical Studies* decided
to produce a testimonial volume of the journal dedicated to Crawford,
and historians as diverse as Manning Clark, Hugh Stretton and Sir
Keith Hancock paid tribute to his scholarship, to his administration
of the Melbourne history school, but mainly to his influential teaching.
Clark remembered the lectures Crawford gave on his arrival in 1937,
and wrote that he and his fellow students 'had been given that feeling
of being taken up on to a high mountain, and promised that Clio
would help us to see "all the kingdoms of the world" '.[75] What needs
to be explained is not merely the interpretation of Clio's purpose that
Crawford held, but also how it proved so influential, and why his
successors moved off in the directions that they did.

Born at Grenfell, N.S.W., in 1906, Crawford was educated at
Sydney High School, then at the universities of Sydney and Oxford.
During the 1930s he worked as a schoolmaster, and subsequently
lectured in the history department at Sydney University before being
appointed to the Melbourne professorship. At an ANZAAS conference in January 1939, shortly after taking up the chair, he delivered
his credo of history, published in pamphlet form as *The Study of
History: A Synoptic View*. In this he began by attacking traditional
political history for its assumption that it is the elite who determine
history, on the grounds that this view robs man of his freedom to
decide his future. There is no single and readily identifiable end
towards which history is moving, argued Crawford, for human history
is confused and complex. To analyse the past, the historian therefore
has to be 'synoptic', that is, to view his objects as interrelated rather
than discrete. Crawford simultaneously rejected the economic determinism of Marx and enlisted marxist social theory to his 'synoptic'
history, on the rationale that Marx had taken factors other than the
overtly political into account. This was an adroit example of intellectual co-option: while Hancock had simply refused to concede ground
to Marx (or Freud), Crawford strove to incorporate marxism into his
own variety of social theory.[76]

Three years later, Crawford was appointed first secretary to the Commonwealth Legation at Moscow, where he served from 1942 to 1944. A decade later Brian Fitzpatrick was to refer to this experience of Crawford's as a 'practical preparation' for writing history.[77] However, at the time, Crawford might have felt his experience in Moscow less a practical preparation and more a traumatic experience: although he has never recorded this Moscow episode in print, there is a clear shift in his theoretical stance in the mid-1940s. Notably, in an address entitled 'History as a science',[78] given in August 1946, Crawford flirted briefly with Carl Hempel's attempt to establish that historians should use general laws of history.[79] This momentary search for a more mechanistic view of history seems to indicate that Crawford was no longer so optimistically confident about the dichotomy between freedom and necessity. It was possible, Crawford had argued in 1939, for the historian to make a value judgement about a particular turning-point in the past by considering the various options open at the time: 'If it could be shown of an historical situation that more than one course of action was available, then moral assessment would be valid'.[80] This was a precise formulation of the moral conception. But after Moscow, the question of freedom (in philosophical terms, as a counterpoint to necessity) often brought Crawford to the very brink of despair: 'from time to time situations develop that are intractable in themselves. The effect of increased knowledge of such situations may prove to be a clearer understanding of their intractability'.[81] On this issue he sought guidance from his colleagues in the department of philosophy, notably George Paul. By the end of the 1940s, Crawford had moved from the positivism of Hempel to the linguistic philosophy of Wittgenstein: to a philosophy of history, in other words, which saw no need to be dissatisfied by uncertainty. Reminiscing in 1971, one of Crawford's former pupils claimed that he was not a mechanistic theorist: 'Set to draw a sheerly mechanical inference, Max was quite likely to get it wrong'.[82] According to A. L. Burns, 'speculation was free' in the Melbourne history school: he then regarded Crawford's 'searching out for a social-scientific conception of history' to be mistaken. Although the school had the reputation of being marxist in the 1940s, 'our approaches moved through and then away from marxism'.[83] One unfortunate corollary of this shift, however, was that by the early 1950s the Melbourne school had accepted 'the mystique of history as a craft *sui generis*', and had begun to content itself with a process of debate over sources as the means of getting closer approximations to historical truth.[84] This retreat into self-justification also spelt, it seems, an end to Crawford's vigorous theorizing about the intellectual validity of history as a discipline and weakened the vitality of the department's liberalism. In 1956 Manning Clark, still in close contact with the Melbourne school, contended that liberalism had become a 'bankrupt' political doctrine.[85] Given this ideological vacuity, it is hardly surprising that Crawford's history department 'produced academics by the score, clerics, some civil servants, but very few politicians'.[86]

Some important aspects of Crawford's view of history can be discerned in his school-text, *Ourselves and the Pacific*, which by 1967 had already gone into five editions and nine reprintings. Crawford drew heavily on Portus for those chapters of the book that dealt with Australia, adapting the prose into a form suitable for older children, but he attempted to place the history of the continent within the larger context of the Pacific Ocean. This is Hancock's idea of 'span'—refurbished as the 'synoptic view'—in practice. This bird's-eye view of the Pacific pays dividends a number of times throughout the book: by considering the geography of migration as an historical process, for example, Crawford is able to conceptualize an 'Oriental Emigration, 1850-1924': the reader is persuaded to see how Chinese on the Ballarat goldfields in the 1850s are not strange oddities but part of a global pattern of exodus from Canton.[87] But there is no attempt at a systematic explanation of the political cross-currents within the region, which would take up the issues of war, racism and imperialism in a rigorous and consistent manner. The countries whose shores are washed by the Pacific are treated as separate cultures and their interrelatedness is of secondary importance:

> Until recent times both Australia and New Zealand went their ways little aware of their Pacific setting. Indeed there are chapters in this book dealing with both countries . . . in which there is scarcely any reference to the Pacific at large.[88]

Crawford also applies the moral conception of history at significant points of his analysis. As *Ourselves and the Pacific* was revised five times between 1941 and 1967, Crawford was provided with opportunities to make magisterial pronouncements on each of the important changes in the Pacific. In the 1952 edition, for example, he reported that the Communists had overrun China—mentioning Chiang Kai-shek but not Mao Tse-tung—and claimed this victory was 'moral' rather than 'military':

> China had been betrayed to its communist minority by its anti-communist leaders who had been unable to inspire loyalty themselves but had repressed and exiled those democratic liberals who might have done so.[89]

These were brave words to write at a time when Australia was following the U.S. in recognizing Taiwan rather than mainland China, and
when Australian troops were being committed to Korea. It is reminis-
cent of the stand Crawford's mentor, G. A. Wood, took on the Boer
War issue. But again the liberalism implied in such pronouncements
was constrained within certain limits: Crawford preached the virtues
of Australia's 'democratic tradition', which he defined as the use of
'reasonable compromise' rather than recourse 'to a preconceived
ideology'.[90]

What therefore was Crawford's influence? To begin with, he
revitalized Hancock's social theory. Hancock himself has stressed the
degree to which their views of history were consonant: 'Our
approaches to history are so much in tune that his *Per Quale Iddio*—
to cite one example—gives me the feeling of taking up with him again
an interrupted conversation'.[91] Secondly, like any great teacher, he
posed problems for his students which bedevilled some of them (and
set the terms of debate) for some time after. Noting this phenomenon,
A. L. Burns calls it an 'anticipation';[92] but it would be more accurate
to say that this prefiguration of later controversies pertained to
certain flaws in Crawford's theory of history. Crawford's eventual
abandonment of the search for general laws of history, for example,
helped erect the supposed dichotomy between the quantifiers and
those historians who regard their task as primarily literary. A more
crucial flaw in Crawford's idea of 'synoptic' history was that it
provided no criteria at all for establishing the relevance of each of the
factors: this dilemma remained with Hugh Stretton, who accepted as
a postulate that Crawford gave a 'personal exhibition of the correct
relations of science, art and conscience', but proceeded to rearrange
the correct approach to 'conscience'. Whereas Hancock and Crawford
had argued that it is possible to suspend judgement until the options
of each historical situation are known—and then to make the necessary moral evaluation—Stretton argues that the principles of selection
(of what factors are to be seen as relevant) spring from the value
structure of the historian. This twisting around of Crawford's methodology took Stretton at least a decade to formulate.[93] The third
facet of Crawford's influence, which was probably the most important,
was that as a former schoolmaster he did not neglect the teaching
of history in secondary schools. His textbooks, *Ourselves and the
Pacific* and *Australia*, were still selling strongly as recently as 1971,
and Victorian high schools were staffed for three decades with history
teachers who had graduated from his department.[94]

Although Melbourne was the focus of historical research in the
1940s and 1950s in Australia, producing an almost missionary

orthodoxy exemplified by Crawford and other liberal patriots, the shape of historical inquiry at the University of Sydney under professors S. H. Roberts and J. M. Ward was somewhat different in important respects. Two key assumptions implicit in Ward's thinking mark him off from this orthodoxy. The first of these is his conviction that Australia is to a large degree best seen as part of a world which exerts pressures on it; the conception of the relative autonomy of the island continent, which lies at the core of even the most internationally minded of earlier historians, Hancock and Fitzpatrick, is all but denied by Ward. This assumption means that Ward cannot be a nationalist in the strict sense of most, if not all, of his fellow historians. Ward is 'unpatriotic' to the extent of arguing in 1975 that no distinctively 'Australian' person had emerged 'until the last decade or so'. [95] While Hancock envisaged his fellow countrymen as *'independent* Australian Britons', for Ward the question 'What is an Australian?' would have been meaningless before 1945 at least, because (by implication) until then Australians were to all intents and purposes derivative Britons. To gain some sense of the differences between Ward and Hancock and their understanding of nationality, one can look at Ward's review of *Country and Calling* in 1955. Ward begins by asking a most pertinent question: Why should Hancock have written his autobiography at the age of fifty-six? Why choose to write it two-thirds through his academic career? If Hancock wrote it as an *apologia* for not pursuing Australian history because 'it did not raise enough general questions', Ward's query remains unanswered. 'Is it merely insensitive', wrote Ward, 'to suggest that Hancock's autobiography has not explained sufficiently why the conflict of *Country and Calling* should have been so important to him?' [96] The insinuation seems to be that Hancock had begged the question of whether Australia had cut its umbilical cord with Mother England; if not, the 'country and calling' dichotomy was a false one. The second key assumption which occasionally comes to the surface in Ward's scholarship is that there is always the need for some kind of lawful elite whose task it is to provide 'good government': the elite must anticipate and respond to consensual values, aspirations and expectations in order to promote a common good. Reminiscing in 1975, Ward stated that at the end of the 1930s:

> I was already pragmatic, impatient of dogma, and sceptical of dreams but, I hope, humane. The way to reform seemed to me to be through the intelligent action of those lawfully in power, through the resources of lawful action open to them. I distrusted attempts at total social or political engineering almost as much as I later disliked total war. The

best and most lasting reforms were those achieved with an eye to stability, not sudden reversals of established trends.[97]

These two assumptions, which are both integral to his social theorizing, are reflections of Ward's legal training, especially his interests in Anglo-Australian constitutional and administrative law.

A brief sketch of Ward's life will serve to locate the origins of this sceptical legalism. Born in Sydney in 1919, he endured what he termed 'a strict Presbyterian upbringing' and spent five years (1931-1935) at the intellectually and socially aggressive Fort Street Boys' High School.[98] The young Ward had the particularly middle-class view of education as a series of 'gates' to be passed through down the corridor to a comfortable job. This view was reinforced by the economic conditions of the period, of course, and by his schoolteachers, although Ward commented that the school itself was never merely repressive: 'It had a strong tradition of independent thinking and of free speech, provided that speech was reasonably courteous and that protest did not cross the hazy line that separated intelligent observation from active disobedience'.[99] Reflecting on this pattern of socialization, Ward seemed aware of the 'repressive tolerance' which provides the life-force for elite schools:

> Intelligence, intellect and power of communication had all been prized at Fort Street, and the barbarian aspect of life at that school, that is, the constant injunction to succeed lest we perish, was never corrupted with proposals that we should take short cuts, endeavour to defeat the examination system, or otherwise try to succeed in our academic business without really trying.[100]

Having scaled the educational escalator adroitly throughout those years, Ward entered Sydney University in 1936, encountering at first Crawford (the year before he migrated to Melbourne), then Roberts (who had succeeded Wood in 1929 as Challis professor of history), and finally J. Anderson. All three men seem to have left their mark on Ward's thinking: 'Many were our speculations about the future of certain intellectual activities in some of the teaching departments of the faculty of arts, if ever they were subjected to Communist, Freudian, or better still, Communist and Freudian criticism together'.[101] Ward graduated with an arts degree in 1938 and entered the law faculty in 1940. Unable to serve in the war effort because of his deafness, he took on a number of journalistic jobs in areas as divergent as textiles, life insurance and the lend-lease programme. He now believes that five years away from the faculty of arts proved a useful thing, as he was exposed to all sorts of experience. Unable to pursue a legal career—again because of his physical disability—he was nevertheless admitted to the N.S.W. Bar in 1948 and, scratching around in Australian constitutional history, found the whole field 'to be totally misconceived'.[102] This insight—that the colonial contribution to Australian constitutional reform had been woefully exaggerated in the interests of Australian nationalism—embarked Ward on his academic career. In 1949, at the age of thirty, he succeeded Roberts as the Challis professor of history at the University of Sydney, a chair he continues to occupy. In 1939 'Roberts solemnly warned me to expect no opening whatever in history', Ward noted drily. 'Ten years later almost to the day he had to welcome me as his successor'.[103] It seems that Ward's additional law degree held him in good stead for the appointment.

This legal training has shaped Ward's research interests, which are primarily concerned with British colonial policy in the nineteenth century. Australia is, from this perspective, merely one of a number of imperial possessions whose management was entrusted to various groups of men based in Downing Street. Before accepting the professorship he had written *British Policy in the South Pacific (1786-1893)*, and his major works since then have been *Earl Grey and the Australian Colonies, 1846-1857: A Study of Self-Government and Self-Interest; Empire in the Antipodes: the British in Australia: 1840-1860;* and *Changes in Britain, 1919-1957. Earl Grey* is probably his most polished book, dealing with an important aspect of the major changes in British colonial policy at mid-century. Earl Grey, himself, 'a man of faith' according to Ward, is the central character and much of the book is devoted to understanding his work as secretary of state in terms of his attempts to implement certain high-minded policies within the limits of the possible. These limits are circumscribed by his fellow Whig colleagues in cabinet and the colonial situation. Ward warms to his theme precisely because he sympathizes with the principles which guided Grey, interrupting the narrative occasionally to express a judgement about Grey's perception of events and personalities in the Australian colonies: some colonial leaders, for example, were pressing for a governor-general, or some 'superior functionary', in the late 1840s and Grey urged the adoption of a federal constitutional structure. Ward believes that in advocating this structure Grey 'was pressing on the colonists large changes for which they had never asked'.[104] The fundamental weakness in Grey's federation proposals, according to Ward, is one of poor management: he had been oblivious to the intense localism of the colonies and their lack of enthusiasm for federal union, which was caused by differing economic conditions, poor communications and disagreements over immigration policies. He came close, but not quite close enough, to displaying the degree of tactical skill necessary to cope with the irascible, short-sighted colonists.

There is, then, a homily about 'good government' implicit in Ward's history, as there is also a mode of social theorizing, both shaped by his sceptical legalism. His conception of society and social change emerges vividly in an address he gave to ANZAAS in January 1975 on the post-war objectives of the nation. The 'great acts of national choice' decided upon in the late 1940s enumerated by Ward in this address were:

   i) Increase of national strength, economically and in an international sense politically.
  ii) Preservation of vital traditions of politics, law and administration, including national identity sense.
 iii) Rapid economic growth, which would assist the first objective, provide proper foundations for guaranteeing the second objective, and, hopefully, produce that limited degree of social equality that Australians have traditionally desired.
  iv) Generally, the building up of a powerful and peaceable nation, enjoying high standards of living, guaranteeing opportunity to all its people and preserving in the main English ideas of liberty, law, order and good government . . .[105]

(Australians had rejected proposals for the further centralization of government and Labor plans for nationalization, argued Ward, at the 1949 elections.) It was his contention that the lawful elites who have governed the country since that time should have had these objectives in mind. The business of the historian then, presumably, is to judge the management of the country in terms of the extent to which it takes account of 'national' wishes. This is a crisply defined variant of the moral conception of history. Ward's judgement is that Australian post-war governments have neglected two aspects of the national objectives: the increase in foreign investment has affected 'our external relations, which are no longer primarily political and diplomatic', and the phenomenon which Galbraith identifies as 'private affluence—public squalor' has led to a deterioration of living standards.

The chief problem with Ward's formulation pertains also to his social theory, for it presupposes popular 'desires' such as 'limited social equality' which are highly abstract in nature. A marxist conception of 'class interests', for example, might lead to a rather different conclusion, namely, that the 'limited social equality' which may be gained is not a consensual value but rather the outcome of working-class demands. Ward, however, does not seem to see this point of view: he once wrote that one of Humphrey McQueen's aims in *A New Britannia* was 'to show that lower-middle and working-class standards have prevailed in our history'.[106] This *faux pas* more accurately reflects Ward's social theory than McQueen's, for McQueen's argument is more the opposite of this. Ward is on much firmer ground when he attempts to analyse the ways in which benevolent elites endeavour to frame legislation to meet majority opinion. Here some critics would protest that 'majority opinion' is better described as 'ruling culture', the imposition of values and aspirations which reflect the interests of the 'ruling class'. Yet very few of Ward's students have overtly objected to his theory of history: a notable exception is T. H. Irving, who has since undertaken a class analysis of Australian history.[107] Although he recognizes that post-war governments have not lived up to his ideal of 'good government', Professor Ward still believes that current problems can be 'put right' by a benevolent elite. His next historical study will be a trilogy of Australian conservatism concentrating on Macarthur, the 1890s and the 1930s. This will undoubtedly provide insights into an area which has been neglected by most Australian historians, especially the radicals, to their detriment.

Ward's two chief interests, then, both flow from a sceptical legalism: the nature and functioning of elites and the pattern of legislation and administration—the main themes in his scholarship—relate precisely to the type of contextualist theorizing which Ward represents. Anglo-Australian legal theory embodies a series of general principles which are the conceptual equivalents of the highest level of generality discerned in Hancock's *Australia*; lawyers then seek to establish in practice how these general principles apply to particular circumstances and cases. It finds an automatic justification in the existence of a 'lawful elite', for these people are guardians of the general principles enunciated by legal theory. The general principles retreat from view and—like the proposition that all persons are equal before the law—seem innocuous enough; their practical application and the legitimacy of their practitioners do not appear 'artificial' because the connections between the general and the particular are real, not hypothetically constructed. Ward's history, therefore, operates not only within this English juridical tradition but, more significantly, within a larger paradigm: the contextualist mode of perceiving social relations.

J. M. Ward's history can therefore be seen as an extension of the paradigmatic conception of the Australian past which had developed within Melbourne University's department of history and among its graduates. Ward fashioned a view of the Anglo-Australian past which drew both from the sceptical legalism of the English juridical tradition and from the moral conception of history. His history pronounced on the degree to which colonial governments were able to meet the expressed desires of those they ruled. It did not, therefore, in any way challenge the notion embedded within liberal patriotic historiography that the general background—in Ward's history, the legislators—and the foreground—those under English rule—should be seen as linked concretely rather than abstractly. However even before Ward had begun his academic career, an older historian had argued the case for seeing the relationship between England and Australia in rather different terms: this man was Brian Fitzpatrick, a radical by inclination, who ultimately inspired a school of historians now known as the Old Left. But the Fitzpatrick school, as will be seen, did not present a diametrically opposed view of Australian history to that of the liberal patriots.

The Old Left

Fitzpatrick's rich and complex marxist analysis of Australian history lacked contemporary impact. In the first place, it was not even understood. Only specialists in economic history—such as N. G. Butlin, J. W. McCarty and W. A. Sinclair—appreciated and debated his interpretation (in the late 1950s and 1960s).[108] A long line of hostile critics consistently if not deliberately misinterpreted him. In the 1940s most academics and intellectuals regarded him as something of a prejudiced oddity. 'It is difficult for a man who feels so strongly as he does not to betray his feelings'.[109] There was no attempt at a sustained critique of his social theory, simply a positivist conviction that readers ought to 'balance' their interpretation of Australian history by considering his view amongst other possible ones. By the mid-1950s the epithet 'disappointed radical' had begun to be attached to him, a caricature which was revived in 1970 by Humphrey McQueen.[110] Other historians were profoundly moved by the depth of Fitzpatrick's work, but sought to apply his insights in a rather piecemeal fashion: Russel Ward, R. A. Gollan, Ian Turner and Geoffrey Serle are the more conspicuous of these. It was only in the 1970s that the implications of Fitzpatrick's work came to be fully understood.[111]

In the second place, Fitzpatrick's lack of influence was probably a consequence of his inability to exploit *institutional* mechanisms for the social distribution of his analysis. The fact that many of his critics seized upon one of his lesser works, *A Short History of the*

Australian Labour Movement, highlights this problem, for this particular book was his best-known and best-circulated, especially through the Australian Army Educational Service.[112] The resounding manifesto with which it opens—'I have taken the view that the history of the Australian people is amongst other things the history of a struggle between the organized rich and the organized poor'— conveys a 'vulgar marxist' tone which is absent from his four main volumes of history. Fitzpatrick seems to have missed a wonderful opportunity for diffusing the full richness of this theory of Australian history through the soldier—education programme. He also appears, in retrospect, to have relied too heavily on the networks of progressive thinking in the 1940s, for such groups were isolated and did not exert strong counter-hegemonic pressure. Even if Blainey is correct in asserting that Fitzpatrick enjoyed wide influence in the 1940s,[113] there were solid institutional limits to this influence: *The Australian People* set out 'points of view not usually shown in the daily press or in school histories', according to a contemporary observer.[114] Despite a welter of pamphlets, newsletters and *Smith's Weekly* articles which attest to his burning activism, Fitzpatrick had either renounced the use of the mass media and the educational system after leaving the Melbourne *Herald* in 1935 or was shut out of them. His exclusion from university appointments suggests that the latter was more often the case. Any discussion of his work, however, which does not take account of the depth of his anger, the breadth of his understanding and the sincerity of his commitment, is missing the point.

Brian Fitzpatrick was born near Warrnambool in 1905 to poor parents, but was able to enter the University of Melbourne by diligent part-time study, and as an undergraduate supported himself with scholarships, prizes and casual employment. The fire within him bade that he rise each morning of his life at six, work until lunchtime and then spend the rest of the day drinking, mixing socially or otherwise living life with gusto until all hours, and then be at his desk the next morning.[115] Those who met Fitzpatrick were impressed by his courtliness and tolerance for ideological adversaries. He had established his intellectual credentials with two highly original volumes of economic history researched in the mid-1930s: *British Imperialism and Australia, 1788-1833: An Economic History of Australasia* and *The British Empire in Australia: An Economic History, 1834-1939*. These were written in a serious neo-Ciceronian style which obscured to a large measure the heart and mind of their author, and it is difficult to read into them the complex of factors which impelled Fitzpatrick at this stage of his career. But two pages of *The British Empire in Australia* suggest one important factor: the death of a brother-in-law, struggling against the unrelenting Mallee and an insensitive government to 'make a go' of his soldier-settlement property.[116] Fitzpatrick restrains himself superbly; the year-by-year details of this forgotten Anzac's forlorn battle to plant wheat are recited bloodlessly from a letter (correctly footnoted) the author had received from 'his sister, Mrs A. W. Maxwell, then of Underbool, Victoria'. The immediate reason for this sudden digression from a general economic history was to offer evidence against F. W. Eggleston's argument that the closer settlement scheme had failed because it was an example of 'State socialism'. Fitzpatrick quietly responded that:

> there was not the faintest flavour of 'State Socialism', in any ordinary meaning, or of any other kind of Socialism, about the Victorian or any other state scheme of closer settlement . . . [indeed] the schemes, with whatever motives designed, had worked out as systems exploitative of large numbers of industrious individuals.[117]

The words are calm and precise, as precise as his description of his brother-in-law's inability to repay the government or to raise a second mortgage from the banks: 'His savings were all used up, and, through deflation of land values, now (1933) even his equity in the property was gone'. [118] That the People did not own the Land was to be a recurring theme in Fitzpatrick's writings.

This was a populist demand which Fitzpatrick regarded as a 'natural right' amongst others; yet he glimpsed that if he were to understand how the majority were deprived of their rights he would need some general social theory. In short, he wedded Rousseau to Marx. The materialist conception of history freed him from the dominant mode of history represented by the 'patriots' (he had disagreed with Scott while an undergraduate) insofar as his value standpoints informed and flowed from his variety of marxism. But, although the ideological implication of his scholarship was further to the left than that of Crawford, Hancock and others, there were still remarkable continuities between his social theorizing and theirs.

This can perhaps be best demonstrated by examining the internal logic of Fitzpatrick's best work, *The British Empire in Australia*. 'He did not hammer his pessimistic interpretations into his readers' in this book;[119] rather, his ideological position is incorporated into the analysis in two ways: his choice of a marxist framework and the implications of the argument, which a careful reader would draw out. The underlying dialectic of Australian history for Fitzpatrick turns on

British capital and Australian labour. The antagonism built into their relationship is the chief determinant of Australian history, and the unifying factor which binds these contradictions together and will decide—he implies—the outcome of their struggle is the availability of Australian land. There are obviously a considerable number of intervening factors in this process, and the model works best when Fitzpatrick is able to handle them all. Probably the single most brilliant example of this is his analysis of the reasons for the temporary cessation of transportation in the late 1830s. The basic narrative is organized around the divisions among the colonial pastoralists and among the English administrators, mainly over the issue of whether the emigration into Australia of both free and bond labour could be simultaneously increased in volume. The mediating factors which come into play—and are seen increasingly throughout the debates as significant factors by the personalities themselves—are the state of the colonial labour market, the growth of the pastoral economy, and the 'condition of England'.[120] Developments in each of these areas intersect to change imperial policy on the transportation of convicts during the 1830s. This example also illustrates Fitzpatrick's acute sense of time as the essential axiom of the historical imagination. His use of time is not merely chronological ('B happened after A') but also diachronic (because B occurred after A, C was the result rather than D). One instance of this, which also reveals an important postulate of Fitzpatrick's thinking, occurs at the end of the gold-rushes:

> We may put it that the pastoral industry had been confirmed in its occupation of Crown land just before political democracy was instituted in the Australian colonies, and thus barely escaped expropriation; that the industry, ignored by the natives and immigrants who preferred to look for gold, had under the pressure been able to lessen its dependence on labour; and that economic conditions overseas had stimulated its growth at the time when the availability of labour and the improvement of internal and external transport facilities provided the necessary conditions of a large development of production and marketing. The Crown, the capitalist, and the resentful colonial himself, had inadvertently worked together to preserve and strengthen the pastoral base of the Australian economy.[121]

The elegant flow of the prose, each clause fitting neatly into place before the argument is neatly rounded off, matches the elegance of Fitzpatrick's social theory. The significance of the economic interests behind the Order-in-Council of 1847, the beginnings of colonial self-government and the Land Acts of the 1860s, is most succinctly put. Fitzpatrick attached great importance to these events, as he made clear in his next major work, *The Australian People:*

> Probably a proletariat was never created so quickly . . . The Land Acts of New South Wales and Victoria . . . were the hinge on which the door of opportunity swung shut on the mass of Australians . . . It was in the early 'sixties of last century that the shape of most things to come for many a long day was determined for Australia . . . The pressure for land for the people . . . made little impression, because of the interposition of a well-established overseas capital interest which imperial policy had made strong before colonial self-government.[122]

According to this view, working-class mobilization in the latter half of the nineteenth century proved powerless to overthrow the existing hegemony and during the strikes of the 1890s private capital was able to call on the State for assistance. Fitzpatrick, however, discerned a measure of popular resistance to subsequent attempts by the State to regulate the society in the further interests of capital, partly because so many referenda had been defeated. As a consequence, his overall understanding of the attitude of Australians toward the State is arguably more fully developed than that evidenced in Hancock's *Australia.*

Fitzpatrick also showed a flair for situating particular individuals in the process of class formation, such as in the case of Angas.[123] But Hancock could also situate historical actors in his handling of the general and the particular. There were inherent flaws in Fitzpatrick's marxian analysis, and some of these (besides the questions raised about the data itself) were clarified as a result of N. G. Butlin's reappraisal of Australian economic history from a non-marxist viewpoint.[124] As Butlin's work suggests, Fitzpatrick clearly underestimated the importance of urbanization as a shaper of class patterns and paid too little attention to the development of an Australian bourgeoisie whose activities were not immediately circumscribed by English capital. In addition to Butlin's criticisms it also seems clear that he allowed a fairly unspecified definition of the 'working class' to float over a large segment of the national history.

These three flaws were a direct result of certain weaknesses in his social theorizing; indeed many of the problems in the contextualism of the liberal patriots recurred in Fitzpatrick's writings about history and politics. Indeed, Crawford and Fitzpatrick shared enough common ideological ground for them both to be involved in the late 1930s in the Australian Council for Civil Liberties; the professor thought so highly of Fitzpatrick that he even secured some research funds for him in this period. The civil libertarian element of Fitzpatrick's world view was succinctly summed up by Manning Clark in 1970: his Marxism was 'enlivened and indeed saved from the 'greyness' of doctrinaire history by his own nostalgia for the life of the fearless, the free and the bold'.[125] Clark perceived the tension in Fitz- patrick's social theory between the inevitability of class struggle leading to the achievement of socialism and an admiration for the determined way in which most Australians were anti-authoritarian. This is essentially the same paradox which Helen Bourke dis- cerned in Fitzpatrick:

> How can we preserve personal liberty while allowing to the state the degree of centralized power needed to curb those interests which exploit the people, without incurring that 'regimentation' which Fitzpatrick so abhorred?[126]

Although Fitzpatrick's active personal involvement in the mainstream of political struggle from about 1935 was more than sufficient to persuade him of the degree to which hegemony and class power are maintained through such institutional means as repressive legislation, the use of the State apparatus and the class domination of the media, he continued to write history and act it as if the battle were partly or (sometimes) wholly to be won by an appeal to the demo- cratic 'instincts' of the Australian people and more generally to 'public opinion':

> Fitzpatrick believed that there was an important function for a grouping of intellectuals, such as that gathered in and around the Council for Civil Liberties, in so far as it could quickly create a public opinion, and with a fair show of credibility purport to represent it.[127]

Despite the ideological gulf between them, then, Fitzpatrick was as optimistic as Hancock in the appeal of sweet reason to affect the power-holders, whether they were Labor Party men or members of the Lyons ministry.

Fitzpatrick had sought to present an alternative view of Australian history to that of the patriots. He was followed by a group of historians who saw themselves as a school of radical nationalists. They are perhaps the best known Australian historians, partly because of the attacks made upon them. They were already being described as the 'Old' Left in 1970 when Humphrey McQueen launched an abrasive attack on them in the introductory pages of *A New Britannia:*

None of these historians would object to being described as socialists; indeed, some have welcomed the title marxist. As I do. The difference between us is that for them socialism is a thing of the past; something to lament, and lamenting, paint in lurid rose ere the pall of death become too apparent. Their tale is a sad one. A tale of decline, of a once radical people corrupted by their own victories. In essence they picture radicalism, and with it socialism, as chances gone for ever. There is nothing to look forward to except king-making and wire-pulling in the A.L.P.[128]

What the Old Left historians have in common, as McQueen implies, is the belief that marxism is not just an ideological stance but more importantly an analytic method for understanding the Australian past. Although their social theorizing is by no means unitary or monolithic, it is this fundamental belief which connects the scholarship of Russel Ward, R. A. Gollan, Ian Turner and (to a lesser extent) Geoffrey Serle. There is also a significant paradox built into their understanding of marxism and, in turn, their understanding of Australian history: they all come from relatively privileged backgrounds which ensured them a 'good' education, but were profoundly distressed by the nature of Australian society during the 1930s and 1940s. This led them to adopt the marxist theory of history and, with the exception of Serle, they all joined the Communist Party of Australia. The works of Brian Fitzpatrick became a symbol of their enterprise. They graduated from different universities (Melbourne, Adelaide and Sydney) and entered academia in the 1950s via universities (A.N.U., Adelaide, Monash, the University of New England) where, curiously, the orthodox moral and patriotic conception of history was not dominant. These four men were not the only radical historians who emerged during this period, but Noel Ebbels died in 1952 and Noel McLachlan was out of Australia for most of the 1950s; nor were they the only marxist academics (Lloyd Churchward, Stephen Murray-Smith and Geoff Sharp moved into different fields), but Australian history seemed the area of intellectual endeavour most amenable to their interests.

The nature of their common interests can be roughly divided into two areas, which, when combined, threw up problems about their own role as intellectuals (by the early 1960s) and also shaped the quality of their marxism. Their first area of interest was also seminal to the work of Fitzpatrick as they understood him: the organized working-class or 'labour movement'. This interest was to find institutional expression by 1962 with the founding of the Australian Society for the Study of Labour History and its Bulletin (later called

Labour History), and has led to later allegations that the Old Left are 'labour historians' to the extent that they misunderstand the overall class structure and class relations within it. For example, Stuart Macintyre argued in 1972 that Ian Turner concentrated on the labour movement to such a degree that its relation to Australian society as a 'totality' was seriously neglected; that he assumed a simple and unmediated relationship between economic circumstances and working-class activities; that when this simple model broke down he could only resort to irrational factors in his explanation of particular events or to moral outrage rather than serious analysis (especially in *Sydney's Burning*); and that this limited focus made it impossible for him to see 'the Australian legend' in its specific socio-economic context.[129] This final criticism raises the second interest of the Old Left: Australian 'culture'. By 'culture' the Old Left tended to mean (before about 1968) those folk-songs, novels, poems and other cultural forms which were an incipient or fully fledged expression of indigenous conditions or ideas, values and aspirations. Australian 'culture' was also important for Fitzpatrick but not as important as it proved to be for those who followed in his tradition. *Overland, Meanjin* (and later *Arena*) were the journals which provided a forum for this second interest—an intense interest which some later commentators have entirely missed. For example, in 1976, Neil McInnes wrote that

> there is no doubt that Australian nationalism is a creation of the labour movement. It was a creation that the right bitterly scorned and opposed, and which the communists, with their subservience to yet another foreign power, did nothing to assist.[130]

The implicit assumption that in its halcyon days the Communist Party of Australia was hostile to the development of a nationalist literature and 'culture' is wrong: the reverse was true, and it was partly this commitment to a counter-hegemonic culture which attracted so many local writers and artists to the communist cause.[131] The Old Left historians, in fact, took Australian 'culture' to mean some spontaneous proletarian culture; in this they were partly misled by Fitzpatrick's dichotomy between British capital and Australian labour, which implied a demarcation between the traditional (foreign culture) and the original (or indigenous). The problem was partly a consequence of the almost complete absence of conservative novelists, poets or dramatists of that period (a notable exception being the late James McAuley), though some were liberal or anarchist rather than strictly radical. At times the Old Left historians seemed aware

that their annexation of 'culture' for the radical cause was somehow
based on a faulty jump of logic, but the generalization remains true
that for most of the 1940s and 1950s a nexus was assumed between
radicalism, nationalism and Australian 'culture'. From the late 1950s
this nexus no longer seemed to 'fit', and the relationship of intellectuals to the labour movement suddenly became an important item on
the Old Left agenda. Significantly, the interests of the Old Left were
taken up by the New Left in the 1970s, though in a greatly modified
form and, as it will be argued later, with the aid of a much more
sophisticated theoretical framework. McQueen may be said to have
originally concentrated on the 'cultural' aspect, while Connell and
Irving are primarily concerned with the issues of 'class structure',
though there are indications that both themes are becoming less
separate. How these two preoccupations of the Australian Left are
reflected in the scholarship of Ward, Gollan, Turner and Serle will be
analysed by reference to each of them in turn.

Russel Ward was born just after the beginning of the First World
War and educated at a number of schools in different states; his
father was a schoolmaster who assumed the headmastership of
increasingly distinguished schools in Queensland, Western Australia
and South Australia. After graduating from the University of Adelaide
in the mid-1930s, Ward also became a schoolmaster, teaching at
Geelong Grammar, Sydney Grammar and, following war service in the
second A.I.F., working as an assistant master for the New South
Wales Department of Education until 1952. In that year he published
a school textbook, *Man Makes History*, which eventually sold
200 000 copies, and in which he acknowledged his debt to one of his
'old history teachers', G. V. Portus.[132] Whereas Crawford had
differed from Portus by broadening the scope of Australian history
to incorporate its Pacific setting, Ward took the opposite course
and showed how Australian history fitted in with the broad march of
civilization over the past 8 000 years. In order to do this, he employed
an ingenious literary device: he began with Arnhem Land Aborigines,
'who know almost no history', and suggested that Western man was
as civilized as them only 8 000 years ago. Most of the text is the
tale of civilization, and it ends with Dampier sighting Aborigines
on the north-west coast in 1688:

> You have now finished reading the story of Man's climb from
> savagery, and so you can understand how and why there was such a
> tremendous difference between the culture of the Aborigines and that
> of the first British visitors to our country.[133]

This is an elaborate homily indeed, and it is doubtful whether many of the young schoolchildren reading Ward's book throughout the 1950s and 1960s would have grasped this message of tolerance. It is far more likely that the terms 'civilization' and 'savagery' would have reinforced existing prejudices. But it perhaps shows the influence of V. G. Childe, the Australian socialist who, after leaving for an overseas career in archeology, had sought to synthesize the development of civilization according to a marxist framework. Ward had embraced marxism as a result of a general curiosity to know how the world 'ticked', and to understand 'proletarian culture' or what the majority of Australians thought and how they saw themselves. As an undergraduate he specialized in English Literature, and he vividly recalls a conversation with his professor at the end of the course. Ward asked why no attention had been paid to Australian literature: 'Australian literature!', came the reply from J. I. M. Stewart (the author 'Michael Innes'), '*What* Orstralian literature?'[134] This remark lingered in Ward's mind and he eventually came to reject the Anglocentrism implied in it, researching his Ph.D. at the Australian National University (1953 to 1955) on the subject-matter of *The Australian Legend.* Ward's general intellectual interest over these two decades was the relationship between literature, his original undergraduate study, and society as a whole—a combination which edged him toward an appreciation of the historical specificity of literature. Marxist theory proved an obvious and attractive guide in this process, especially as Ward's past nomadic existence had given him a strong appreciation of those values which comprised what he would later term 'the national mystique' and which he associated with the down-to-earth Australian worker. Ward had the necessary sensitivity and lacked the conventional academic blinkers to pursue this quarry into the outback folk-songs, ballads and bush-inspired short stories.

The result, *The Australian Legend,* was at once so strikingly original in its theme and in its use of source-material that many of its vociferous critics completely misunderstood the book. In an anguished tone, Ward responded to one line of criticism in a foreword to the second edition of 1966:

> At the risk of tedious repetition: *The Australian Legend* does not purport to be a history of Australia, or even primarily an explanation of what most Australians are like and of how they came to be that way. It does, as the title suggests, try to trace and explain the development of the Australisn self-image—of the often romanticized and exaggerated stereotype in men's minds of what the *typical,* not the *average,* Australian likes (or in some cases *dis*likes) to believe he is like. Typical and not average because, in the nature of things, such a

national self-image can be built only on those character-traits which differ most dramatically from the general English-speaking, or even European, norm.[135]

If the measure of a book's worth can be judged in terms of the number of reviews, articles and monographs it provokes, *The Australian Legend* would rank high on the list. Most of Ward's adversaries have until recently been non-marxist, and this has shaped the nature of the debate. For it has meant that none of them (until McQueen) were prepared to argue on the same terrain, that is, to assume a common marxist ground. This is not entirely the fault of the critics, however, since Ward occasionally moves away from the marxist approach of, say, Raymond Williams or Richard Hoggart, and his book lacks the overall theoretical sagacity of their contemporaneous efforts. He is not much concerned with the actual production of this literature, for example.

The Australian Legend contains an argument which advances in four stages. Firstly, Ward argues that there is something identifiably *Australian*, a proletarian 'mystique', which is described in the opening pages. Secondly, this mystique evolved out of bush life, especially out of the conditions of labour and leisure of the nineteenth-century nomadic bushmen: the drovers, shepherds, shearers, bullock-drivers and others in the pastoral industry. Thirdly, this set of values was transferred to city people by osmosis, especially through the fiction of popular writers such as Lawson and Furphy. Finally, the advent of socialist ideas in Australia after about 1880 was accepted by these men quite quickly, since mateship—an integral part of the mystique —was a 'natural socialist ethos', and this led to the mushroom growth of bush unionism.

There is little point in the conventional empiricist critique which dwells on particular aspects of Ward's case, such as his selection of one document or source rather than another, his use of those documents he does select, or relatively minor quibbles about the internal consistency of his argument, for none of these criticisms reveal the inner logic of the book. Rather, the implicit social theory—which claims to be marxist—is the fairest yardstick by which the book should be assessed: each and every stage of Ward's argument, in fact, is vulnerable to criticisms which are sympathetic to his general approach. Firstly, one could argue that the idea of hypothesizing a 'mystique' is rather dubious on at least two grounds: it accepts the whole bushman-digger legend handed down by Bean and later historians without providing any critical lever on that tradition (it tends to assume what needs to be proven) and then the concept of 'mystique' itself seems to be an amorphous amalgam of 'ideology', 'self-perception', 'community-perception', 'set of values', 'social reality', 'class consciousness' and other jumbled concepts. Secondly, Ward never quite makes clear how and whether the difference between bush life as such and the life of the itinerant bushmen made for varieties *within* the mystique (the concept cannot handle such variations, in fact) or different mystiques altogether. A more rigorous class analysis of the social structure of the outback would have clarified this problem somewhat. Thirdly, the implicit relationship between town and country is at best left rather vague: communication theory might demonstrate the processes of filtering involved and the essentially two-way nature of the interaction. Finally, the relationship between union ideology and the bush ethos fails to take into account the operation of the 'ruling culture', those components of unionism such as racism which do not necessarily spring spontaneously from some aspect of proletarian life but may owe their origin to the ideological dictates of broader social forces. Very few of these criticisms could possibly have been foreseen by Ward in the mid-1950s; it is therefore grossly unfair to criticize him (rather than the argument itself) for theoretical insights which have developed within Australian marxism only during the 1960s and 1970s.

The Australian Legend exhibits considerable technical virtuosity in its handling of disparate and often fragmentary source-material; it also makes an important breakthrough in terms of what can be regarded by Australian historians as 'respectable' evidence. Although Hancock had used all sorts of evidence (including some primitive sociological data) in *Australia*, the thrust of historical inquiry during the long reign of the patriots had been an emphasis on the written historical document. Russel Ward almost single-handedly broke that rigidity.

In 1957 Ward was appointed to a lectureship in the department of history at the University of New England, Armidale, rising to a professorship ten years later. The 'McCarthyite virus' had blocked his attempt to seek a post at the University of New South Wales,[136] and the provincial university gained as a consequence a man with considerable flair for teaching and communication. The question of 'national identity', broached by *The Australian Legend,* continues to be paramount at Armidale, for example in the work of Miriam Dixson.[137] Ward has subsequently written or co-authored collections of folksongs, a general history, and two coffee-table books on the nineteenth century. In 1977 he published a political history of twentieth-century Australia, *A Nation for a Continent.*

R. A. Gollan has traversed much the same ground as Ward, but has emphasized the political and organizational aspects of the later nineteenth-century working class. Born in the year of the Russian Revolution, Gollan was a contemporary of J. M. Ward's at Fort Street High School, studied history at Sydney Teachers' College in the late 1930s, served in the R.A.A.F. during the Second World War, and, after a part-time M.A. at Sydney University from 1946 to 1948, went to the London School of Economics on an A.N.U. scholarship. His thesis, which was the foundation for *Radical and Working Class Politics*, was supervised by Harold Laski. But, besides British influences such as Tawney, Gollan (having joined the C.P.A. in 1936) was also greatly influenced by Australian marxists such as Guido Barracchi and Brian Fitzpatrick.[138]

Gollan has also written a study of the origins of the Commonwealth Bank, a history of the C.P.A. from 1920 to 1955 and *The Coalminers of New South Wales: A History of the Union, 1860-1960*. The last mentioned is probably the best single monograph Gollan has written, for reasons which R. W. Connell suggests:

> The book is principally a history of industrial relations in the coal industry and the politics surrounding it, and this takes it beyond a history of the miners as it requires also an analysis of the employers and the interaction between the two. Particularly in his discussion of the nineteenth century, where he is able to draw on the records of the Australian Agricultural Company (the leading miner, despite its name), Gollan is able to give an illuminating account of the relationship between working-class and ruling-class economic organisation—showing *inter alia* the importance of the union in promoting employer organisation.[139]

The Coalminers stands out from the rest of Gollan's scholarship—and most 'labour history'—for its attention to class relations and to class formation, although in this respect it dwells too much on 'work' and not enough on 'home', including the role of women and family. Perhaps more than other Old Left historians Gollan has (modestly) accepted the general tenor of the younger Left's criticism; his future work may show traces of cross-generational influences.

Ian Turner originally shared with Gollan an emphasis on the organizational aspect of the working class, but he is the most versatile of the Old Left historians and has moved through a number of fairly distinct stages in his outlook. The first stage began with his involvement in the Melbourne University Labor Club (originally founded by Fitzpatrick) as an undergraduate in the late 1940s and his commitment to revolutionary socialism.[140] During the second period, between 1959 and 1968, Turner was in a state of considerable flux, unsure of his ideological position and the study of history, though this uncertainty was not directly reflected in his scholarship. His third period may be dated from 1968 and marks his shift of interest from an exclusive concern with the labour movement to a study of Australian culture.

After leaving Melbourne University in .1949, Turner worked as a communist activist in various manual occupations; he was finally expelled from the Party in the late 1950s. In 1959, thoroughly disillusioned with the Soviet regime and no longer so confident about the Leninist road to socialism, he embarked on a Ph.D. at the Australian National University, following in the footsteps of Ward and Gollan. Truer to liberal principles than most academics in the late 1950s, Sir Keith Hancock allowed Turner to pursue research on the labour movement in eastern Australia from 1900 to 1921. An article in the fledgling *Labour History* followed, then the thesis was published and Turner taught first at Adelaide, then at Monash, where he still remains.[141]

Industrial Labour and Politics included a chapter on the twelve Wobblies imprisoned in 1918 for conspiracy and arson, which Turner later expanded into a book, *Sydney's Burning*. The following year he and L. J. Louis published a source-collection on *The Depression of the 1930s*. The central theme of these works is the labour movement's attempt to effect social change in Australia during the first three decades of this century, and Turner's scholarship over this period from 1959 to 1968 can therefore be seen to follow the work of Gollan, Fitzpatrick and Childe. The (marxist) social theory which underpins this decade of Turner's work is vulnerable to many of the criticisms which have been levelled at the work of his predecessors.

One of the central assumptions of *Industrial Labour and Politics*, as Turner himself acknowledges in the Introduction, is that 'in Australia the labour movement has been the principal initiator of social change'.[142] This argument, advanced originally by Hancock and others, had already been attacked by Henry Mayer in his famous article in *Historical Studies*.[143] The subsequent 'initiative—resistance' debate has shown the complexity of the problem and the difficulty of always presenting the A.L.P. as initiators of social reform and their opponents as obdurate conservatives. (But in the early 1960s the issue seemed much more clear-cut.) A second explicit assumption is that the internal dynamics of the labour movement deserve serious scrutiny in relative isolation from the rest of society, an insufficient argument in support of labour history. But the most crucial of all his assumptions is his definition of labour history. Inspired by British historians such as Tawney, Turner set out the historiographical premises on which his work was based:

> Labour history is history of a new kind: it introduces the concept of masses rather than *elites* as the moving forces in the historical process . . . . Labour history has a special attraction because of the high aspirations of the movement, which traditionally seeks not just to change governments but to change society . . . It is this concern with values, and the conflicts this engenders, which insists that labour history is almost necessarily partisan: not only are the historian's sympathies engaged, but his work affects present circumstances and is often written with answers to present problems in mind.[144]

Are there no conservative values? As is often the case in his writing Turner's rhetorical style clouded one vital implicit premise:

> Labour history is concerned with modern industrial society—with the creation of a class of wage-labourers . . . with the formation by this class of organization to protect their immediate economic interests, to participate in government, to change the structure of society; with the formulation of a general theory of society and an ideology which at the same time explains their condition and guides and justifies their action.[145]

This is a succinct definition, but it fails to explain the existence of conservative labour historians who do not accept the connection between the people they study and the validity of their revolutionary goals.

By 1968 Turner had rejected his exclusive commitment to the study of working-class organizational forms, and taken up a scholarly interest in the second strand of Old Left thinking: the study of Australian culture. The Soviet invasion of Czechoslovakia and the May revolution in Paris that year, together with the rise of the Australian student Left and the local anti-Vietnam movement, go some way towards explaining this rather abrupt change. But he had obviously been dissatisfied since the late 1950s: he recently described his departure from the Communist Party in that period as analogous to the situation of a devout Catholic who finds himself excommunicated.[146] By 1968, however, he no longer believed the description of the working class offered by its leaders, and set about investigating indigenous culture for himself in a rather haphazard way. The first and most obvious question to ask was: what were the aspirations of Australian people? This involved drawing out the genuinely indigenous visions of the Australian future (not all of which were 'proletarian') and relying on the ideologues and the intellectuals as articulators of popular desires. The result was *The Australian Dream*, an anthology published later in 1968, which gives some indication of the early steps its author was making away from his doctrinally pure marxism.[147] To begin with, the book was dedicated to Manning Clark in terms that would make an egotist blush:

TO MANNING CLARK
who taught me and many others
that knowledge comes from doubt,
and love from understanding.

Turner is undoubtedly referring here to his undergraduate days at Melbourne, where he had been among Clark's favourite students. In the early 1950s, indeed, Clark and Turner had protested outside the U.S. Embassy in Canberra against intervention in Korea. It is instructive to read the two selections from Clark which Turner included toward the end of the anthology. 'A Letter to Tom Collins', one of Clark's earliest statements (1943), is a penitent young man's letter to Joseph Furphy, ending with the poignant lines: 'When we see Dad and Dave we feel angry with you and Lawson. When we contemplate the alternative we are thankful for you and your ideal. I wonder what we will do'.[148] Turner's decision to include this 'letter' seems to suggest that he had returned to the peculiarly Old Left dilemma of what constitutes 'culture'. The choice seemed to lie between the work of quality produced by an elite or the levelling tendency of 'mateship'. He also reprinted with some approving editorial notes an article by Clark, which argued that because of general affluence the Australian people had abandoned ideologies of any variety.[149] This was also the conclusion Turner reached in his introduction:

Is it possible to dream any more? . . . The nation tolerates rule by conservative and incompetent elites who offer the people scarecrows for thrills and featherbeds for relaxation. The clenched fist, shaken in the face of injustice, has abdicated to the indifferent shrug. The inadequate satisfactions of work, the inanity of plastic culture, the spangled hollowness of the economy, the boring pretentiousness and stupidity of the political and social elites, might as well be tolerated; self-expression becomes a mindless use of individual leisure.[150]

It was perhaps inevitable that the sort of existential questioning

Turner was embroiled in at this time should lead him to a deeper reading of Clark, the great doubter, and two years later he published a fairly incisive interpretation of the 'voice of prophecy'.[151]

An existential approach to history enables the practitioner to view aspects of popular culture and social history in a relatively disengaged manner. After 1968 Turner moved closer to but did not accept Clark's proposition that not all questions are reducible to politics (a phrase Turner used to paraphrase Clark), that some phenomena can be observed free of ideological implication. So Turner accepted an invitation to write a general article on the history of Australian women, published in 1969. Only four years earlier he had dismissed women workers as 'not relevant to a study of the labour movement since they gave rise to no significant trade unions'.[152] So clearly he was now beginning to think himself beyond the canons of 'relevance' imposed by the labour movement. He also took an active academic interest in what could ponderously be described as a highly important aspect of proletarian culture, Australian Rules football, which other historians such as K. S. Inglis and W. F. Mandle were also beginning to regard as significant. From 1967 on, he has delivered the Ron Barassi Memorial Lecture to his students at Monash, but no publication has yet ensued. A collection of children's nursery rhymes followed; *Cinderella Dressed in Yella*, and then an assessment of the importance of the Russian Revolution in 1970. Turner argued that since other revolutionary movements have not pursued the Leninist model successfully, its chief significance lay in its use as a 'moral touchstone': it demonstrated that the benefits of material progress belonged to the society at large rather than a privileged few. 'Whether material progress . . . will also make people happier or better is, as Professor Manning Clark has pointed out on a number of occasions, another question.' 'Lennonism' (the philosophy of the Beatles and the counter-cultural movement) was now as important as Leninism:

> Only when men have ceased having to think about filling their bellies is it possible for them to separate themselves from survival and to think of their human capacity to develop themselves in new and rich and rewarding ways, to seek new kinds of relationships and communication, to investigate new possibilities of experience and new ways of perceiving their world.[153]

Little of this new interest in proletarian culture (expressing the dreams, values and beliefs of ordinary Australians) has yet to surface in Turner's historical scholarship. His account of the First World War written in late 1973 and early 1974 for F. K. Crowley's narrative history of Australia, to take one example, reads remarkably like those in any other general history (although perhaps the editor wielded his blue pencil with a heavy hand).[154] In 1975, Turner co-authored a study, *Australian Graffiti*, with photographer Rennie Ellis, 'Australia's oldest hippy'[155] : this was an ingenious attempt to collect evidence of popular feelings from a reticent social group.

After the Liberal victory of November 1975, Turner felt completely justified in turning his back on revolutionary socialism, because:

> given Australia's political traditional and present political climate, a revolutionary resolution of the conflict between public, political and private economic power is not a real possibility . . . The democratic process leads to cumulative rather than immediately comprehensive change; movement beyond the present radical consensus requires establishing the legitimacy of that consensus rather than seeking to outflank it with a revolutionary critique.[156]

Turner advocates that radicals should be less critical of the sort of democratic socialism exemplified in Hugh Stretton's *Capitalism, Socialism and the Environment*, as it provides a coherent guide towards a possible future. This represents a remarkable shift for an Old Left historian, and hints at a possible ideological direction his studies of proletarian culture might take.

Geoffrey Serle is a somewhat enigmatic Old Left historian in the sense that he is usually listed among their number yet himself claims not to be a marxist. He claims to write 'in the liberal humane tradition . . . to suggest a variety of alternative interpretations which more committed historians may advance according to their lights'.[157] In the late 1940s he, also, was involved in left-wing political discussion, and was even persuaded to preside over the Melbourne Labor Club one year; but he prefers to remain detached from vigorous propagandizing in his history. There is little doubt that he was as persuaded of left-wing views as his friends at Melbourne University. In 1946 he concluded a defence of socialism published in the campus magazine *Shop* with the sentence, 'The facts are on our side', and in the same year his father wrote to Nettie Palmer:

> My boy Geoff walked with 70 other University boys in the May Day procession. He is a good chap & very sensible about his Socialism & I think realizes he must not expect to bring it about quickly.[158]

But while Turner became a Communist Party activist during the 1950s, Serle turned to more orthodox historical concerns, writing on the history of the Victorian Legislative Council and co-authoring a documentary book on various aspects of the social history of Melbourne.[159] Then, during the early 1960s, while other intellectuals connected with the Old Left set up the Australian Society for the Study of Labour History and the journals *Labour History* and *Arena,* Serle seemed content to restrict his attention to suggesting reforms of the university departmental structure and research for his work on later nineteenth-century Victorian history.[160]

The Golden Age (1963) was the first product of this research. His work on Eureka had been foreshadowed in an article published a decade earlier,[161] but the ten or so years which had passed between the book's publication and the completion of Serle's studies at Melbourne and Oxford give some indication of the seriousness and thoroughness with which he ransacks the archives. The Eureka article had emphasized the 'confused causal situation' but in his chapter on 'Sir Charles Hotham and Eureka' in *The Golden Age*, Serle was much less concerned with giving a detailed narrative of events leading up to the rebellion than with presenting a critique of the secondary accounts. For example, he argued that one contemporary observer in particular was 'commenting from inadequate information':

> Karl Marx summed up the diggers' agitation as a 'revolutionary movement' of the 'workers' and in doing so started a hare which some left-wing writers have since pursued to exhaustion. Such an interpretation breaks down because of the near-absence of revolutionary political aims by the Eureka men and the difficulty of placing the diggers in standard class-categories.[162]

If 'standard class-categories' are partly or wholly absent from Victorian society in the 1950s, what alternative stratification does Serle find in its place? Also, what sort of social structure does Serle discern in Victoria in the 1880s in his second general history of the colony, *The Rush to be Rich*.[163] It is mistaken to conclude that there is no such model implicit in Serle's history: it is present in each book but Serle uses his considerable literary skill to keep it incorporated within the narrative: 'I take a great deal of trouble to revise out, to eliminate, the explanatory scaffolding of argument for literary advantage'.[164]

Occasionally Serle attempts the mechanist ideal of formulating general laws of historical process, but these attempts are low level in their theoretical significance, only loosely related one to another and fairly infrequent. For example, in at least two places in *The Golden Age* he asserts a nomothetic correlation between migration and increased egalitarian consciousness: 'The very fact of migration tends to make men equal, in so far as they reject aspects of the society from which they flee and determine to start afresh'.[165] And, '. . . the tendencies of migrants to think in levelling terms is generally underestimated; inherent in the process of migration was the assumption that all should start again from scratch'.[166] But it is more pertinent to examine his conception of the class structure in Victoria during the 1850s and 1880s: the best method for analysing the social theory implicit in the work of any historian—marxist or not— who professes explicitly to use the concept of 'class' is to direct attention to the viability of such usage.[167]

The social structure of Victoria at the beginning of the 1850s, according to Serle, can be characterized in terms of clear class divisions. Class antagonism existed between the 'exclusives' (those who regarded themselves as colonial aristocracy) and the 'democrats' (a term which embraces not only lower-class politicians but the working and lower-middle classes at large).[168] It is evident from this ambiguous definition of 'democrats' that the tension between a class-in-itself and a class-for-itself is not very well worked out: Serle cannot handle this tension at the level of theory. So he avoids the use one contemporary commentator, Marx, makes of 'standard class-categories' in the passage already quoted, and usually prefers to employ occupation-based aggregates in order to define social groups. In two places he argues that after 1861 the basic social conflict was between the squatters, merchants and bankers on one side and an alliance of mining, farming, manufacturing and working-class interests on the other.[169] Interestingly, Serle often peppers his discussion of social structure with the judgements of contemporary observers; he is well qualified to do this as he knows the primary documentation of the period in exceptional detail.[170] But this seems to provide an escape from the necessity of vigorously analysing these theoretical problems: he is occasionally forced to take recourse to such terms as 'working class' or 'ruling class' to refer to a particular consciousness which is either absent or present. For example, he is dismayed at the degree of 'working-class acquiescence and subservience' he detects in 1861. What is this if not a direct appeal to 'standard class-categories'?[171] By jumping between these two sorts of class definition, then, he thereby sidesteps the essential task of analysing class formation as a process. In one passage, which details working class mobilization and the re-emergence of certain unions in the mid-1850s, he recognizes implicitly that this process is not necessarily linear and progressive, but devotes very little space to it.[172]

To go one step further, it is clear that Serle does not, in fact, systematically explore the connections between conditions of existence and class consciousness: there is very little discussion of this in *The Golden Age,* except where Serle deals with the old theme of life on the goldfields—but this is an isolated example. The central thrust of Serle's history is not to establish connections between economic life and social life; rather, his characteristic nexus is that between the social and political spheres. He is most comfortable when there is a particular and unique political event which he can trace back to its social and (sometimes) economic origins. Politics is thereby held up as the ultimate legitimizing agent, whereby events surface from the swirl of detail and lay claim to historical significance. It is too easy a criterion of significance and it forces Serle to put predominant emphasis on the overtly political, such as the Eureka rebellion and the achievement of manhood suffrage.

These problems recur in *The Rush to be Rich.* One of the more generalized features of the 1880s is the urban land boom, yet this is inadequately covered by Serle in terms of its class aspect, probably because he neglects to examine the concept of the nuclear family and its obviously crucial role in suburban expansion. Instead Serle is happier dealing with the explanation of particular events, such as the Victorian contribution to the London Dock Strike of August 1889 and the 1885 Factory Act.[173] In the latter example he traces a causal chain between the sweated conditions in factories, the moral concern of the liberals, the mobilization of 2 000 women into a Tailoresses' Union, this union's strike, a commission of inquiry and the passage of the Act. It is a copybook example of how 'democratic processes' operate—including details of conservative reaction—but fails to account for the more generalized features of the social structure, which are not always to be explained merely by such unusual and unique events. In addition, *The Rush to be Rich* does not advance much further than the aggregate idea of class to be found in *The Golden Age.* The later work is probably a better piece of history, despite Serle's introductory disclaimer that it is 'not as thorough a study as *The Golden Age*',[174] because it is more richly textured: Serle interweaves the impressions of novelists and travellers more skillfully and enlarges his scope to include aspects of colonial life, such as its sexual mores, which he does not deal with in the earlier monograph. This probably reflects changes in history-writing between 1963 and 1971 rather than life in the colony he is describing.

Towards the end of *The Golden Age,* Serle quotes approvingly Brian Fitzpatrick's contention that the ambitious diggers were mostly turned into a proletariat by the 1860s because of an 'enforced conversion to wage earning'. This in turn meant a 'return to the accustomed old-world economic relations of capitalism [which] generated tensions which for long exacerbated Victorian politics'. [175] This theme is picked up in *The Rush to be Rich:* by the 1880s, says Serle, Victorian society was settling into a stable mould with little chance of individual mobility, and class consciousness would not be awakened by the leaders of the labour movement until the following decade. The main determinant of class was not birth or education, but material success—and working-class consciousness would only come when opportunities were denied it. [176] The way in which Serle here mixes together marxist with non-marxist ideas about class suggests the same uncertainty about the differences between a class-in-itself and a class-for-itself discernible in *The Golden Age.* In some instances Serle implies that the aggregates which made up the 'governing class' were divisible along occupational lines (such as the manufacturers who set up their own bank because of their suspicion of other banks [177]), but he also declares that there existed a unity of bourgeois opinion because of a homogeneous ruling class—an important insight which should have been spelt out. [178] In one sense Serle's rich texturing of colonial life brings him closer to a fuller understanding of the intricacies of class differences: his detailed descriptions of housing and living conditions, wage structures, farming life, religious persuasions and factory conditions give something of an insight into the discrepancies of lifestyle. But Serle cannot explain the ideological supremacy of the bourgeoisie and does not seriously examine the forces making for hegemony: 'shrewd and simple alike were bemused by the notion of the inevitability of progress . . .' is the closest statement towards this end. [179]

The Rush to be Rich inevitably invites comparison with Michael Cannon's studies of the same period, and Serle has acknowledged Cannon's assistance in providing a 'framework' to be 'broadly adopted or modified and filled out'. [180] But there are substantial differences of approach between these two authors, as Cannon suggests in his review of *The Rush to be Rich:*

> Struggle as he may, his [Serle's] notions of orderly history crumble before their manifold rogueries, their hot-blooded intrigues, their daily lust for life, and their obsession with individual success or salvation . . . [theirs] was an era in which individuals were expected to flex their muscles, and, in greedy pursuit of wealth, proceed to change the face of the earth without suffering much interference from governments and officials. [181]

This is less a description of the book under review and more a statement about the reviewer's own convictions in attempting to summarize the later nineteenth century, for, as will be discussed later,

Cannon's history is essentially organicist rather than contextualist.[182]

Another interesting aspect of *The Rush to be Rich* is Serle's endeavour to assess, at some length, the role women played in colonial society—notably in terms of their (often perceptive) comments on contemporary issues, their participation in the paid labour force and their treatment as sexual beings. Serle is one of the first male general historians to devote some attention to sexual mores.[183] He observes that women were by and large expected not to enjoy sexual intercourse, and tries hard to remain morally impartial. But he makes one awkward slip: he gives an occupational breakdown of women in paid employment—2 000 domestic workers, 5 000 governesses, and so on, in one section of the book—then later discusses prostitution in a general discussion of sexuality and states blandly that there were upwards of 2 000 women engaged in that profession, quite oblivious to the fact that he had thereby made a distinction on 'moral' grounds between these different forms of employment.[184] (Regretfully, he also does not discuss women in unpaid employment.)

In general, then, Serle's history moves towards a marxist approach and then away from it. The lack of ease with which Serle draws on marxist social theory can be attributed to a number of causes. Perhaps he is unable to reconcile a marxist approach with what he takes to be his 'professional' obligations as an historian.[185] Perhaps his love for Melbourne (except for three years in Oxford, he has lived nowhere else) blinds him to the class patterns that have arisen there. Most probably, however, his intense passion for Australian 'high' culture and his intimate knowledge of late colonial sources have overwhelmed his model-making capacities. His most recent monograph, *From Deserts the Prophets Come*, a generalist history of Australian culture, simultaneously displays his wealth of learning and his retreat from explicit theorizing. The latter is manifest in his very use of the concept of 'culture': sometimes it is used to mean 'high culture' (ranging from scientific discoveries across the cultural spectrum to creative art) while at other times (especially in the colonial period) it embraces all forms of cultural expression down the scale to 'low culture'. Serle also has great and unresolved difficulties in deciding whether all or only some intellectuals are *déclassé* or whether they inevitably represent social groups or classes. The simplest route out of all these dilemmas would have been to apply a rigorous class analysis to Australian intellectuals and their work, but, in keeping with the traditional Old Left assumption that Australian culture is almost invariably proletarian if it is indigenous, Serle avoids this task. Indeed, it would be fair to comment that Serle has been moved more by marxist expectations than by marxist methodology.

What has been the significance of the Old Left in the manufacture of Australian history? In general, they exploded the moral conception of history (unwittingly) by positing that it was possible to study history 'scientifically' once a commitment to a certain partisanship had been announced. This was rarely stated as openly as Turner did in 1958 when he wrote that it was impossible

> to absolve historians from the need to apply a scientific method to the study of the growth of Australian society, the need to seek for a 'science of society'. [In addition, the conflict of labour and capital is] the most productive way of looking at our history.[186]

The Old Left brought Australian 'culture' to the fore, thereby sharpening the debate about how the force of ideas may affect the historical process. They also established the legitimacy of 'labour history'. But this breakthrough was actually a compromise with the existing orthodoxy; the founding of the journal *Labour History* in 1962 did not amount to a strictly marxist challenge, as the editor (R. A. Gollan) made clear in the very first editorial, because

> all the trends of opinion within the labour movement itself are represented by people writing labour history. There are also some interested in labour history who are opposed to labour. This is as it should be for it imposes on all the need to work conscientiously . . .[187]

Labour history was a 'safe' specialism which did not impel its practitioners towards the critical examination of non-marxist social theories, whether those of the liberal patriots, with their emphasis on the universal and the particular, or those put forward by later schools of historians. This paradox is captured neatly in a symposium held in 1967 on 'what is labour history?' Among the speakers were J. A. La Nauze, N. B. Nairn and T. H. Irving, each of whom represents a different school of Australian history: each prospectus for labour history faithfully reflected their different allegiances. La Nauze urged labour historians not to prejudge the moral issues which he saw as inherent in their task: there was a danger, for example, that they 'are likely not only to be interested in the activities of a group as aspects of human behaviour but to believe that they are, by and large, good or right'.[188] N. B. Nairn, who has subsequently 'explained away' any trace of widespread radicalism in the Australian labour movement, challenged Ian Turner's view, mentioned earlier, that labour history had to be partisan. Nairn adroitly interpreted this 'partisanship' as 'radicalism' and continued:

> There is no real reason to lament this, for once the strife goes so does radicalism, which would be sad for both the labour movement and Australia. At the same time, the disagreements should from time to time be kept within the bounds of decency. Labour, too, must aspire to a measure of respectability and power.[189]

Finally, T. H. Irving foreshadowed a major New Left argument by stating that in nineteenth-century New South Wales 'wage-earners did not create a working class', and arguing that a more rigorous theory of class was needed by labour historians.[190] The different viewpoints expressed at this symposium, then, summarize the impact of the Old Left on Australian historiography: much of what they advocated was co-opted, their ideological implication was rejected, and most of their theoretical foundation was dismissed by the impatient New Left historians. Irving's mechanist history and Nairn's organicism will be more fully understood in the context of subsequent chapters.

The argument in this chapter has turned on two fundamental propositions: that despite some diversity of theme the liberal patriots and the Old Left shared an essentially contextualist mode of social theorizing; and that despite their ability to bypass the moralism implicit in patriotic scholarship the Old Left remained within this contextualist framework. The patriots developed a style not merely of explaining the Australian past but of understanding history generally. This mode of social theorizing was contextualist and broke from the history written by formist chroniclers such as Battye and Jenks, and organicists such as Jose and perhaps Shann. Whereas Battye was concerned to narrate the biographies of Western Australian pioneers, such as the original pastoralists in the North-West, the new group of historians insisted that individual lives had to be placed within a larger context. The general became as important as the particular. And whereas organicists like Jose had emphasized the careers and visions of the leaders, implying that all beneath them were, or should be, infused with the same concept of 'progress', the contextualists were much more democratic. Their mode of social theorizing, as in Bean's treatment of the common soldier, enabled them to make sense out of the lives of everyday folk. The A.I.F. private became as important as the general.

It might be supposed that almost all history depends on an understanding of both the general and the particular. This is not so: it will be demonstrated later that neither formists nor organicists need to make explicit reference to both general and specific phenomena. Much of the biography written in Australia employs a formist concentration on its subject and little else besides; other formist history, notably Manning Clark's, sees individuals as representatives of collectively shared faiths and character traits, concentrating on those particular individuals rather than on the larger groupings. Organicists typically work from the opposite direction: they conceive a general direction, or end, to the past they are describing and tend to flatten out differences of detail in narrating the events which make up that history. Contextualists both emphasize the intricacies of connection between the general and the particular and employ a distinct rule of combination for understanding this connection. Unlike the organicists they do not construe general teleological principles: Crawford, for example, specifically enjoined his students not to imagine an end towards which Australian history was inevitably moving. Nor can this be discerned from Hancock's *Australia*. The closest any liberal patriot got to defining such an end was A. C. V. Melbourne's Whiggish argument that Australian political institutions became progressively more democratic during the nineteenth century and, as noted earlier, this view was not widely shared by other patriots. Hancock's espousal of the theory of political initiative and resistance can indeed be seen as a sophisticated answer to unilinear Whiggism. Just as there was a party of resistance to wild experiment there was also no inevitability about the Labor Party's policies, for it contained both useful idealists and hard-headed pragmatists. Similarly the Old Left school was not convinced of any inevitable direction or conclusion to Australian history: none of them, for example, took the view that a socialist revolution was definitely going to take place. Their training as historians, rather, led them away from the vulgar teleology of many contemporary marxist pamphleteers and agitators.

The dominant rules of combination characteristic of contextualism avoid laws of history as well as teleological thinking. Crawford came close to mechanistic theorizing in the 1940s but moved from it before the end of the decade. This is not meant to imply that there was no trace of determinism in the contextualist historiography of this period; indeed, a thread of environmental determinism ran through much of this history from Bean to Russel Ward. This thread was important in establishing a connection between the generalized features of the Australian environment as each historian in the tradition understood them and the particular aspects of social life which were supposedly related to them. For Bean the rigour demanded by bush life produced the Anzac, for Hancock the transplantation of a fragment of English civilization into a novel environment created a tribe of independent Australian Britons and for Russel Ward those character-traits which are ordinarily thought of as distinctively Australian arose out of the patterns of work and play upcountry. In each of these arguments there is no commitment to invariant and universal laws of history. For example, Ward did not develop a hypothesis about the relationship between rural folk heroes and urban mythologizing. Ten years later a mechanist historian, J. W. McCarty, would raise the tantalising similarities between urban perceptions of bushrangers in Australia, cowboys in North America and gauchos in Argentina, a comparison which gestures toward the proposition that the process of urbanization generates a need for romanticized individualists in a non-urban setting..[191] This proposition is an example of a low-level historical law and is quite outside the usual parameters of contextualist thinking.

Contextualist theorizing in liberal patriotic historiography was able to deal with the general, the middle-ground and the particular without a commitment to invariant laws of historical change; it was also able to synthesize large aspects of social life. Crawford, who enunciated more clearly than the others what this mode of history was about, made this point specifically: the historian had to be 'synoptic', not merely concentrating on elite politics but seeking to understand how general features of a polity—such as 'the common good' related to the needs and beliefs of individuals. So there were Great Men in the traditional sense in this history, but there were also collective Great Men, notably the Anzacs, and there also was an emphasis on the elite's duty to understand and respond to popular demands. In J. M. Ward's history, for example, it was shown that a homily about 'good government' existed, and probably his planned trilogy will assess the degree to which conservatives have met the needs of their constituents, their employees and their communities in general.

Conversely, the radicals of that period, the Old Left, though able to dispense with the need to moralize in as much as their adoption of a marxist approach was regarded as 'scientific', were unable to penetrate the orthodox social theory, despite their concentration on two important areas: working-class organizational forms and the examination of Australian 'culture'. But the paradox was that their understanding of marxism did not provide a critical lever on what were assumed to be the important themes and periods of the subject-matter of Australian history, a reflection of the essential similarities between their social theory and that of Hancock and other patriots. This can be demonstrated by the degree to which they accepted as important the issues raised in *Australia,* or accepted its chief underlying assumptions. The British Empire, so important to the internal logic of *Australia,* was translated by Fitzpatrick into 'British capital', a concept which led him to underplay the importance of local capitalists. He fell in line with Hancock's (implied) view that there did not exist an aggressive Australian bourgeoisie, though he saw the role of the State rather differently, as authoritarian and choosing to side with British capital in the strikes of the 1890s. Hancock's emphasis on the Australian environment was reflected in Ward's study of *The Australian Legend,* providing a handy explanatory device whenever the more immediate focus on the conditions of life and leisure of the nineteenth-century bushmen receded from significance. Hancock's concepts of 'prevailing ideology' and 'public opinion' were either tacitly accepted by the Old Left, or, in the case of Fitzpatrick, openly celebrated as anti-authoritarian. Ward modified them into something he called the 'national mystique'. Most crucially, Hancock's (revamped) conception of the major political parties as parties of initiative and of reaction was accepted by the Old Left historians, although they realized that the Labor Party was not monolithic: Fitzpatrick observed that Labor could be as authoritarian as the conservatives when in office. But Hancock's view that laborites could be divided into 'idealists' and 'pragmatists' was never challenged by the Old Left. Nor was his contention that classes (except in an economic sense) did not exist in Australia, despite the Old Left's identification of 'Australian culture' as proletarian. Finally, the White Australia Policy—which Hancock saw as a cornerstone of Australian legislation—was not closely investigated by the Old Left; odd remarks occasionally show their disquiet about the racism of the Australian people, but overall they regarded it as a touchy subject which was better left alone.

So the variety of social theorizing implicit in the scholarship of Hancock and the teaching of Crawford in the Melbourne department of history was largely untouched by the Old Left. Crawford legitimized this mode of explanation in the theory and method classes he pioneered, to the extent that his social theorizing came to be accepted as 'natural'. But three alternative modes developed in the 1950s and 1960s which were to challenge the orthodoxy: these will be examined in the following three chapters.

3 Evoking a person, a period, a place

3   Evoking a person, a period, a place

Manning Clark

The first challenge to the orthodoxy of patriotic historiography was
sounded in the mid-1950s. In a series of articles beginning with
Manning Clark's manifesto of 1956, 'Re-writing Australian history',
a younger group of historians attacked what they discerned as
Whiggism in both liberal and radical history. Some commentators
called it a 'counter-revolution' against what had gone before: the term
was coined by Peter Coleman, who in 1962 edited a symposium on
'the new Australia', *Australian Civilization*. In the introduction to this
book, Coleman argued that 'the Australianist legend' had been
dominant until a post-war challenge by 'disinterested' (ideologically
neutral) historians, such as A. W. Martin, Peter Loveday and Bruce
Mansfield. More than anyone else, however, Manning Clark was the
chief figure in this countervailing tendency.[1]

But despite Coleman's acute resumé of the situation (indeed, he
foreshadowed a major New Left argument), there are two inaccuracies
in this account. As the previous discussion has shown, the orthodoxy
was characteristic not only of radical scholarship but, more importantly, of the liberal patriotic tradition. The radicals, far from
establishing this orthodoxy, were still contained within the logic of
discourse set up by the liberals. Secondly, there was no unanimity
among the new historians.[2] In August 1962, Martin defended himself
against the implied charge of being a conservative in an ANZAAS
paper, 'The Whig view of Australian history'—two months after
Coleman's book was first published.[3] As subsequent developments
have made clear, not all of the counter-revolutionaries were conservatives. Martin, and others who were members of the immediate
post-war generation, went on to become a new type of liberal
historian, as will be discussed in chapter 5; some contemporaries such
as A. G. L. Shaw (who also contributed to Coleman's symposium)

became 'syncretic conservatives', as chapter 4 will make clear; and the sole distinct cause of all the mischief became Manning Clark.

This epithet, borrowed from the chapter heading of volume II of Clark's *A History of Australia,* serves to emphasize two important attributes of Clark's historiography: his singularity amidst the pantheon of Australian historians, and his provocative insistence that historians should be concerned less with formulating grand over-arching explanations of the past and more with probing the intractable universal questions about human nature which emerge from its study. In this chapter it will be argued that Clark and his emulators have been working within an essentially formist problematic, pushing that mode of social theorizing to its furthest limits, and that a second and larger group of historians has, less successfully, been employing the same historiographical style with very different ideological implications.

Born in Sydney in 1915, Charles Manning Hope Clark was the second son of a devoutly Anglican family. Various relatives, his father, an uncle and his elder brother all became Anglican clergymen; but Clark decided as an adolescent that such a career was not for him. Not surprisingly, his childhood was suffused with Christian teachings, and his autobiographical short stories suggest a young man determined to test these precepts' applicability to the outback conditions of Phillip Island, in Western Port Bay, where the Clark family lived during the early 1920s. Sir Keith Hancock romanticized the bush career of his clergyman father in *Country and Calling;*[4] Clark, on the other hand, was much more sanguine about the efficacy of his father's attempts to transmit God's message. The young Clark also detected certain inconsistencies of principle and practice in the adults around him. This realization that the world was not quite as his father described it was intensified by Clark's schooldays at Melbourne Grammar in the late 1920s and depression years. There he felt alienated from his wealthy classmates and discerned in their behaviour an absence of affection for the modest and loving Christ he knew.[5]

His undergraduate days at the University of Melbourne during the 1930s brought Clark into contact with young radicals whose Freudian and socialist ideas explained much of the alienation he felt. He recently described himself at this time:

> . . . at Melbourne University some of his teachers, much reading of Left Book Club books, and conversations with students in the Old Melbourne University Cafeteria had converted him to the belief that a change in the ownership of the means of production, distribution and exchange would produce ultimately a change in human behaviour. By

removing the main cause of the domination of one human being by another, one of the main causes of human vileness would disappear. It was not clear to him then what human beings were going to be like in such a new society. It was all left delightfully vague. There was that prophecy that in such a society the distinction between brain and manual labour would disappear, and the freedom of each would be the condition of the freedom of all.[6]

His history teachers at Melbourne included Scott, whose insistence on the importance of the original source left a lasting impression, and Crawford, whose crisp definition of the moral conception of history exhilerated Clark. Christianity and marxism had given him some partial explanations of the behaviour of those around him (and, indeed, of himself), but growing up in a clerical household had alerted him to the danger of playing the smug intellectual who used this understanding to mock others and berate them for their human weaknesses. A sensitivity to the vantage point of others emerged in his M.A. study of de Tocqueville and this also produced within him a certain degree of reserve about embracing too vigorously the theories of his radical peers.

This reserve perhaps also resulted from his experiences in Europe in the late 1930s, especially his fortuitous arrival in Bonn the morning after Nazi stormtroopers had smashed up every Jewish business-house one night in November 1938.[7] Returning to Australia in 1940 to take up a teaching appointment at Geelong Grammar School Clark was still a radical-nationalist in the Old Left tradition but a somewhat chastened one. In 1943 his short 'Letter to Tom Collins', published in *Meanjin*, suggested a man who was already doubting the worth of 'mateship', the very keystone of the radical intellectual edifice.[8] (But the complete break did not come until the early 1950s, and it proved to be a break not with radicalism as such, but with orthodox radical historiography.) In 1939 Clerk married Dymphna Lodewyckx who, like her Belgian father, was a gifted linguist and widely read in the literature of Western civilization. The Lodewyckx family had emigrated to Australia but remained uncomprisingly European in their intellectual outlook. His association with this family deepened Clark's interest in the classical European theoreticians, novelists and playwrights of the nineteenth century, and broadened his understanding not only of Marx and Lenin, but of Dostoevsky, Tolstoy, Dickens, Hardy and Ibsen.

In 1949, after teaching political science and history at Melbourne University, Clark accepted a professorship at the Canberra University College, a dependency of Melbourne University until its amalgamation into the Australian National University a decade later. The defeat of the Chifley government and the subsequent anti-Communist hysteria of the early 1950s which led both to the Korean intervention and the Petrov charade, eroded his radical premises about the dominant ideological outlook of the Australian people. This disillusionment about the prospects for real change was underlined by personal tragedy: in 1951 one of his best friends, Dennis O'Brien, was killed serving in Korea; and in 1952 Noel Ebbels, perhaps the brightest of his students at Melbourne, was killed in a highway accident near Gundagai. Something of the change within Clark can be discerned by comparing the first volume (begun in June 1949) of his *Select Documents in Australian History* with the second (published in 1955) and the subsequent 1957 one-volume sourcebook. The first is matter-of-fact in its selection and arrangement of documents, and Clark's editorial comments are threadbare and prosaic; the second and third are much closer to what is now regarded as 'vintage Clark' in the prose style of the editor. More importantly, the author's anguish about the radical-nationalist tradition emerges forcefully; for example, in his criticism of the late nineteenth-century optimists such as Lawson:

> They were tainted by assumptions of European superiority: they had accepted, too, a shallow conception of human nature. 'The heart', says the book of Jeremiah, 'is deceitful above all things'. The confidence of these nationalists and improvers, and their snarls for the outside world, especially Asia, can be explained as the product of ignorance, and the dead hand of the European past in Asia.[9]

Having taken a gamble that Australian history was worth researching Clark turned to the possibility of setting out his revisionism in the form of a general history. He first entertained the idea of writing a two-volume narrative textbook which would encompass all of the history. But after some deliberation in the mid-1950s he rejected this plan and started to write what was the first volume of *A History of Australia* in May 1956 while at Oxford. He decided to write this history primarily in terms of three traditions: Protestantism, secular humanism and Catholicism. The first two traditions had directly influenced his outlook and for some understanding of the third tradition he visited Ireland in the (northern) spring of 1956. Reading newspaper accounts of the treatment of the Irish during the 1840s, listening to the English at Queen's College, Belfast, propounding the virtues of their race and seeing Irish political slogans daubed on Ulster walls, started Clark on a serious contemplation of the Irish question. His head thumping with excitement he sat down at Oxford to write. The first sentence came out: 'It was all there in the beginning'.

> Then fatally he paused to ask the academic question: what was there in the beginning? He thought then it might be more prudent not to risk putting down on paper what he was really interested in, but rather to write an academic work characterised by caution, judiciousness and balance, with that gale inside him not audible to the reader.[10]

The first two volumes of *A History of Australia* were careful orchestrations of Clark's preoccupations at the time. One of his students of that period, Michael Roe, described him as an 'alienated rebel of the Cold War years',[11] and it is clear from *Meeting Soviet Man,* an account of his visit to the USSR in 1958, that Clark had not entirely despaired of the view that the world could be improved by changes in the ownership of the means of production.[12] Clark's ideological position has rarely been straightforward: to some he has appeared an iconoclastic radical, to others a reactionary conservative. This is mainly a consequence of his language and style: partly aphoristic, partly metaphoric, his inimitable prose does not readily reveal the inner thoughts of the writer.

Language, style, structure of narrative, mode of social theorizing: these all run together in Clark's history. He concentrates on the evocation of people, their value-systems, their environment and their perceptions of the period in which they lived. At one level, then, he is interested in the unique and the atypical, but by personifying the broader faiths and conflicts of each age he is also striving to posit connections between individuals and the larger questions of their day. A surface reading of Clark's history is sufficient to establish that his habitual mode of social theorizing is formist, but Clark is not content to limit himself to the mode of the chronicler. By fusing together the individual and the world-view Clark's history achieves a good deal more than run-of-the-mill formism. To understand how this works in practice, in the creation of his history, and to discern the ideological nature of his work, it is necessary to penetrate beneath the surface of his narrative.

Clark regards history as a branch of the arts and certainly his narrative exhibits a studied artistry. Perhaps the artistic activity most analogous to Clark's history-writing is musical composition, which relies largely upon the arrangement of sounds into themes and the juxtaposition of those themes into some overall pattern of harmonies and discordances. This partly explains the popularity of

Clark's history with the general reading public: changes in mood, rhythm and tempo punctuate the narrative, adding depth to the meaning of the story. Rapid, short sentences in one passage contrast with long, sombre descriptions in another; a staccato character-sketch of a governor is followed by a more leisurely narrative, then sometimes by a frenzied cacophony of argumentative sounds as the antagonists in the overheated penal colonies bicker and squabble, reaching either a sudden dénouement or a drawn-out coda. Clark's most important device in structuring his narrative is his use of the overture, usually at the beginning of a chapter:

> After 1800 the outlines of two societies began to take shape in the settlements of New South Wales. One drew its wealth from trade, the other from land and sheep. One laid the foundations of bourgeois society, the other created the ancient nobility of New South Wales. At the same time the Protestant ascendancy continued to dominate the civilization in the colony, despite some desparate and anguished protests from the Irish Catholics; the relations between Europeans and aborigines rushed headlong towards their final tragedy; new settlements were begun at Port Phillip and in Van Diemen's Land. All these tendencies were strengthened when Philip Gidley King was Captain-General and Governor-in-Chief of the colony of New South Wales.[13]

This overture foreshadows the main themes of the 'King, Flinders and Port Phillip' chapter. The last sentence enables Clark to proceed with the first theme of the chapter, biographical details of King, details which are in turn carefully chosen with a view to what King represents (the social group and set of ideas personified). The rest of the chapter follows fairly closely the pattern set out in the opening paragraph, taking up each of the themes of the overture in turn: King and his officers, European attitudes toward the Aborigines, Irish protests (especially the Castle Hill revolt), the exploratory voyages of Flinders, the attempted settlement of Port Phillip Bay and (next chapter) Van Diemen's Land.

Clark organizes his narrative into chapters along conventional lines, according to governorships, but there is no set pattern to the musical composition, as overtures are often replaced by climactic paragraphs which sum up at the end of a chapter. The themes of each chapter are expressed in separate groups of paragraphs, which are juxtaposed contrapuntally. Thus the Castle Hill rebellion represents the 'Protestant ascendancy' at its blackest in suppressing the Irish Catholics; directly following (despite the chronological inaccuracy) are the exploratory voyages of Flinders, to symbolize the scientific and material achievements of English civilization. Then the chapter closes, poignant once more, with the Port Phillip Bay débacle, without Clark needing to pass judgement directly on the Protestants. Far from exhibiting the randomness usually characteristic of empiricist historiography, Clark's narrative is tightly structured, his biographical portraits have a point, and the world-views of the period (Catholicism, Protestantism and the Enlightenment) are integrated into the social context.

It requires slow, careful reading of the text to ascertain the depth of Clark's ideological commitments. His anger at the treatment of the Aborigines, for example, cannot be discerned at the level of the text itself, because he uses contemporary accounts—often transposing whole sections of primary source-material into his own text—in order to let his characters speak for themselves; words like 'savages', 'lubra' and 'nigger' cannot be taken at face value. It is by his choice of timing in introducing the theme of injustice toward the Aborigines that Clark's attitude is revealed. By multiplying examples and by juxtaposing those examples alongside certain other themes he is able to build up a general picture of their treatment.[14] It is not a tale of uninterrupted despair, however, as some of these vignettes make clear. At least one group of newcomers was able to live with the natives during the 1820s:

> Early in 1826 there were upwards of two hundred people on Kangaroo Island who were about to elect their own king and pass their own laws. [At this sealing settlement] convict bolters compelled their women to hunt and fish while they sat on the beach and smoked and drank. They often flogged their women, finding that fun, too, and from time to time exchange their seal skins for food, grog and tobacco with parties from any trading vessel prepared to risk a visit to such desperadoes.

This is not Clark's observation of these people; it is taken from the *Hobart Town Gazette*. In the next paragraph an alternative point of view is presented, that of a French ship captain who visited Kangaroo Island six months later: 'He thought that the Aboriginal women found life with European men more pleasing than with the men of their own race because the Europeans had much more respect for them'.[15] This faint suggestion that leader-writers and journalists cannot always be relied upon, that the historian must look for conflicting accounts in order to get closer to his characters, is a hint that Clark believes the ship captain. Exceptional examples like this one are presented by Clark for the same reasons a composer alters the volume of his music:

they are diminuendos which accentuate what went before and what further barbarism lies ahead.

Few of Clark's reviewers have detected in his history this overall coherence, this notion that his narrative is tightly structured to produce a specific literary and ideological effect. The first volume of *A History of Australia* was published in 1962, and Clark was criticized trenchantly for empirical inaccuracy, gross imbalance in his selection of themes and for neglecting some important primary sources. The Malcolm Ellis review in the *Bulletin*, entitled 'History without facts', remains the most vituperative book review ever published in Australia. In his lengthy catalogue of factual errors Ellis found it impossible to mention any commendable aspect of the book:

> The First Fleet [according to Clark] sails out of Portsmouth Harbor— it was never in it. It sailed from the Motherbank off the Isle of Wight. The officers and marines landed in Sydney Cove and the Union Jack was hoisted there and toasts drank shortly after noon on January 26, 1788. Actually the landing was made early in the morning and the ceremony took place near sundown. D'Arcy Wentworth was *not* an ex-convict or a descendant of the Earl of Stafford . . .[16]

And so on, for two whole pages of the *Bulletin*. Other reviewers have been puzzled by the unobtrusive way in which Clark presents his themes. One reviewer of the second volume (1968) was left bewildered:

> There seems a discrepancy between the stated theme and the actual one followed in the text. The stated theme of the second volume is the movement of Australian history from darkness into light . . . The theme actually pursued throughout the book is the more well-worn one of the development of political and social groupings in the colonies, and the resulting conflicts between these groups and the governors.[17]

Yet part of the greatness of *A History of Australia* stems from the lack of direct authorial comment in the text. He is dealing with personalities, dates and events which are indeed quite well known, but there is a studied selectivity and arrangement of the 'facts'. The 'errors' which creep into the text are almost always of a mundane kind: in the fourth volume, for example, a check of some of Clark's sources (such as Dickens' *Household Words*) would show that page references are occasionally a page or two awry. But these slips pale beside the ability to weigh contemporary accounts and judge which one is the most reliable.

Above all, one must recognize the significance of Clark's use of formist conceptualization in the structuring of his narrative. He has come to emphasize two dimensions of history: the foreground actors, their ideas, values and activities; and how these historical characters reflect or respond to the broader aspects of the historical process, such as Catholicism, the physical environment, the Aboriginal way of life, secular humanism, and so on. Each of these world-views provides an answer to one of the questions which Clark sees as eternal: Is evil an innate human characteristic? Do changes in material circumstances affect men's consciousness? What is the best way for men to live? Under what sort of conditions do men and women live amicably? For Clark, history is partly the search for snatches of an answer to these moral issues. This aspect of his thinking is also apparent in his reviews of other historians' work: when reviewing Anne Summers' history of women in Australia, for example, he was looking for some personal insight, some guidance as to how men should behave towards women.[18] In the quest for such an understanding, for some transcendental morality, formism is a particularly suitable mode of theorizing: it brings into sharp focus how real men and women behaved toward one another, how one race treated another, how farmers and explorers perceived their physical environment, how Protestants treated Catholics. The faiths by which these people lived, their ambitions and beliefs, provide partial answers to these ethical problems, and, in turn, give the tolerant historian some way of understanding their motivations.

The flaw in such a model is Clark's reluctance to admit the validity of middle-ground processes. One important example of such a process is the Old Left concept of 'mateship'. On numerous occasions Clark questions the importance of 'mateship', sometimes by characterizing it as a 'comforter', sometimes by insisting that it no longer existed and sometimes by denying that it has ever existed at all, except in the minds of men like Lawson or Furphy. Patterns of class formation and the role of social institutions such as the family are some middle-ground processes which receive inadequate treatment in Clark's account. When Clark does draw reasonably explicitly on some model of social processes, he tends to rely on argument by repetition; he multiplies example upon example, and the result is a static understanding of the process in question. For example, in his chapter, 'Country gentlemen and bush barbarians', in the third volume,[19] Clark judiciously selects details of the rural social structure to depict how social relations were controlled by the gentry; but the processes by which they exercise this control are not elaborated and there is no prescriptive power in his description. Would these social relations remain frozen in the mould of the 1840s? What sociological factors operating within or without the rural setting would break up this status quo? This lack of a centre makes Clark appear sometimes Hegelian, sometimes vulgar marxist: the problem is most acute whenever he tries to explain the origins of a particular world view or the dialectic of ideas, and sometimes ideologies, in particular, are rather absurdly held invariant over time.

This problem should have increased rather than diminished in the third (1973) and fourth (1978) volumes, because Clark is here dealing with more densely populated periods of history: he has to cut short some of his biographical sketches in order to economize on room. But in these volumes he is more often the authorial voice stepping into the narrative to explain to the reader what is going on. This compromises his aim of letting the nineteenth century speak in its own terms and may explain why he has taken advantage of his retirement from teaching at the A.N.U. to commence a number of biographies. *In Search of Henry Lawson* was published in 1978 and two other biographies, of W. C. Wentworth and Sir Henry Parkes, are planned. The Lawson monograph concentrates on the man and his fiction and places little emphasis on his social context; it is therefore securely in the formist tradition, but free of the conservative ideological implication characteristic of most biography written in Australia. It takes Lawson's confused ideological vacillations seriously, attempting to locate them within the different steps of his perilous journey toward some understanding of himself and his fellows that he never finally reached.

It is Clark's two-sided perspicacity—the ability not only to evoke persons, places and periods but also to see into the hearts of men— which has attracted younger historians to his style of presenting history. Yet none of Clark's emulators have been able to match their mentor's skill.[20] Michael Roe's *Quest for Authority in Eastern Australia, 1835-1847* (Melbourne, 1965) traces out the pattern of ideological cross-currents in the late convict period, a theme which owes an obvious debt to Clark. Other historians have been influenced by Clark's work and have developed Catholic historiography (these include J. J. Eddie, J. N. Molony, T. L. Suttor and P. J. O'Farrell), not merely concentrating on a theme which is of interest to Clark but, more significantly, approaching it in a similar mode. Of these historians, P. J. O'Farrell, now professor of history at the University of New South Wales, has been most concerned to ponder the theoretical issues involved in choosing to concentrate on religious history, asking questions which Manning Clark has not always directly raised, such as: Is the believer likely to be a better religious historian? Is it possible or even desirable for such an historian to judge the success of the churches in what is, after all, their fundamental task, namely, the salvation of souls? Why have so few historians in Australia taken up religious themes? In a paper published in 1977, O'Farrell tentatively suggested an answer to the last question: '. . . my arguments are related to the judgement that a large section of the profession is effectively dehumanized, either by deliberate choice or lack of developed capacity in its approach to the discipline . . .', and echoing Manning Clark, he continued: 'We are obsessed with technique, grossly negligent of the need to understand the character of the fundamental datum of history, the living human being'.[21]

Neither Roe nor this group of Catholic historians have attempted a large-scale history of Australia which would equal the breadth of Clark's endeavour. Perhaps the only general history yet published which takes Clark's approach as its model is a one-volume history by John Ritchie, *Australia As Once We Were*. Ritchie's work is avowedly conservative in spirit and also differs from Clark's approach to the extent that it implies complacent answers to 'the great questions of mind and spirit'. Such a book both highlights by contrast the libertarian open-mindedness, even anarchism, of Clark's kaleidoscopic ideological position (and that of many of his emulators), and emphasizes that the characteristic outlook of most formist practitioners in Australia has been an underdeveloped conservatism.

Empiricist conservatives

In May 1978 a controversy about Clark's history erupted in a number of Australian newspapers. The attacks made on him reflected some of the dominant preoccupations of a group of historians who constitute a school in the sense that they share certain attributes, but who have not recognized themselves as anything beyond 'research historians'. The controversy brought their shared assumptions about the purpose and method of historical investigation into sharper focus, and for this reason alone is worth examining in some detail, for the criticisms levelled at Clark by representatives of this school suggest some of the defining qualities of the 'empiricist conservatives'.

The attack on Clark began with an article in the *Townsville Daily Bulletin* written by Colin Roderick, emeritus professor of English at James Cook University, Queensland. Roderick contended that Clark's biography of Henry Lawson was 'a tangled thicket of factual error, speculation and ideological interpretation'. These comments, and the subsequent flurry of letters, articles and cartoons, were carried in the *Sydney Morning Herald*, the Melbourne *Age* and the *Australian*.[22] Most professional historians who publicly joined in the debate defended Clark's history, but those who supported Roderick's attack —in tea-room conversation or in letters to the editor—took up and elaborated Roderick's three central points, which are all mirror-reflections of the empiricist standpoint. 'Factual error' is a grievous crime for the empiricists because their history attempts to establish the primacy of 'facts' in understanding the past. 'Speculation' is also a cardinal sin, for it challenges their view that history should be written only on the basis of what is known and verifiable, to which the label of 'a fact' can be attached. 'Ideological interpretation' is a third major fault, for it challenges one of their basic assumptions, namely that on the basis of strict adherence to known 'facts' history can be ideologically neutral. Clark became the object of their vilification both in 1978 and in 1962 (when Ellis reviewed the first volume of *A History of Australia*) not only because of his prestigious reputation among Australian historians but also because his formist approach to history made him more vulnerable to this sort of criticism than historians employing one of the other three modes.

There is, then, a fundamental similarity of approach between Clark and the empiricists. They agree that history should concentrate on the unique and the particular, that the historian should attempt to evoke a person, a period, a place. But for Clark there are no such things as independent 'facts'. The empiricists take the opposite viewpoint and this is the first defining feature of the usual empiricist strategy for writing history. Their two other contentions, that 'facts' alone constitute the proper foundation of history-writing and that historians ought to be ideologically neutral, are intimately connected to this first basic assumption.

Just as many other features of Australian history-writing owe their origin to English and American historiographical trends, there is nothing peculiarly Australian about empiricism. But its specific flourish in Australian history-writing appears to date from the post-war expansion of university history departments and the growing importance of higher degree research. It would be difficult to name more than a couple of historians in the inter-war period who were as strongly empiricist as are some of the contemporary representatives of this view of history. From the many recent academic historians who can be shown to employ an essentially empiricist approach, four may be singled out for detailed scrutiny: A. T. Yarwood, L. L. Robson, B. K. de Garis and W. F. Mandle. These men teach in four different universities—New England, Melbourne, Western Australia and the A.N.U. respectively—and come from a range of backgrounds. They all began their research work for higher degrees in the late 1950s and early 1960s and went through the socialization process that often daunts the postgraduate student:

> The perpetual threat of having to satisfy at least two of the three different examiners, whose general views may clash, results in writing innocuous stuff (i.e. moderation, detachment). Interests in turn become more and more narrow in an effort to achieve a situation where you have a more detailed knowledge of your subject than your examiner . . . Most [postgraduates] accept that precision, moderation and detachment are scholarship, and for the rest of their learned lives avoid saying anything.[23]

This is not the opinion of an empiricist conservative. Yarwood explains his experience in different terms:

> Writers of academic theses experience anxiety from the moment they decide upon a general area of study until they define its limits. Particularly when there is a time limit for completion of the thesis, there is an urgent need to choose a subject which is manageable and fairly compact. Chronological limits should not be too wide, nor should the issues or problems be cosmic in scope. If we wish to extend the frontiers of historical knowledge, we need to find what work has already been done, in order to hit upon a period, or an aspect of a question which has been unexplored.[24]

Yarwood's justification seems, on the fact of it, quite unexceptional: historical knowledge can certainly give the appearance of advancing territorially with thesis-writers on the frontier. But this is only one possible way of explaining the advance of historical knowledge among many. It is the metaphoric equivalent of the suburban quarter-acre block. It assumes that the growth of historical knowledge is analogous to the steady subdivision of a large city, expanding outwards in small increments as each generation of home-builders searches for unsettled building blocks which might be theirs to occupy. The grand themes and high-flying generalizations are sky-scrapers or high-rise apartment blocks which have no place in the suburbs. 'The historian's great challenge [sic] is to recreate and interpret from surviving evidence the actions, ideals and motives of the people of a past age', according to Yarwood.[25] It might appear as though this definition of the historian's purpose is modelled on Clark's history, but, to the extent that it supposes that Clark is simply engaged in compressing a series of biographical vignettes into the compass of a general history, it produces a different form of history.

Biography is a favorite genre of the empiricist, for it enables him to imagine a topic of history where the 'facts' indeed are paramount and it seems possible to marshal all the evidence together to form a coherent whole. In an article outlining his plans for his biography of the Reverend Samuel Marsden, for example, Yarwood defined what he saw as the important elements of biography:

> Biography involves five basic processes: the evocation of a past age; the narration of events; the interpretation of the subject's motives; the judgement of his character; and the assessment of his role and impact.[26]

The background which the biographer must understand is determined, argues Yarwood, by the subject of the biography himself; to understand Marsden, 'a solid grounding in eighteenth and nineteenth-century religious history' is necessary, as well as an understanding of many other themes which he lists in detail. Among these is 'the question of Catholic toleration'; Clark had approached this theme with deadpan seriousness, but a note of sarcasm enters Yarwood's description:

> The glorious balance and good sense of the British constitution and the Established Church were measured against the ignorance and poverty of the Irish Papists, the bloody insecurity of Napoleon's Europe and the obscurantism and cruelty of a church which still tortured heretics.[27]

Only themes of European history directly relevant to Marsden's background are seen as important. The 'spirit of the age' is a rather vacuous concept unless it can be related directly to the values and motives of the individual whose life is the subject of the biography.

This suggests the initial empiricist proposition, namely, that the 'facts' of history are parmount. A person's background must be seen in terms of its particularity, and only 'facts' can serve to build the bridges between his life and his times. It is this subsequent step of logic which demarcates between empiricism proper and the type of history proffered by Clark and other historians. Clark had been something of a paragon for the empiricists in the 1950s, but his role as a symbol of the validity of their enterprise diminished during the 1960s as his *History* began to shape up along different lines. It was the younger Clark, who produced *Select Documents in Australian History* in the 1950s, who most excited these men. Yarwood, seeking to isolate a thesis topic, turned to *Select Documents* and found his 'inspiration' in Clark's treatment of the theme of race relations.[28] *Asian Migration to Australia* was the eventual product of this

research. Similarly, Frank Crowley, who during the 1950s was an
empiricist, but whose subsequent work allows him to be categorized
as a 'syncretic conservative'—a development which will be examined
later—was greatly influenced by Clark: indeed, he was Clark's first
M.A. student.

L. L. Robson also came into contact with Clark, while working on his
doctorate at the A.N.U. in the early 1960s. His thesis, which was
published as *The Convict Settlers* in 1965, was a study of the convicts
transported to Eastern Australia in the early period, which relied on
detailed statistical analysis. Robson's motivation for pursuing this
topic was his dissatisfaction with the generalizations propounded
about the convicts by earlier generations of Australian historians,
Clark included, and his belief that thorough quantificatory techniques
would produce more meaningful generalizations. This interest in
quantification is a marked feature of the empiricist style and is shared
by B. K. de Garis in his study of the transition toward party politics
in Western Australia at the turn of the century.[29] Robson and de
Garis contend that before one can generalize about the past one
should begin with a thorough understanding of all the relevant
'facts', 'facts' such as the known attributes of convicts—their sex,
age, place of origin, nature of criminal offence—or the parliamentary
voting patterns of Western Australian politicians. It is this concern
with the primacy of 'facts' that provides the first defining characteristic of the empiricist historian, and suggests why they were among
the first Australian historians to appreciate the importance of quantificatory techniques.

So Roderick's claim that Clark's biography of Lawson was vitiated
by 'factual error' is, for the empiricists, a savage comment. His
second criticism—that the Lawson book was full of 'speculation'—
also contravenes an important empiricist tenet, for these historians
not only insist that historical inquiry must begin with the known
facts but are loath to make any statement which does not have an
irrefutable 'fact' behind it. The underlying rationale here is that the
past is revealed by 'facts', that the historian's job is to arrange
those 'facts' in some order and sequence, and that where there are
no surviving records the historian should not speculate about them—
'facts' should not be 'invented' by the historian. The degree of uncertainty is thereby reduced: no leaps of faith are ever required. Only
'facts' provide the basis of generalizations: reconstructions of the past
before the 'facts' are understood are by their very nature fallacious.
This antipathy towards premature 'theorizing' is at the heart of
empiricism.

In common parlance empiricism usually means that real knowledge

is based on experience; in historical inquiry it means that only knowledge based on verifiable 'facts' is to be trusted. The older historian
can therefore ordinarily write better history because he has had more
time to research the 'facts' and because he is more 'mature'. This
belief accounts for the common empiricist claim that biography should
be the province of the older historians: they can bring to the study
of another individual's experiences the benefit of their own experiences; they are much better equipped than the younger historian
to 'understand' or to 'empathize' with the subject of the biography.

As Stretton would argue, extreme empiricism can lead to excessive
trivialization of history, for what can be said without speculation of
any kind is always miniscule in significance.[30] But even where the
empiricists embark on reasonably ambitious projects they are limited
in their endeavours precisely because of their unwarranted trust
in 'facts'. Whenever there are 'errors' in the status of the facts
themselves rather than, say, inconsistencies between different
'facts', the empiricists are surprisingly oblivious to them. The facts
of history do not merely help explain the past; they were created
by it. By asserting the primacy of 'facts', and the necessity to avoid
excessive speculation by strict adherence to the factual record, the
empiricists can often find it difficult to escape from their thickets of
facts. Two examples of this tendency may be given: Robson's use of
statistical analysis in *The Convict Settlers,* and Yarwood's comments
on the usefulness of the *Sydney Gazette* as source-material for his
biography of Samuel Marsden.

In his research for *The Convict Settlers*, Robson took a statistical
sample of the known 'facts' about the transportees and, with the
aid of a computer, he was able to produce quantitative statements
about their ages, the ratio between male and female convicts, the
exact location of these people in various parts of the United Kingdom
at the time of their arrest, a detailed analysis of their crimes, and so
on. The generalizations thus produced were, to his mind, quite
factually correct:

> There's a sort of beauty about mathematics and the procedures . . .
> You can see something working out in front of you, and you can be
> pretty sure that what you've got is basically—I won't say
> unassailable—[but] if your methodology is correct, it's very difficult to
> go wrong in a sense . . .[31]

This was certainly the case with *The Convict Settlers* up to a point,
for Robson was indeed able to establish certain generalizations which
challenged earlier theories about the convicts. He not only took
convict women more seriously than earlier historians, for example,

but was able to show that only one-fifth of them had originally been convicted of prostitution, a conclusion which immediately cast doubt on the hoary myth that the convict women were habitually 'immoral'. Other historians would have challenged this myth in a completely different way. They would have accepted that the crimes committed by these women and men did indeed occur, and that the punishments meted out to the convicts are also indisputable facts of history. But then they would have asked how these crimes and punishments were defined by the English legislators and what legal theory underpinned the definitions. Then the ideology of the British government of that period would have been more seriously scrutinized. Instead Robson states that his purpose was to ignore these questions:

> Anyone who is bold enough to generalize about why 150,000 people committed crimes is asking for trouble but the great object of drawing the sample was to base speculation firmly on facts, to show what did in fact occur, and not what someone said was supposed to occur, to set the record straight, and reduce levels of generality as much as possible.[32]

Here in crystalline form is the empiricist obsession with 'facts', the desire to narrow the field of study down so sharply as to permit low-level generalization, and the marked distrust for 'ideas' ('what someone said was supposed to occur'): Robson finds it 'tempting to laugh at nineteenth-century ideas that offences were caused by 'moral destitution' . . . '[33]

Similarly, Yarwood's attitude to primary source-material is equally empiricist. In his article 'Writing an ecclesiastical biography' he describes sources for his biography of Marsden and contends that the *Sydney Gazette* 'conveys the texture and spirit of the times [1804 – 1838] more vividly and comprehensively than any other single source'.[34] This is an absolutely extraordinary claim. The *Sydney Gazette* conveys very little more than the news and advertisements of interest to the literate minority: for the historian using it as a source it does not even contain much information about the activities and ideas of the women within that elite; even its jokes deride women, which suggests that the humorous sections were masculine views of the world. Perhaps what Yarwood really meant by his remark is that the *Sydney Gazette* contains more 'facts' for the historian than any other single source of the period—since it was the only colonial newspaper until the mid-1820s this is hardly surprising. But none of the 'facts' printed in the *Sydney Gazette* can be accepted without a recognizing the selective nature of what the *Sydney Gazette* regarded as newsworthy.

The third defining feature of the empiricist school is also vulnerable to criticism. Roderick criticized Clark's biography of Lawson for its 'ideological interpretation' because it contravened one of the empiricists' cardinal tenets: that it is possible to write ideologically neutral history. This can be achieved by testing the veracity of each 'fact', relating them to one another without excessive speculation and drawing only such conclusions as can be reasonably deduced. Such professed neutrality is, in fact, a form of conservatism, as a number of social scientists have argued. Perhaps the most cogent of these arguments is that put forward by Hugh Stretton in *The Political Sciences* which, amongst other things, amplifies the pithy dictum attributed to George Orwell that not to commit oneself politically is in itself a political act.[35] But the more immediate questions are how does this conservative ideological position flow from the empiricist preoccupation with 'facts' and how does it limit their understanding of the past?

In propounding the importance of 'facts' the empiricists are prone to be cynical about ideas, because these are not 'hard fact'. They tend to regard their subjects' values and ideas either as unnecessarily over-complicated or, sometimes, as mere rhetoric which must be 'stripped away' so that the 'facts' might be laid bare. Ideas are not the stuff of history; they are 'soft facts', or, in Robson's words, 'what someone said was supposed to occur'. This distrust of concepts and ideas has at least three consequences in most empiricist scholar-ship: the ideas held by historical actors can never be regarded as a significant explanatory factor; theories of why something happened must be suspended until all the 'facts' of the situation are known; and the conservative implication of empiricist history comes to be regarded as neutral scholarship. Each of these three consequences will be discussed in turn.

An example of the first consequence has already been cited: Yar-wood's sarcastic reference to the 'glorious balance and good sense of the British constitution and the Established Church'. It might cer-tainly be 'tempting to laugh', in Robson's words, at such bigotry, but the historian presumably has to take all ideas seriously, to explain how they arose, and to explain how they affected people's behaviour. There is almost a note of approval in Yarwood's description of Marsden subscribing to 'no nonsense' about 'the noble savage' in his estimation of the Aborigines and the Polynesians.[36] But approval or disapproval is, strictly speaking, irrelevant: the historian must understand the values and beliefs of his characters in order to under-stand their motivations. Without this, history is robbed of any motivating force. Robson, for example, finds it difficult to accept that there has ever existed a 'labour movement' in Australia.[37] This contention may sound odd, but it follows on quite logically from empiricist logic: if the labour leaders' speeches and pamphlets advocating 'brotherhood' and 'solidarity' are regarded as mere rhetoric, then the notion of a 'labour movement' is an empty one. B. K. de Garis makes a similar point, by implication, in an article describing the Fremantle disturbance of 1919.[38] A mob gathered in protest at the employment of non-union labour on the wharves, shots were fired and one man was killed. For many Western Australians this was a 'riot', a demonstration of working-class 'solidarity' in the face of conservative opposition; for de Garis, once the rhetoric has been peeled away, it is a mere 'incident'. He uses police and newspaper reports to demythologize the event, omitting, for example, the autobiographical account Xavier Herbert gives in *Disturbing Element,* which de Garis would no doubt regard as an embellishment long after the event. Herbert's story is almost certainly factually 'incorrect'—but it serves to reflect the mythic power of the event for later generations, a not inconsiderable 'fact'.

The empiricists also exhibit discomfort whenever they attempt to introduce the theoretical insights of other academic disciplines in order to make sense of the data they have diligently collected and assembled. Theory, especially for Robson in the case of *The Convict Settlers,* is something which can be turned to for guidance only after all the available 'facts' about the convicts are known and tabulated. The final chapter of the book is a wild pursuit of various types of theory, a breathless long-distance run through the fields of psychiatry, sociology and criminology. Robson does not appear to see that these theoretical constructions are not 'givens' which can be applied to his facts at whim, but are themselves the intellectual products of their time and culture. This is nowhere more evident than in his discussion of the family life of the criminals.[39] It is rather hopeful to expect twentieth-century models produced from the experience of middle-class North American sociologists to explain much about the late eighteenth-century kinship patterns of London criminals. (It might have been more helpful to read John Gay's *The Beggar's Opera.*)

Few conservative intellectuals in Australia have openly declared their ideological standpoint. But if historians like Yarwood, de Garis and Robson are professed neutral observers of the Australian past, their critics are vociferous in their condemnation of empiricist history. This condemnation was taken to excessively dualistic lengths in the late 1960s by the New Left. For example, a leading historian of the British New Left argued a thesis which his Australian counterparts also subscribed to:

... historians have been particularly prone to the empiricist delusion that the data they use are the sole basis of the generalizations they deduce. The task of producing the concepts adequate to historical explanation is abandoned in favour of the deceptive obviousness of chronological succession.[40]

Part of the purpose of the present discussion has been to imply that such a dichotomy between 'empiricist' historians and those who explicitly advocate the use of theoretical concepts is summarily over-simplified. Instead the term 'empiricist' should be reserved for those, like Yarwood, de Garis and Robson, who combine a formist pre-occupation with the evocation of particular persons and periods with an ideologically conservative world-view.

It is, as an American critic recently observed, impossible to demarcate rigidly between theoretical and non-theoretical or empiricist history:

> ... even empiricism is a theory and the exercise of a model, and ... even the plainest unreflective history—the sheerest, most 'mindless' enumeration of 'facts' of annals or a chronicle—implies a whole metaphysic and constitutes through its mere enunciation a whole philosophy of history in its own right.[41]

But the conservative empiricists in Australia do not explicitly espouse the view of history implicit in their work. Instead, as one of Manning Clark's defenders in the Roderick controversy pointed out, they remain nit-pickers:

> Those who defend the more conservative traditions of historiography can afford ... to quibble over the minutiae of historical 'facts'. Their whole perspective on historiography is such that their work appears to be largely concerned with the mere presentation of 'facts' whilst interpretation, or in Roderick's view speculation, performs only a minor role. When history is *written* as if the status quo is unchanging it appears 'natural' to all who *act* as if the status quo is unchanging.[42]

This reluctance of the conservatives to proclaim the intent of their history may be changing. In his introduction to *Going It Alone* W. F. Mandle stated his position frankly:

> I am not, as will become clear, an historian of the left ... Conservative history in Australia has not flourished, despite the asserted individualism of its people. I do not lay claim to be a revisionist, or to be deliberately setting out to redress a balance in Australian historiography. My approach springs, as all historians' approaches

must, from my own beliefs. The conservative historian has his
principles no less than does the radical.[43]

Mandle's book is empiricist, but it can also be categorized as 'syncretic'. It is empiricist in the sense that it provides an episodic treatment of twentieth-century Australian history: Mandle selects ten
topics, ranging chronologically from the battle of Pozières and the
1916-1917 conscription controversy to the Poseidon boom of 1969-1970,
and examines the 'facts' of each case. Liké other empiricists he
attempts to cut through the mythologies surrounding various events,
such as the deaths of boxer Les Darcy and Phar Lap in the
U.S., to get at the real truth.[44] But the book is also 'syncretic' in the
sense that its ten separate vignettes of twentieth-century Australia
are linked together by the deduced theme of nationalism: each topic
mirrors some aspect of this search for an Australian identity. The
result somewhat approximates the vision of Australian nationalism
enunciated by the Old Left historians, especially Russel Ward;[45]
but Mandle's approach is markedly different: his book reveals the
transition from empiricism proper to a higher order of conservative
history, the 'syncretic' organicism, which characterizes the work of
historians such as N. B. Nairn, F. K. Crowley and A. G. L. Shaw.
This version of conservative history is the subject of the first half of
the next chapter.

4   History as a circular argument

4 History as a circular argument

Syncretic historians

> The Australian story is something like a fun-fair. The same things happen again and again. Ferris wheels go round and round, hurdy-gurdies grind out the same tunes, swings and see-saws move up and down. Everyone appears to have something to spend. Worries are left behind and troubles are forgotten. People press from one sideshow to another eager to sample everything. The biggest crowds throng around the lucky dips where anyone may draw a winning ticket. From outside the scene appears featureless and dull. The shouts and laughter are too carefree and light-hearted. Apart from the showmen no one seems more important than anyone else. What is the purpose of it all? How can a fun-fair give a young nation an inspiring history?[1]

This description of the Australian past was written in 1962 by the late Douglas Pike, formerly professor of history at the University of Tasmania. He was not arguing that all Australian history should be seen in these terms. Further comments in the same chapter—the final chapter of a general history of Australia, with the provocative title *Australia: The Quiet Continent*—make it clear that Pike believed that the metaphor of a fun-fair could be used to illuminate Australian history only from about the 1880s onwards. There had been colour and excitement in the story of the early pioneers, and in the lives of the restless frontiersmen who opened up the outback, but by the 1880s a pattern had emerged which would have been immediately familiar to his readers in the 1960s. The labour movement, partly nurtured by this bush environment, had put an end to the 'self-dependence' of the sturdy yeoman by casting its fortune with the interests of capital; the ideas and visions of the local cultural elites were beginning to take on an Australian flavour (although the intellectuals were unable to wean the great majority of their readership away from the traditional notions derived from their British ancestry); and by the late nineteenth century it had become clear that sport was one of the few areas where Australians had a distinctive contribution to make. Moreover, amidst the noise and hubbub of the fun-fair, only the leaders stood out from the crowd. [2]

Pike's history is an example of organicist history, and, within this category, it is syncretic. Organicists, unlike formists, do not view historical events as unrelated to one another: they seek to establish connections between events, persons and ideas. But they do not establish these connections by positing causal links—as a mechanist would—nor by employing the contextualist strategy of locating historical events within their period or social context. Instead they organize their history around a specific theme, which assumes greater significance than its constituent parts. This theme may be something like 'progress', 'community' or 'plenitude'; and since it might be used to crystallize any number of themes or events, there is a real danger that the historical argument will become circular. Syncretism is a type of organicism which fuses together a cluster of themes to produce this effect. Syncretic historians in Australia have typically concentrated on one or more of the four themes mentioned by Pike in 1962: the symbiotic relation between capital and labour, the irrelevance of high culture for most Australians, the importance of sport and the continued dominance of the political elite—weaving them into an organicist account of the Australian past. Underpinning their history is the intractable assumption that the story of Australia is best seen as a merry-go-round, set in motion at some point in the past. Some other historians who emplicitly employ this motif are F. K. Crowley, A. G. L. Shaw, N. B. Nairn, Bruce Mitchell and Michael Cannon. In his preface to *Australia in the Victorian Age,* Cannon takes this essential circularity of history to its logical endpoint: 'It is chastening', he comments, 'to see how many topics are merely nineteenth-century mutton dressed up as twentieth-century lamb'. [3] Built into this view of history is a conservative prognostication about the impossibility of substantive changes in the social ordering of Australian life. At some point in the past, organicist historians would argue, the essential features of Australian society were set; there has been no fundamental change in the underlying nature of that society since then: any apparent changes are part of the working out of a logic in social relations, established by the experience (usually) of mid or late last century. This conception produces a history which is hung on one theme, and flattens out difference, conflict and antagonism. Viewing history in these terms can only lead to two responses in the heart of the author: a sense of passive acceptance and positive endorsement (the conservative position), or a sense of alienation and the desire to escape the forces which hold Australian society in a unidirectional trajectory. This second response is primarily anarchistic, and is most thoroughly worked out in Australian historiography in the work of the feminist historians.

As the second half of the chapter will demonstrate, the leading feminist historians share the syncretic conservatives' circular view of history, for they too see Australian history as a merry-go-round. They believe that the conditions which determine women's role in Australian history were set in motion at least three generations ago. Anne Summers, for example, argues that the sex-role stereotypes of 'damned whores' and 'God's police' were fully operative late in the nineteenth century, and have continued to oppress Australian women ever since. Miriam Dixson's *The Real Matilda* purportedly covers the period 1788 to 1975, but the narrative ends at about Federation; the twentieth century is simply a postscript to the more formative years of the previous century. It would be difficult to imagine two groups of historians more ideologically and thematically distinct than the feminists and the syncretic historians, but both schools draw upon the image of Australian history as a merry-go-round. The difference between them is that for the feminists the merry-go-round is a joy-ride which women should get off.

The syncretic historians do not exhort their readers to jump off the merry-go-round. Their ideological stance is similar to that of the empiricists, and their history can be considered as a higher stage of empiricism proper. W. F. Mandle's *Going it Alone* represents a half-way transition toward syncretism: it is topical and concentrates on unique events of the twentieth century; but it is also thematic in its identification of a movement toward nationalism as the dominating motif of more recent Australian history.[4] Fully-fledged syncretic historians organize their narrative around such a dominating motif, and the details they select from the past are incorporated in it to the extent that their history circulates around one point rather than moving in any particular direction. Some vulgar marxist history resembles this description. When crude marxists contend that all history is the history of class struggle their argument is also circular, because every aspect of human existence is seen as revolving around this one proposition. Such history also assumes a definite end towards which all history is moving. Circularity and teleology are marked features of organicist strategies, but seldom have the leading Australian marxist historians written other than contextualist or mechanistic narratives. Organicist histories are more commonly written by conservatives. N. B. Nairn's history is a good example of this. In a series of articles, and in *Civilising Capitalism*, Nairn has argued that the role of the organized working class has been to tame the worst aspects of capitalism, rather than to confront it directly with the intention of overthrowing it; and that this state of affairs (which promotes J. C. Watson to the status of hero and denigrates W. G. Spence) is a desirable one.[5] This line of argument is a straightforward example of conservative organicism, for it postulates a symbiotic relationship between labour and capital: the two can grow together amicably for the general good. Nairn and some other syncretic historians emphasize the relationship between labour and capital, but this need not be the central theme of a syncretic history: other conservative organicists treat different themes as fundamental to explaining the merry-go-round. Nor is the ideological implication always so explicit.

Nairn's ideological position is more sharply expressed than that of A. G. L. Shaw, Michael Cannon and Bruce Mitchell, all of whom strive for a kind of neutral agnosticism. Shaw is the best example of the conservative as sceptic, in books such as *The Story of Australia* and *Convicts and the Colonies*. He is self-proclaimedly apolitical, and prefers not to be seen to be attached to any one political party, religious cause or school of history. He comments:

> I think once you commit yourself to a school . . . you look at everything from that point of view. Well, what I like to do is get people looking at things . . . I would find a Catholic historian or a New Left historian and a Liberal and a Labor and a marxist—you name it—and nearly all of them will say something to me that I think would be useful. Nearly all . . . and I suppose you then get a sort of eclectric picture.[6]

A similar eclecticism is advanced by Michael Cannon, who has recently completed his three-volume series, *Australia in the Victorian Age*. Unlike Geoffrey Serle, who has written two monographs of Victorian history in the same period, Cannon makes some attempt at explicit class categorization.[7] He organizes his narrative into chapters which deal with the 'working class' and the 'middle class', but uses these only as organizing categories within which to structure his vivid descriptions of nineteenth-century life in Australia. Cannon has an ex-journalist's eye for the telling detail, and his histories capture vividly the sights, sounds and smells of 'glorious Smelbourne'. But he does not look for a pattern which would explain how these marked differences of lifestyle came to exist and continue to change over time: they are thus reduced to static categories which the reader must presume will continue as such into the twentieth century.

The same implication is evident in syncretic school-texts. One of the first of these was Bruce Mitchell's *The Australian Story and Its Background,* an interesting text for at least two reasons. Mitchell attempted to move beyond earlier interpretations of Australian history, by paying much more attention to the condition of the working class and the role of the State in political struggles than had been the case with earlier school-texts. He also introduced what were then, in 1965, relatively new aspects of the fabric of Australian history: the development of housing, the relation between local and national history, and sub-themes such as the history of the press. These fresh themes, however, were not very well integrated with the rest of the book and its overall structure. For example, 'How a free press was won' sits uneasily towards the end of a concluding chapter on the old subject of constitutional development: after discussing the early newspapers and Forbes' decision to permit freedom of the press, Mitchell abruptly cuts the story short, taking refuge in a few platitudes about the 'rights and responsibilities' of the mass media.[8] Similarly, the chapter on 'Changes in housing' deals merely with changing architectural styles, and shies clear from suggesting connections between these and the development of the nuclear family, the building industry and the class structure, as other historians might have done.[9] Finally, Mitchell's chapter on 'Local history and the growth of Sydney' represents a brave attempt to establish the connections between local, state and federal history; but rather than attempting even the most elementary analysis of the dynamics of the city or its regional stratification, Mitchell concerns himself only with discussing the city's infrastructure, its transport system, water supply, drainage and so on. Mitchell's assumption that twentieth-century Australia has been reasonably egalitarian is the critical one for understanding how he treats the larger themes of the book: the condition of the working class and the role of the State in political struggles. Interestingly, Mitchell devotes chapter 4 in its entirety to economic changes in nineteenth-century Britain, then two chapters to parallel changes in Australia; chapter 8 to the condition of the British working class and chapter 9 to 'Workers and the State in Australia'. It might be argued that this is a rather excessive emphasis on the British background, but it is even more pertinent to suggest that the separation of economic development from the conditions of the workers is a rather unreal one, which mystifies the way in which working class political struggle stems from the conditions of work experience. It also leaves Mitchell with very little room to explore the development of these themes in the present century. He justifies this with the contention that all the ground rules for the conflict between capital and labor were set in the later part of the nineteenth century, then meekly admits that there have been such social groups as the Wobblies and the Communist Party in more recent times, and that inflation and the increasing automation of industry also affect the pattern.[10] The reader can only conclude that the events at Barcaldine in 1891, and Broken Hill in 1892, and the Factory Acts and Arbitration legislation, have led to an equilibrium, based on an irresolvable conflict of interests, which divests Australian history of any real dynamic.

Another popular textbook, published two years later and concentrating solely on the present century, is far more explicit in its portrayal of recent and contemporary history as humdrum, bland and uncontroversial. A. G. L. Shaw and H. D. Nicolson's *Australia in the Twentieth Century* is perhaps the most persuasive secondary-school textbook written from the syncretic conservative viewpoint. It is crammed full of empiricist bits and pieces; besides a main text running to fifteen chapters, Shaw and Nicolson included a note on the use of illustrations as historical evidence, twenty-eight line drawings, two appendices, fifty-nine photographs, an epilogue on Canberra, eight biographies of prominent Australian men and three time-lines. Like most other syncretic historians, however, the authors emphasize the overt political processes, and this emphasis determines the treatment of topics ranging from foreign affairs and economic depression to involvement in the wars and state-federal relations. The authors' justification for this is given at the beginning of chapter 3: 'The Federal Government has to discover and regulate the pace and direction of development so as to satisfy public opinion which can show itself at election times'.[11] No attempt is made to define 'public opinion', nor is any effort made to consider whether crucial instances of its exercise, such as the Petrov affair, may have been open to manipulation. Instead there is a calm assurance that the Australian people are always moderate and sceptical of any -ism; religion, ideology and 'high culture' are notably absent from the volume, save for a biography of William Dobell which gives the authors an opportunity to deny the force of ideas in Australian history:

> Norman Lindsay and his friends painted pictures with innumerable naked mythological and human creatures in an effort to shock Australians out of their provincialism. But his hundreds of naked nymphs could not fill the vast empty spaces of Streeton's purple valleys or persuade Australians not to take their art seriously. Even the lighter-hearted beach-side Australians did not recognize themselves in Lindsay's fancy dress.[12]

According to this reading of their history, Australians have never been moved in the twentieth century to ask the larger questions, nor has their society been anything but stable. (Part of this is an argument by comparison: stresses and strains in other countries are observed, to such an extent that Australia is made to appear almost entirely devoid of conflict.) At each and every critical juncture, few Australians are immoderate or raise their heads from the pursuit of the humdrum. At the end of the First World War:

> Wounded soldiers, delayed marriages, new motor-cars, the influenza plague, money and the future—such were the concerns of many at the dawn of the twenty years' peace.[13]

Again, during the 'jazz age',

> though the 'fast set' of the 'twenties with their cocktails, fox-trots, movies and speed liked to think of themselves as typical of their age, most people were neither 'fast' nor 'wowsers' and laughed at the extremes.[14]

At the height of the Depression, some people formed a:

> 'New Guard', ready by physical protection to defeat the designs of revolutionaries and disloyalists'. All this agitation might have caused rioting and fighting, but it was not necessary. No one wanted a revolution.[15]

Australians at that time were much more concerned with cricket.[16]

The same image continues even into the 1960s, at the time of writing:

> The daily life of the average Australian of the 1960s would be well understood by those who worked in the 1920s, as they lived in the same sort of houses, and enjoyed the same sort of pleasures. Most Australians paid only passing regard to the fact that science and technology provided great abundance after than before World War II, though some found a very great difference in their daily work.[17]

Shaw and Nicolson are not only unmoved by the passions and excitements of twentieth-century Australian history, but also have an agnostic eye for the irony to be found in what others see as major events. For example, at the close of their description of the proclamation of the Constitution, in Sydney's Centennial Park on 1 January 1901, they record that:

> the ministers took their oaths, the 'Te Deum' was sung, and the official party left. Then a sudden storm brought rain, and the crowds

rushed to get away. There was quite a crush and many children's good new clothes were ruined.[18]

Similarly, Shaw and Nicolson's account of Gallipoli is far more prosaic than that of most Australian historians; they also give credit to the strategic skill of the Turkish commander, Kemal Ataturk—whom earlier textbook writers had not even mentioned.[19] Another consequence of this theme of the humdrum is that Shaw and Nicolson state their doubts as to whether many Australians are interested enough in politics even to know the parliamentarians,[20] a contention which raises one critical question about their social theory. If, as they suggest, Australian history should be understood primarily through the formal political processes, how can this approach enable the historian to understand the deeper trends of a society which is professedly apolitical?

A general difficulty with the syncretic approach arises at this point, for it becomes plain that such a concentration on the underlying harmony of Australian history, which flows perfectly logically from the intrinsic assumptions of syncretic historians, occasionally leads to patently erroneous conclusions:

> There has been little racial feeling as such in Australia. Most Australians were delighted at the success of Aborigines where they have done well as soldiers, sportsmen or, occasionally, in the professions; but in some towns there has been opposition to Aborigines moving into houses in certain districts, or to their using the local swimming-pool.[21]

The syncretic historians are so concerned to establish the naturalness and self-regulation of Australian society that they are caught flat-footed whenever they seek to explain away apparent abberrations such as racism.

The syncretic historians understand the Australian past as dominated by one set of mutually interacting social processes which follow on naturally and logically from conditions in the late nineteenth century. They have emphasized four stock themes which tend towards reducing history to a circular argument. All of these themes may be detected in the work of Nairn, Shaw, Cannon, Pike, Mitchell and Mandle. They are brought together in their most highly articulated form in the work of F. K. Crowley.

A few details of Crowley's life may throw light on his view of history. Crowley, like Hancock and many other Australian historians, was a minister's son. Indeed he was born, in 1924, in the very vicarage (in the Melbourne suburb of Brighton) of which Sir Keith Hancock's father was in charge. Crowley's father had been sent to this parish as assistant curate, but this was only one way-station in the family's journeyings from one vicarage to another. Crowley therefore had an adventurous, nomadic childhood, growing up in a number of towns and suburbs of South Australia and Victoria. He entered the University of Melbourne in 1943 and, after graduating, became Manning Clark's first M.A. student, sharing Clark's excitement about the possibility of pursuing Australian history as a discipline in its own right. Throughout the 1950s Crowley taught Australian history at the University of Western Australia, and it was here that his view of this history seems to have set.

It is illuminating to read the accounts of Western Australian life Crowley wrote during the 1950s. He took an active interest in local politics, and contributed a blow-by-blow narrative to the 'Political chronicle' section of the newly formed *Australian Journal of Politics and History*. He also published a pamphlet on the defeat of the Hawke Labor government in the state election of 1959. (Hawke's government had taken office in 1953, but was defeated six years later by conservative politicians, led by David Brand and Charles Court, who promised the Western Australian electorate an acceleration of economic development through the more extravagant utilization of Western Australia's natural resources.) Crowley watched the Labor government's efforts to effect even the most mild-mannered reforms come to nought in the conservative upper house. He saw that Western Australians were excited only by minor political squabbles, such as the regulation of bookmakers, and cared nothing for the larger issues, raised by town planners, reformers and academics. His pamphlet, *State Election: The Fall of the Hawke Government*, appeared within two months of the poll being declared. His preface was sarcastic in tone, referring to the machinations of the three conservative organizations which brought Hawke down:

> I am indebted to the Editor of the *West Australian* newspaper, who on 23rd March, 1959, declared that election post mortems are only of academic interest . . . I am also indebted to the Democratic Labor Party and the W.A. Trade Bureau for making the story so interesting.[22]

It is unlikely that this pamphlet would have attracted a commercial publisher, for it was written with a cheeky irreverence and cynical scepticism which almost, at times, erupted into open support for the A.L.P. Crowley ridiculed, for example, the 'anti-socialist' campaign mounted by the conservatives: there was no question of farmers and businessmen not getting government aid. The pamphlet concluded on a prophetic note:

> . . . it remained to be seen whether the new government was able to offer the wage-earner and the salaried voter as much as the Labour Party had done. It was fully committed to dismantling those governmental enterprises which had been the means of bringing about 'socialism by stealth'. Was its confidence in the business community to be justified?[23]

Crowley has subsequently written many books and articles, but none of them in such an impassioned prose style. As one critic has said of a more recent book: 'Crowley does have occasional flashes of inspired prose, but they never extend beyond one sentence'.[24]

The difference in style between Crowley's earlier writings on Western Australian politics and his history 'proper'—beginning with *Australia's Western Third*—is symptomatic of a deeper change within him, reflected in his history as a movement towards fatalistic syncretism. With the defeat of the Hawke government, Crowley became cynically resigned to the fact that those families who had ruled Western Australia since the 1890s would continue to rule it during his lifetime. He still has some admiration for the non-conformists who attempt to challenge the status quo—as a book he more recently published on marihuana-smoking testifies[25]—but he has generally become resigned to the hopelessness of any non-conformist creed in suburban Australia. The sunny skies of Perth would bleach out any incipient radicalism: its residents are too fond of the turf, of yachting on the Swan River, of the barbecue on the patio, to be moved by idealism of any sort. Crowley can detect no movement or dynamic in Australian history which would ever shake this suburban lassitude.

However the lassitude which infects his prose style quite probably says nothing about Crowley's personal outlook. In September 1974, for instance, he made front-page headlines in the Sydney press, by complaining publicly when he discovered that his signature had been forged on a postal vote in the Botany Council elections.[26] And occasionally a note of genuine concern about injustice creeps into his academic prose. In that chapter of *New History of Australia* the volume on '1901-1914', which he as editor of the anthology allotted to himself, Crowley concluded on a quixotic note: 'In 1914 Australians celebrated 126 years of material progress. So far, only the Aborigines had suffered'.[27] But Aborigines, women and other less powerful groups received scant mention in the pages of his history: they were pushed put onto the edges of the historical stage in the past, and historians should bear this in mind.

Crowley defends this view of 'general history' vigorously. In an interview in 1975 he was asked:

> . . . *if you were sitting down to plan your* New History *now . . . would you take notice of what feminists have been saying over the last couple of years?*

No.

You don't think that women are part of the new interpretation?

Yes.

But not in the way that they see it?

I don't think either statement is incompatible. Well, I think Aborigines would get the same answer. In the history of white settlement, between 1788 and about 1975, *yes*, the Aborigines were insignificant. [Insignificant] as a labour force except in the Kimberleys in Western Australia? Yes. Important in a few country towns? Yes. That's my view of general history. In my opinion, women in Australian history became important about five years ago, when they started making a noise, and started getting difficult . . . I have a lot of material on Aborigines from about the 1840s because they were a part of the life of the people living at that time. Murdering people and being murdered, they were the cause of military posses in the country districts. And they were again important in the parliament of Queensland, because they started to chop up the miners. But when they're not important, they're not in . . . People complain I've not put enough in about Aborigines:that's not a complaint, to me that's a simple observation. It means they've got the message. Our message is that the Aborigines just were not important in the early history of white settlement.[28]

For Crowley, women are also only as important in his history as they were to the contemporary observers in the past. And in the 1 300-odd pages of his two-volume source-book, *Modern Australia in Documents,* women are featured directly or indirectly (as in the birth-rate controversy) on a mere 153 pages, less than one-eighth of the total.[29]

Like many other Australian historians, Crowley claims to have no preconceived model of how society works, yet his attempt to write 'general history' is that of a syncretic conservative: it is History From the Top Down, or how the elite views and moulds social themes—for Crowley, social consciousness is defined from and by the leader ship. The basic problem with his social theory is that where social dynamics are not glimpsed by the ruling class and its spokesmen, they are automatically regarded as irrelevant: so Crowley often fails to understand divergent movements and lower-class cross-currents. Syncretism is the organizing principle of his two-volume *Modern Australia in Documents,* and the result is merely headlines history, with only fleeting glances at deeper and broader trends.

The syncretic historian, however, is capable of adroit synthesis, and it is not surprising that it was Crowley who was able to pull together a rather disparate group of academic historians to produce *A New History of Australia.* Careful editing and firm leadership ensured an amorphous but well-conducted orchestration. However the outcome was no more than 'the state of the argument in their particular intellectual sport', a mere company report from 'Academic Enterprises Proprietary Limited', as Manning Clark succinctly put it, 'the work of men who do not seem to have heard the angry knocking at the door by the youth of today'.[30]

A close analysis of Crowley's published work on Western Australia brings the problems inherent in syncretic conservative social theory more sharply into focus. The rise of the labour movement, for instance, merits only an occasional sentence in his *Short History of Western Australia.*[31] Crowley prefers to emphasize those factors which encouraged the growth of material wealth, such as the discovery of gold, the expansion of the rural sector and the arrival of convict labour:

> As an economic expedient the convict system had been a great success. To begin with, the total population of the colony had soared from 5,886 in 1850 to 22,915 in 1869, and clearly the arrival of so many convicts had a lot to do with this . . . The presence of so many more people to feed encouraged farmers to increase production, and the area of land under crop increased more than six times over between 1850 and 1869. In the same period the number of horses increased sevenfold, cattle more than threefold, pigs fourfold and sheep fivefold.[32]

This is Animal Farm with a vengeance! It might have been more intellectually honest for Crowley to have admitted frankly that this view of history simply does not allow for an explanation of social change, but instead he seizes at outward signs of difference to 'explain' the dynamics of change in Western Australia:

> Further evidence of social change could been in the appearance of the city of Perth. The first cinematograph film was shown at the Cremorne Theatre in 1896, the first motor car seen in 1898, and typewriters and cash-registers were coming into general use.[33]

The antagonisms which occurred are either ironed out or omitted altogether, in favour of an end clothed in such terms as 'state development' or 'community progress'. There may well be such an organic self-image carefully nurtured in Western Australia, but it is suggestive that Crowley has not attempted another state history. One reviewer of *Australia's Western Third* contended that occasionally its readers 'are almost taken into the realm of official propaganda'. That reviewer was A. G. L. Shaw, himself a syncretic historian, but one who has attempted a synthesis of the history of the entire continent, not just its western third. Commented Shaw: 'The Western Australian story is very similar *mutatis mutandis* to the story in other states'.[34]

Organicist frameworks within Australian history-writing are either anarchist or conservative in their ideological implication, and, in Crowley's case, it is clearly the latter. He has the classic conservative hallmark of professing to be non-ideological, at least in his public persona. Human existence is fickle and emphemeral: the only constant Crowley can find is that those who ruled Western Australia in the last century still govern it. His world-view assumes a future identical, with only minor variation, to that which has gone before. Society, if it moves, is moved forward by the elite: the force of ideas is regarded only as so much drum-banging by the politicians and pulpit-preaching by the clergy. Australians viewed collectively are motivated only by self-interest and the pursuit of the humdrum. The socialist utopia is denied absolutely, since the lower classes can be manipulated to do anything. In socio-historical terms, Crowley's world view is not merely the mirror of petit-bourgeois ideas; it can more narrowly be isolated to Australian suburbia of the 1950s and early 1960s. It encapsulates the monotonous regularity of Friday night at the pub and Sunday morning behind the lawnmower. Nothing changes or breaks into suburban tranquility, and yesterday is much the same as tomorrow: history is reduced to a circular argument.

Feminists

The flourish of new feminism in the first half of the 1970s produced two general histories of Australia which sought to demonstrate and explain the essentially patriarchal nature of its White settlement. These two histories, Anne Summers' *Damned Whores and God's Police* and Miriam Dixson's *The Real Matilda*, had the combined effect of assailing the masculinist assumptions upon which almost all previous Australian history had been grounded. Despite the ideological and theoretical differences dividing them, virtually all the leading professional historians at the close of the 1960s were male; and few of them had paused to consider that their canons of relevance had excluded Australian women from their models of explanation. Many of them remained unconvinced by feminist argument during the 1970s and continued to maintain that because women had been regarded as insignificant in the past they ought to be insignificant in historical explanation. Russel Ward, for example, concurred with F. K. Crowley, when he wrote in 1978 that 'women have always figured on the historical stage pretty much to the extent that they did in the *public* life of the past'.35 This comment assumes that the task of historical explanation is to reconstruct the past as closely as possible to the image it presented to contemporaneous observers. Feminist historians, however, ask a question which runs entirely against this notion: why were women denied the full expression of their talents in the Australian past? Merely to pose this question requires a certain level of abstraction, for it is one which would hardly have occurred to nineteenth-century men and women; indeed, it stands outside the set of patriarchal beliefs about the supposedly innate potentialities of women, and is not necessarily dependent on any masculine definition of human 'talents'.

Such a level of abstraction does not derive logically and inevitably from any one of the four archetypal modes of social theorizing in particular, but it is remarkable that the two general feminist histories were demonstrably organicist in character. Why this was the case, will be explained with reference to the nature and outlook of the women's movement in Australia during the early 1970s. Just as it was historically contingent that feminist history should have originally taken an organicist shape, it is not inevitable that it should always remain within this problematic, for changes in feminist ideology from the mid-1970s have begun to alter their explanation of the past and present of women's oppression in Australia. Brief reference will be made to the work of Beverley Kingston, and certain other feminist intellectuals in order to suggest the salient features of this transition toward a more mechanistic account of women's history. Feminist questions about the Australian past, it will be implied, are highly important; but the questions and the methods these entail will need to be reframed before feminist historians can force a more thorough reconsideration of Australian history.

It was not inevitable that feminist intellectuals should have turned to the study of Australian history; rather, feminist historiography developed naturally out of the needs and interests of the women's movement around 1970. Feminists were quick to embrace historical inquiry as an essential part of their endeavour to explain women's lot under patriarchy, largely because they followed Germaine Greer and others in rejecting the biological determinism they detected in Freud's work. Juliet Mitchell's resurrection of Freud in *Psychoanalysis and Feminism*, though published in England in 1974, was not absorbed by Australian feminists until after Anne Summers' and Miriam Dixson's general histories had appeared. Marxist theory also received short shrift, partly because many of the leading feminists had reacted against the sexism they had experienced in left-wing organizations during the 1960s. The result was that the feminist understanding of the position of women in Australian society drew largely upon a fusion of traditional sociological and historical methods, in the service of the new questions. [36]

Anne Summers followed this perspective, in general outline, in the conceptualization of *Damned Whores and God's Police*, which she began researching in earnest in 1972. She was then 27 years old and a recent graduate in political science from the University of Adelaide. Early in 1970, while still a student, she had helped establish the Women's Liberation Movement in Adelaide, after an involvement in left-wing politics stretching back to 1965, the first year of her (broken) university career. Her dissatisfaction with the New Left, and her active participation in the women's movement in both Adelaide and Sydney, placed her in the centre of Australian feminism of that period; and *Damned Whores* came to represent the dominant strand of this feminism. [37]

The book itself was a vigorous and imaginative presentation of what most Australian feminists saw as the explanation of women's oppression. Structurally, the book was organized in two parts: the first, sociological half advanced a model of this oppression, viewed in contemporary terms, and the latter half was a historical analysis of how this present situation was arrived at. The tone of *Damned Whores* was suitably iconoclastic: Summers spared little of her trenchant prose style in putting forward her case. Indeed the argument remorselessly castigated almost every aspect of men's involvement in the structures of patriarchy, to such an extent that even friendly critics felt permitted to regard some of her statements as 'extreme'. Many of her statements about rape and about prisons, to cite two instances, seemed to be of this type. [38] However the domain assumptions of the argument remain unshakeable. Foremost among these is the hypothesis that two stereotypical views of women, the Magdalen and Madonna images, were powerful determinants of women's lives in Australia. These images, though usually recognized as embedded within Western culture generally, are detected by Summers in an Australian setting as 'damned whore' and 'God's police' stereotypes. These concepts are, of course, ideological in nature, and are therefore constantly reproduced by the cultural conditions of Australian patriarchy. On the face of it, this is a slippery argument. It carries with it the inherent danger that, in attempting to use these stereotypes as categories of analysis, Summers will reproduce them herself: just as women have been slotted into these two categories historically, Summers also uses them constantly as descriptions of women. In other words, it is very difficult to keep separate the prescriptive and descriptive aspects of the stereotypes. The final chapter, an outline of the 'prospects for liberation' facing women in the present, fails to resolve the difficulties of this position.[39] By this time, Summers has so effectively demonstrated the stubborn persistence of these stereotypes throughout much of Australian history that she cannot now suggest to women how they might escape them, except by lamely enjoining women to 'transcend' the duality. She cannot even urge them to adopt a 'damned whore' gesture, for, as she recognizes, this is a role devised by patriarchal structures anyway.

Closely linked to this problem is the way Summers explains the origin of the two stereotypes in Australia.

> Although basic sexist assumptions about women and men were transported from England with the First Fleet, social and economic conditions in the first fifty years of colonization of this country gave rise to an indigenous variety of the ideology of sexism.[40]

The position of convict women within the penal regime produced the stereotype of 'damned whore' because most of these women were given little option but to rely on their sexuality. The agitation for the moral improvement of the colonies from about the 1840s, led by skilful campaigners such as Chisholm, Lang and Wakefield, produced an immigration scheme and a bourgeois ideology which fostered the development of the nuclear family. The normative ideal of 'the Family' thus became the means by which women could be stereotyped as either its guardians, the 'God's police', or its detractors, the 'damned whores'. Far from freeing women from the vicissitudes of convictism, then, the mid-century campaigners unwittingly circumscribed the lives of Australian women within the narrow choice offered by this duality. This formulation raises a great difficulty: at the centre of the feminist interest in historical inquiry is the assumption that if women's oppression is of historical origin it is then capable of historical resolution. But by locating the critical determinants of women's oppression in these nineteenth-century conditions, Summers does not advance a universal understanding of the cause-and-effect mechanisms involved. Instead she concentrates on specific historical conditions. Since those conditions no longer apply, her final chapter has to appeal to extra-historical factors, in suggesting ways out of the oppression for individual women.

Whether it was read for an understanding of the origin or the perpetuation of women's oppression, *Damned Whores* was limited as an argument to the needs and interests of the mainstream liberationists of the early 1970s. The crux of the case was that, in the very important matter of personal consciousness, it mattered a great deal that women should not be blinkered by patriarchal ideology. The conclusion reached was that women needed to think themselves beyond the duality of good-bad generated by this ideology, and then to act upon this heightened level of self-awareness. This approach provided more than sufficient justification for the efficacy of 'consciousness-raising groups', a characteristic strategy of early feminism (and a highly important vehicle for the development of female culture) but little else besides.

The other major feminist reading of Australian history was provided by Miriam Dixson in *The Real Matilda.* Although written at much the same time as *Damned Whores,* it was not published until six months later, in early 1976. Dixson's background differed from Summers'. Her academic career had been comparatively straightforward, beginning with a B.A. and M.A. in history at Melbourne, a Ph.D. at the A.N.U., tutorships at the University of New South Wales and at Monash, followed by a teaching appointment at the University of New England in 1967. During this period, Dixson's publications were mainly on labour history, especially that of New South Wales in the 1920s and the career of J. T. Lang. This interest continued alongside her developing interest in women's studies: in 1974 she initiated a course in 'Problems of women, family and identity in the Western tradition' at the University of New England. Not only was Dixson's feminism of a more academic kind, it originated within the traditions of Australian history. Summers had not studied history as an undergraduate; Dixson came from an Old Left background and had been impressed with the framework offered by Russel Ward (a colleague) in *The Australian Legend.*[41]

Dixson's understanding of feminist history was also powerfully moulded by her interest in the neo-Freudians, particularly Erik Erikson. She saw the question in terms of 'identity', a concept which held the promise of linking individual psychological identity (as formulated by Erikson) with national identity (following Ward and Michael Roe). Her enterprise was therefore quite ambitious: she aimed to join social with psychohistorical accounts, to explore male-female relationships in the settlement of Australia. If Summers was to produce a work which represented the main tendency within the women's movement, Dixson's style of argument was much more eclectic, given Freud's bad name at that time. Yet both histories were limited by a common weakness: at base they reduced themselves to an unfalsifiable organicism, which rendered Australian history undynamic and devoid of meaningful dialectic.

Precisely how this eventuated, in the case of *Matilda*, was principally through Dixson's use of two essential concepts, 'identity' and 'community'. Her understanding of individual identity owed little to Freud's theory of the psycho-sexual development of the human personality and much more to the neo-Freudian emphasis on the 'imprinting' effects of the social environment. Following Louis Hartz's 'fragment' thesis, Dixson argued that the definition of male and female derived largely from the transposition of nineteenth-century English and Irish folkways into the new environment. Although she often used diaries and personal letters to great effect, in reconstructing how these individual and ethnic identities were reproduced in the antipodes, Dixson lost sight too often of the moral and class biases that recur throughout her primary evidence. For example, she took at face value the 'concern' of some women that convictism was responsible for widespread prostitution, and interpreted this 'concern' as founded upon a genuine desire for 'community'.[42]

Dixson's emphasis on 'community' sometimes took on the status of a personal commitment, for it was part of her conviction that men and women 'finally' belong with one another. This commitment to community sometimes shaped her description of the penal colonies, and flattened out the differences between various social groups in that 'entire society'. Such homogeneity also required a unitary view of 'human nature'; for Dixson, this is the view that an androgynous spirit is 'well locked in the dungeons of every psyche', a view which strongly implies its own teleology. It was to this complementarity, between masculine and feminine, that Dixson most often referred, rather than to the obtrusive differences between men and women, rich and poor. This explains her sudden discovery that the 'lack of commitment to community' on the part of the colonial ruling class was 'baffling'.[43] It can only be 'baffling' if one were to begin from the assumption that such commitment ought naturally to exist. Rather than consistently treating issues of class as central—as, indeed, one might expect from a labour historian—Dixson habitually concentrated on the ways in which oppressed men compensated themselves by exploiting 'their' wives and daughters in turn. However, rather than rescuing her from the problems thrown up by the intricacies of the relationship between personal and national identities, this compensatory argument threw up two major difficulties for Dixson. It obscured the role of institutional agencies of socialization, the importance of which she recognized only in passing.[44] So the social changes wrought by the industrial revolution (which Dixson in her conclusion claimed to have treated as central) were only cursorily noticed: there was no mention at all of the sexual division of labour, a rather remarkable omission.[45] Secondly, the compensatory argument could not thereby explain the oppression of elite women—whose husbands and fathers are exploiters, rather than exploited—and this propelled Dixson toward two contradictory solutions: that there was not really a fully-fledged bourgeoisie anyway; and that oppressive attitudes 'permeated' the entire society, which meant that elite women were bound up in this value-structure despite their advantage of rank.

Those facets of women's oppression which Dixson dealt with in *Matilda,* enabled her to explain it solely by reference to nineteenth-century conditions. Although the book's subtitle promised an account of the period '1788 to 1975', very little of the narrative referred directly to the twentieth century. Dixson's espousal of a psycho-historical method contained its own justification for exploring in detail only the 'formative' years of Australian history; the rest was supposed to flow on from this period. Dixson thus shared with Summers the critical assumption that women are still trapped on the same treadmill set in motion a century ago.

Both Dixson and Summers, then, set forth an account of Australian history which remained within an organicist framework. By hypothesizing the existence of a universally androgynous psyche, and by postulating some innate preference for a harmoniously self-regulating 'community', Dixson's interpretation of the Australian past was constrained within the teleology implied by such assumptions. By concentrating on the ideological shackles which fettered women to two mutually defined stereotypes, Summers' history advanced an argument which contained its own built-in self-justification: as one reviewer put it, 'it runs the risk of being unfalsifiable'.[46] This is, not to say, however, that Dixson or Summers may not produce a general history which would overcome these difficulties. Summers, for example, has subsequently written some provocative and insightful articles, in her capacity as a journalist on the *National Times.* In the opening pages of *Damned Whores* she wrote that 'it is impossible to talk about women's lives without also talking about men', and, to the extent that this statement widens the terms of reference for understanding women's oppression, Summers could progress to producing a more complete picture of Australian patriarchy.[47]

There is, of course, a deeper assumption underpinning most feminist scholarship—the histories of Dixson and Summers included —that would need to be jettisoned before a more complete picture could be achieved: the assumption that, in all significant respects, all men oppress all women and have done so throughout the course of European settlement in Australia. This is the fundamental tenet of orthodox feminism, and indeed is the ultimate cause of their circular view of history. If this proposition is unassailable, then all debate is useless—including historical debate—for the formula provides its own answer to every question which might be raised about the relationship between men and women in Australia. It also generates a circular view of history, because it leads the enquirer precisely back to where she started at the beginning of the inquiry. Feminists should be able to present an account of women's oppression sophisticated enough to explain its most subtle and fleeting forms, but which can also show its rougher edges in bold relief. To achieve this, there must, in the first place, be a thorough understanding of what is meant by oppression.[48]

Summers wrote of a 'nexus of oppression', by which she meant that a number of analytically distinct forces act in unison to create and perpetuate the twin stereotypes. Broadly, these forces may be seen as economic, cultural and 'sex-political'. The last of these is a shorthand description of the power relations associated with the biological differences between men and women: rape, for example, is a manifestation of this aspect of oppression.   Women, according to this model, have been economically dependent on men, culturally impotent in a male-dominated universe of thought, and powerless in the use of their bodies.

This model of the mechanisms of oppression dovetails with the essential assumptions embodied within *Damned Whores*, but it does not readily lend itself to going beyond those assumptions, and it is not the only model available. In 1971 Juliet Mitchell proposed that women's oppression needed to be understood as partly temporal (changing historically), partly atemporal (extra-historical), and partly universal. These three aspects of women's oppression, argued Mitchell, require three different intellectual enquiries: the first could be explained by Marxist theory, the third by Freudian and the second by a combination of these.[49] Mitchell claimed three years later that Freud, far from being a victim of his own culture, had developed a competent understanding of women's psychology within patriarchal societies.[50] By the late 1970s, many Australian feminists were beginning to break with the organicism characteristic of early feminism, largely thanks to Mitchell's influence.

This prompted a return to a work which, although published at the same time as *Damned Whores,* had not created the same excitement: Beverley Kingston's *My Wife, My Daughter, and Poor Mary Ann.* Kingston was closer to Dixson than Summers in background: after a B.A. in history at Queensland, she migrated to Monash in 1964, to undertake a Ph.D. on 'The land problem in Queensland, 1860-1876', under the supervision of G. C. Bolton and Duncan Waterson. A lectureship in history at the University of New South Wales followed, and an ostensibly orthodox academic career. *Poor Mary Ann* was couched in much more conventional prose than the other two feminist histories, and it set out to achieve deceptively limited aims, using fairly well-known primary sources. Kingston aimed to summarize what was known about the kinds of paid and unpaid employment opportunities open to women between about 1860 and 1930: their conditions of work, the productive relations they entered into in their work environment, the ideological conflicts associated with different jobs, the varied relationships between women workers and trade union structures, and the impact of technological invention on these occupations. Housework, domestic service, factory work, teaching, nursing, commercial jobs and several other occupations were the substance of the book. With these objectives in view, it was not surprising that Kingston was directly confronted with the issues of class difference. In treating labour around the home, for example, Kingston entitled one chapter 'She married well and lived happily ever after', and another 'Three pounds a week'.[51]

Although most of her evidence was drawn from sources relating to the history of New South Wales, and her conclusions did not take up all the points raised in the main body of the text, Kingston's approach generated a number of possible mechanisms of explanation which foreshadowed the salient trends of feminist historiography in the late 1970s.

Kingston emphasized the relationship between domestic labour, whether paid or unpaid, and women's labour in the larger economy. She showed, for example, that working-class women could exercise some choice, working as domestic servants or on the factory floor: the increasing shortage of domestics, visible to middle-class commentators of the late nineteenth century only as 'the servant problem', was part of a long-term set of complex processes affecting women's work.[52]

Some of Kingston's tentative conclusions were challenged by later feminists. She had accepted the orthodox feminist view that most trade unions did little for women workers—a view which Summers asserted in her very brief section on women's involvement in the labour movement[53]—and attacked the labourist assumption 'that all men would be responsible for families, and all women provided for by some man'.[54] In an article published in 1977, Teresa Brennan challenged this argument, by claiming that the introduction of the 'family wage', far from being merely another example of unionist sexism, was a considerable achievement for the Australian working class as a whole. The family wage pushed up the net income of each working-class family (though at the longer-term cost of reinforcing the sexual division of labour). Brennan's argument was based on a theory of labour market segmentation, a theory which attempts to show how the working class is divided along lines of sex, race and ethnicity, following the work of Margaret Power and others.[55]

That feminists should have begun by the late 1970s to take such a theory seriously, suggests a keener appreciation of the subtle and quite blatant disadvantages experienced, for example, by migrant women from Southern Europe. Kingston had already been alert to the class differences between women, by not accepting that all women were equally oppressed and by not foreclosing the possibility, indeed, that some women directly exploited others. Since some elite women depended for their public life on the hidden use of other women as domestic servants, suggested Kingston, was it not possible that the declining number of public women, in the early twentieth century, was partly the result of a shrinking pool of these servants?[56] This interesting hypothesis leaves open the question that analyses based on class theory, instead of being merely male-devised schemas which omit women from their reckoning, may be of use to future feminist historians.

5 The search for laws

5 The search for laws

Sociological historians

As a distinct discipline sociology did not flourish in the United Kingdom until the 1950s, despite its acceptance on the Continent from the late nineteenth century onwards.[1] A comparable aloofness towards the new discipline, occasionally taking the form of outright hostility, characterized the approach of Australian historians until the late 1950s. Sociology promised a more systematic method for understanding complex historical processes, but, at the same time, seemed to threaten the discipline of history by positing an abstract account of reality which ran directly counter to the methods used by historians. Sociologists set themselves an essentially mechanistic project: they seek to employ abstract concepts to express general propositions about social behaviour, relationships and processes. Both the sociological historians—in Australia led by K. S. Inglis and A. W. Martin —and later the New Left came to realize that a mechanistic history was possible.

Several young men who graduated from Crawford's Melbourne history department in the immediate post-war period led this sociological reaction against the orthodoxies. Geoffrey Blainey's first scholarly article was an attack, couched in no uncertain terms, on the 'scissors-and-paste' empiricism he detected in most local history.[2] Martin's 1962 ANZAAS paper attacked the 'Whig' view of history.[3] Weston Bate used Crowley's history of South Perth as a chopping-block for his own ideas on how community history ought to be written.[4] Hugh Stretton began by inveighing against the 'measurers', and eventually came to postulate a view of history which overturned the paradigm he had been offered by Crawford.

Later in the 1960s, a new note of criticism was sounded against the same orthodoxies, in a paper given by T. H. Irving, an article in *Quadrant* by R. W. Connell attacking Hancock, and, finally, in 1970, by Humphrey McQueen's attack on the Old Left in *A New Britannia*. A recognizably distinct school, the New Left, was created in the midst of this polemic.

The common theme threaded through these attacks on older schools of Australian history, was that historians had not been sufficiently alert to the patterns and regularities of the past. The search for general laws of history was the constant, if often unobtrusive, feature of this debate, just as it had been the most important question of Western historiography for at least a generation of intellectuals. Could history attain the status of a science? Did this mean that its practitioners could write objective history? Does the study of the past invariably draw upon a search for general laws of cause and effect? Many philosophers of history in North America and Europe propounded a similar answer to this last question, by arguing that historical study could not dispense

> with at least a tacit acceptance of universal statements of the kind occurring in the natural sciences. Thus, although the historian may be concerned with the nonrecurrent and the unique, he selects and abstracts from the concrete occurrences he studies, and his discourse about what is individual and singular requires the use of common names and general descriptive terms. Such characterizations are associated with the recognition of various kinds or types of things and occurrences, and therefore with the implicit acknowledgement of numerous empirical regularities ... And, since historians usually aim to be more than mere chroniclers of the past, and attempt to understand and explain recorded actions in terms of their causes and consequences, they must obviously assume supposedly well-established laws of causal dependence. In brief, history is not a purely idiographic discipline.[5]

In confirming this view that history was nomothetic as well as idiographic, Australian historians, however, derived less from the philosophy of history, and rather more from the techniques and methods of sociology and (especially in the case of Greg Dening) anthropology.

K. S. Inglis is regarded as Australia's leading sociological historian. Inglis was born in 1929 in the Melbourne suburb of Northcote. In the late 1930s he attended North Preston State School, and encountered his first realization of a world larger than his own in the Anzac Day ceremonies, each 25 April. He pursued the study of history from Northcote High School to Melbourne High School, and then at the University of Melbourne, gaining along the way not only a sense of historical perspective, but a concern for the injustices of the world around him. Returning from postgraduate studies at Oxford, he took up a senior lectureship in history at the University of Adelaide in 1956, and this social concern led to his book, *The Stuart Case,* and a number of articles which revealed an impatience to comment on various aspects of Australian society: Catholicism, the press and the Anzac tradition, in particular.[6]

In 1962, for example, he wrote a witty piece, 'The daily papers', which showed a keen eye for the details of how news was presented in the print media, and a sociological interest in explaining changes in newspaper reporting. He discerned a law of history in the development of Australian newspapers, which he jocularly called the Law of Increasing Brightness:

> The headlines have grown higher, fatter and gayer, the display advertisements more seductive and menacing, the photographs larger and more vivid . . . Even the most sedate of the dailies, the *Sydney Morning Herald* and the *Age*, to the dismay of their senior men, have become more skittish during the last few years; 'human interest' stories, often about animals, are likelier than ever before to reach their front pages.[7]

Through the operation of this law, newspaper vocabulary had also become sloppier, reviews of theatre and books had declined in quality, and so on. Inglis also showed a sociologist's eye for the importance of conducting readership surveys, and for understanding the functioning of the news-room; he also pondered the symbolic implication of naming a paper the *Sun News-Pictorial* (Melbourne): did the evocation of the sun, he wondered, signify the sun-baked hedonism of its potential readers?[8]

After leaving Adelaide in 1963, Inglis took up a professorship at the Australian National University, in the mid-1960s, and then accepted the professorship of history at the University of Papua New Guinea in 1966. He was appointed to the vice-chancellorship of that university in 1972. This period of administration, before he returned to the A.N.U. in 1976, slowed down his scholarly output, and it was not until 1974 that the first volume of his planned four-volume general history of Australia was published. This project takes the Anzac landing at Gallipoli as its central point of reference, and the structure of the argument in the first volume closely reflects Inglis's sociological attitude to this event. Gallipoli produced both imperial and national rhetoric, so for Inglis it is important to ask: 'What had Australians thought about themselves before 1915, as Britons, colonists, and members of their nation?'. Similarly, the landing became celebrated as a holiday: so for Inglis it was logical to investigate what holidays Australians had previously instituted. These and other questions occurred to Inglis because they raise laws of history: by exploring the differences and similarities between Anzac Day and other holidays, for example, it is theoretically possible to postulate general statements about the causes and consequences of ceremonial occasions in Australia. Inglis certainly does not present these issues so ponderously; the first volume, *The Australian Colonists,* which takes his story up to 1870, is highly readable. The second volume, *The Little Boy from Manly,* which will take the story to 1900, is planned to appear in 1979.

Even before *The Australian Colonists* was published, Inglis was regarded by many of his colleagues as the best Australian historian to emerge during the post-war period. G. C. Bolton praised his combination of 'historical imagination of a high order, with meticulous sociological technique' to a London audience in 1972.[10] Five years later Russel Ward was even more emphatic: 'I think Ken Inglis is the greatest historian in the country'.[11] After returning to Canberra in 1976, Inglis proposed a 'Bicentennial History Project'—a collaborative, multi-volume history, which would be published in 1988. Australian historians have engaged in very few large-scale team efforts —the *Australian Dictionary of Biography* being the only outstanding example—and it testified to Inglis's standing within the profession, that the Bicentennial idea was seriously considered by many of his colleagues. Some historians immediately raised objections to the details of the proposal (an indication of how the existence of different schools of historians affects the practice of history), but a large number seemed prepared to acquiesce to Inglis' central proposition. He argued that the best method for provoking a novel set of interpretations of the Australian past would be to 'slice' across various points of time—the years 1788, 1838, 1888, 1938 and 1988—and discover 'the texture of everyday life' in Australia at each point.[12] To the extent that this approach would demand a sociological understanding of each of the years chosen for scrutiny, it is clear that the sociological historians' conception of the past will leave a lasting imprint on Australian historiography if the Bicentennial Project proceeds as Inglis proposes.

The sociological historians do not purport to have a grand vision of social theory, that would produce a final mosaic of general laws by which all aspects could eventually be explained. By and large, they seek small-scale insights into the historical process, rather than a 'grand theory' which would provide overall explanations: they proceed atomistically rather than holistically. This, of course, is partly a reflection of the shift in mainstream American sociology, from the gargantuan intellectual edifice constructed by Talcott Parsons to the less wide-ranging theories of the 1960s and 1970s. This was suggested by A. W. Martin when asked if he were committed to any one 'school' of sociology:

> No, not really . . . One of the main reasons I'm interested in sociological history is that I think Australian historians are going to make a breakthrough in social history when they find some way of re-conceptualising what are the important things to attend to in Australian society. Now, it may be that putting on this other [sociological] thinking cap, so to speak, might give one a clue, you know, from time to time. It's like borrowing an idea from somebody else to use as a trigger to fire off something—in your own terms. That's all. No, I'm not committed to any position on that at all, except that I certainly wouldn't be . . . as I once was, really, hopeful of the sort of Parsonian system suggesting insights to Australian historians. I don't think that's on.[13]

Martin first enunciated his advocacy of sociological history in a paper he gave at ANZAAS in 1962. 'The Whig view of history' was never published, for its author's intention was simply to reply to the criticism that his sociological purpose was a conservative one. Martin had been labelled a conservative because he questioned the Old Left view that a line of democratic progress, embodied in the working-class movement, could be discerned throughout the late-nineteenth and early-twentieth centuries. He urged that historians use socio-logical methods to understand class relations, and to explore the network of middle-class associations, in particular, as these un-obtrusive patterns had been neglected in an emphasis on class con-flict.[14] Martin is also interested in political sociology, and has co-authored, with Peter Loveday, a study of parliamentary factions and parties in nineteenth-century New South Wales, a book which has also attracted a fair degree of hostile criticism.[15]

Martin has subsequently been working on a biography of Sir Henry Parkes, endeavouring to bring insights from psycho-sociological theories to bear on the large corpus of papers which Parkes left to posterity. Martin argues that a major defect of previous political biographers in Australia, has been that they do not understand anything by the concept 'personality':[16] using borrowed tools he hopes to show some of the connections between social and individual change, and shifting manifestations of the 'social self'. In the case of Parkes, for example, there is a change in his rhetoric between 1852 (democracy is inevitable and will lead to spiritual and material progress) and 1854 (society is in chaos): this can be explained by social mobility, according to Martin, for Parkes

> has just moved into a sort of respectable businessman's role and in some ways his business activities are threatened by a labour shortage, by the demands for higher wages and so on. Here he is—the champion of the workers—having to walk the tightrope, being on the one hand a *boss* and on the other hand the worker's friend, you know. And his rhetoric in this period is just absolutely fascinating. You can see some of the problems he's facing up to in being effective: the way he talks publicly or write publicly about the social situation of the colony. Now if you didn't know that, I mean you'd simply think that he was jumping on this or that bandwagon . . . There are depths to him for which the rhetoric is being really quite symbolic. It's something very important in his social position and perception of himself socially.[17]

A. W. Martin regards Inglis as the seminal influence on his own work; Weston Bate holds Martin in similar respect, having taught at Melbourne University with him in the early 1960s. Bate was born two years before Martin (in 1924), served in the air force during the Second World War, and graduated from Melbourne University in the late 1940s. He then taught ten-year-olds at Brighton Grammar, so that when Crawford was asked by the Brighton Council to nominate someone to write the suburb's history, Bate was the obvious candidate.[18] The result, *A History of Brighton*, was a considerable success, and is esteemed in many quarters as the first 'professional' suburban history. This was due partly to Bate's use of rate-books as an empirical basis for the study: later urban historians, such as Graeme Davison and Tom Stannage, have developed this technique since. Bate himself, after returning to academe in 1964, has been engaged in a larger study, a three-volume history of Ballarat, the first volume of which was published in 1978. There are significant methodological differences between this work and Davison's *Marvellous Melbourne*—such as Davison's greater emphasis on social structure—but these differences are absorbed within a larger problematic, which the two historians share. Bate has described this problematic succinctly: 'history [is] about producing a model that works'. This purpose lies mid way between 'the whole view' of Michael Cannon (which sociological historians regard as too syncretic), and the marxist social theory of the New Left. The aim of history, for Bate, is not merely to show that individual lives are governed or regulated by institutional arrangements, but also to demonstrate the degrees of freedom within these structures.

Philosophically, my major feeling about history, and what history has committed me to as far as understanding life is concerned, is an eternal pessimism about the hopefulness of people creating society through structures. I think one has to admit, looking back, that there have been successions of groups of people who have believed they have the answer, and who can be shown not to have, and who have enchained people just as much as the chains that they have released. So while I am eternally pessimistic in that sense, perhaps there is where my Christian belief comes in, I'm just very optimistic about people.[19]

The sociological historians, then, write a history which generally has liberal implications; but they do not see themselves as political ideologues, for their exposition of the laws of history which bind societies together is not intended either for the exclusive use of an elite, seeking more sophisticated methods of social control, or for non-elites, seeking programmatic guidelines for emancipation. They tend to prefer a neo-Weberian conception of social structure, rather than a marxist one; and this is primarily what marks them off from the New Left historians. The sociological historians also reject the New Left theory that a society's 'dominant culture' is defined by a 'ruling class', and the syncretic argument that societies are characterized by all-embracing value-systems: instead they subscribe to a pluralist view which sees power (both coercive and cultural) as multi-centred. Social groups are knitted together by common experience rather than by their relation to overarching theoretical constructs, such as the marxist concept of the mode of production.

The attitudes and values of the goldfield diggers, to take an example from one of Bate's lectures at the University of Melbourne, can be traced to their experience first at Ballarat and then elsewhere in Australia. Then a pattern of continental migration—and the spread of certain political attitudes—can be mapped from Victoria (1850s), to New South Wales (1860s), thence to northern Queensland (1880s), north-western Australia and, finally, the Kalgoorlie fields (1890s).[20] Similarly, Bate has argued that Russel Ward's thesis about the evolution of an 'Australian legend' can best be evaluated by dissecting it into smaller components—such as secularism, unionism, chauvinistic nationalism and so on—and locating the specific contexts of each of these. But whereas McQueen followed an analagous methodology in *A New Britannia*, and then located the specific elements in the social group he called a 'petit-bourgeoisie', Bate prefers to employ occupational, geographical and other non-class groupings.[21] This comparison highlights the essential distinction between the sociological historians and the New Left: both schools consciously seek causal necessities and law-observing uniformities, but differ in their models of explanation. The sociological historians contend that 'class', like 'mateship', is a concept which the Left allows to float mysteriously across time and space. They believe that conflict can be explained to a large extent without recourse to a 'class structure', by isolating differences between social groups on the basis of variables which are more empirically sound, such as age, sex, ethnic background and skin colour. [22]

Geoffrey Blainey's scholarship shows that it is even possible for some sociological historians to explain social processes without direct reference to class or class ideologies. Blainey was born in 1930 in the Melbourne suburb of Armidale, three suburbs away from where Hancock grew up and Crowley was born. Like them he was also the son of a clergyman, and like them he also spent much of his boyhood in the countryside, at Ballarat. No doubt he played in the old mine-shafts which he would later recreate in *The Rush that Never Ended;* no doubt he also developed an interest in Australian history and culture from his teachers, especially from A. A. Phillips at Wesley College. Blainey went on to study history in Crawford's department at Melbourne University, in the late 1940s; but unlike Turner, Serle and many of his contemporaries he took no interest in the marxist excitement of that period. It was 'too simple' an explanation of history, he thought. [23] It also ran counter to his individualist faith—some of his later books have shown that he discerns an irreducible gulf between individual initiative and the mind-dimming effects of big government, and that he intuitively believes that governments, or organizations based upon socialist or collectivist principles diminish the capacity of an indvidual to be genuinely creative.

Blainey has been the prospector, the individual searcher, for all of his adult life. Rather than undertake postgraduate studies in history, he left Melbourne University before his graduation ceremony to research *The Peaks of Lyell.* With the help of a research grant, he wrote up the history of the Tasmanian mines, and thereby established himself as a freelance historian. Throughout the 1950s, he accepted commissions to write various company histories and built up a thorough understanding of Australian industrial history. Thinking back, he does not regret this period of his career, but recognizes that he was much more descriptive than analytic in these histories: if he had written *The Causes of War* (1973) in the 1950s, for example, it would have evoked the sights and sounds of warfare, concentrating less on the general pattern of causation. [24] So Blainey has not always seen the search for general laws of historical explanation as the central purpose of his scholarship.

But even as a young historian he was critical of the tendency towards 'scissors-and-paste' that is characteristic of excessively descriptive empiricist history. While putting the final touches to *The Peaks of Lyell* Blainey savagely attacked a local history roughly comparable in scope. This was *Tale of a City*, a history of Geelong, written by David Wild and published in 1950. Wild's history, argued Blainey, was (like most other local histories) produced from 'slabs' of evidence. Six-line extracts from primary sources were incorporated directly into the narrative, regardless of how well they fitted in with other evidence or how trustworthy the original source might have been. Ransacking old newspapers, reports or diaries to find immediately useable 'slabs' was not good enough, said Blainey; instead the historian should collect all the possible evidence, no matter how fragmentary, and assemble it in the form of 'single facts'. One useful way to do this was to follow the system made famous by Beatrice Webb:

> She stipulates that each small piece of evidence should be noted on a separate piece of paper; the sheets to be of similar size (quarto) and written on one side only. 'On each sheet of paper there should appear one date, and one only; one place, and one only; one source of information and one only'. To facilitate the rapid sorting and reading of notes, the date to which the note refers should always appear on the same corner of the sheet: likewise, the heading which describes the subject of the note, and the source in which the evidence was found. A typical sheet might appear as follows:

> | | |
> |---|---|
> | DIGGERS RIOT | 1864 |
> | | 27 November |
> | A dozen German diggers hooted and thumbed their noses at a mounted trooper at Growlers Gully this evening. They ran off laughing when challenged by a shot from his musket. | |
> | | Ballarat Repeater |
> | | 30/11/64 |

> [By shuffling and arranging these notes, the historian] masters and reconstructs the evidence instead of letting the evidence, as arranged by previous writers, be his master.[25]

Using this system would not necessarily have guided Blainey towards a view of history which concentrates on seeking out its inherent laws. Other mechanistic historians—notably Humphrey McQueen—swear allegiance to Webb's system of note-taking,[26] but something else was no doubt needed before Blainey saw his purpose as the search for regularity and pattern, in the mechanistic tradition.

It was probably his decision to return to academe that fostered this development in Blainey's history. In 1961 he became senior lecturer in economic history at Melbourne University (later rising to become professor), and throughout the 1960s his histories gradually took on a more analytic character. In 1963, for example, he published *The Rush that Never Ended,* a general history of metal-mining in Australia. It is a lively, readable book—as most of Blainey's histories are—which concentrates more on formist detail than mechanistic pattern. In a vivid, evocative style, Blainey recounts the experiences of the men who prospected for gold:

> Johns rode in pain, barely able to see or walk, ailing with a paralysis he thought was rheumatism. In tributaries of the Ord they found gold in many places but, being the dry season, they had no water to wash the soil thoroughly. With Johns still in pain they rode into the Northern Territory, reached the overland telegraph at Katherine, and got to the gold diggings at Yam Creek in time for a welcome banquet on 28 October 1882. No men more deserved their welcome . . . [Saunders] was a gold man to the last, dying at the age of ninety-three after falling into his campfire at the gold town of Menzies.[27]

Most of the book is enlivened by descriptions of this sort, adding up to a powerfully conveyed hymn of praise to the plucky prospectors, free-spirited miners and 'alert' managers who built the mining industry. Here and there in the narrative are also glimpses of an explanation for the rise and decline of mines, the development of civilized customs in mining communities and the changing militancy of the miners.

But the measure of Blainey's development can be estimated by comparing this 1963 edition of *The Rush that Never Ended* with the revised edition of 1969, when a new concluding chapter was added to take account of the mineral discoveries of the 1960s. This chapter not only narrates the fortunes of Lang Hancock and the Bass Strait oil-wells, however, but sets out Blainey's theory of mineral discovery. This takes the form of a law: 'if a mineral has not been vigorously sought, it is not logical to argue that the mineral is rare in a country'.[28] In other words, mineral discoveries are not due to luck or accident: when a particular mineral was not in demand or if governmental regulations discouraged its viability, prospectors would not find it or (sometimes) report its existence. Blainey's interest in establishing general laws of history strengthened to the extent that in *The Causes of War* (1973) he generated scores of interrelated general propositions about the origins of hostilities between nations, based on a study of every international war fought since 1700.

Blainey's best-known work, *The Tyranny of Distance*, was published in 1966, and reprinted in a coffee-table format with lavish illustrations in 1974. The original text remained unaltered in the second edition, and reflects the mid-point in Blainey's transition from the empiricism of his company histories of the 1950s to a mechanistic, sociological approach. He took one card out of the historian's pack, the one labelled 'distance', and played it off against the others. Essentially, he argued that the vast distance within Australia, and between it and Europe, shaped the pattern of European settlement in Australia to a much greater extent than historians had previously recognized. In his preface, Blainey explained that he had originally intended to write a history of 'the coming of mechanical transport to Australia' and its effects. It followed that some treatment of Australia's isolation—both internally and in its relation to the Old World—was necessary; hence the factor of distance came to dominate the book.[29] These comments are revealing not only of *The Tyranny of Distance* as an argument, but also indicate something of Blainey's development towards a sociological approach in the mid-1960s; at the outset of the project his aim was, strictly speaking, empiricist but by the inclusion of an abstract explanatory factory the cause and effect relationships of transport innovation formed a pattern.

It was a pattern which, curiously, subordinated the activities and ideas of men to the factors of distance, technological innovation and geography. Blainey had rejected the significance of class analysis —which he saw as central to marxism—but had come to emphasize the material factors which constrained men's lives. ('I think the class struggle and the industrial friction on the metal fields have been exaggerated', he wrote in 1963.[30]) His treatise on distance elevated the role of a material factor almost to the level of a monocausal explanation, in a manner which was strikingly similar to the gauche exaggeration of the mode of production as the ultimately determining factor in some vulgar marxist accounts of Australian history. In Blainey's hands, distance could explain almost anything. Commercial and strategic advantage was the primary motive in establishing Botany Bay in the first place, he argued (following the work of K. M. Dallas), even though the rhetoric of the English government was that their basic aim was to plant a penal colony.[31] Similarly,

> Australia's distance from Europe prolonged the dearth of women. A working man with a young family was reluctant to pay the fares of the whole family to Australia when he could travel more cheaply over the

Atlantic to New York or Quebec; but for a single man the high cost of a berth to Melbourne or Sydney was less forbidding.[32]

The relatively higher number of men in nineteenth-century Australia in turn led to higher conditions of living, to 'mateship' (following Russel Ward's argument), and to an Australian love of sport. Sport is a masculine preference, argued Blainey, and it was partly the demand for increased leisure time which fostered the increased militancy of unions: 'Certainly the success of these demands for more leisure came in considerable degree from the workers' bargaining position, which was fortified by isolation from Europe and the consequent, weaker, flow of European emigrants'.[33] Thus Blainey was able to exclude from his account the role of non-material factors in the rise of unionism, such as the development of radical ideologies, and the growing solidarity between workers, which the Old Left had seen as stemming naturally from 'mateship'. This same sub-theme emerges, by implication, throughout Blainey's scholarship. Chapter 25 of *The Rush that Never Ended* portrayed the diggers as 'redshirt capitalists', for, as long as they were able to make money from prospecting, as self-reliant miners, or from the petty theft of gold in their employers' mines, unions were not of any use to them. The growth of unions after the 1880s could therefore be explained as a result of changes in the mining industry itself, without recourse to the ideology of socialism, which grew up alongside the union movement. Blainey's history is therefore denuded of political passion; for him politics can be explained psychologically: 'Politics is a theatre on which the old grievances and fears and loyalties, made respectable and adult and 'relevant' by ideologies and manifestoes, unconsciously disport themselves'.[34] This is the clearest statement of his view of political ideology that Blainey has yet provided, which suggests that he does not take the style or content of politics as seriously as more traditional historians.

Blainey has most determinedly set himself apart from those whom he regards as conventional historians. He is the individualist, the solitary prospector who searches in magpie fashion across the terrain of Australian history looking for a pattern in the landscape which others have missed; occasionally he finds a nugget. He is something of a loner who personally eschews 'mateship'; friends don't visit him at weekends but let him potter around his East Ivanhoe garden.[35] He is also the impish controversialist who, having thought his own way through a problem, might come to an unfashionable conclusion, such as his defence of the Concorde plane. Although he taught economic history at Melbourne University for over ten years, he had little in common with traditional economic historians; in 1977 he took up the Ernest Scott professorship in the department of history, coming something of a full circle back to the department in which he had studied as an undergraduate.[36] His mechanistic approach had taken him far from the purity of history as taught in the Melbourne department when he was an undergraduate; the career of Stretton, one of his contemporaries, reflects a comparable restlessness with the orthodoxies of that department.

Born in 1924, Hugh Stretton graduated from the University of Melbourne in history, and did subsequent work at Oxford and Princeton. A Fellow of Balliol College from 1948 to 1954, he was appointed to the professorship of history at Adelaide in 1954, at thirty years of age. Asked recently if he was ever a 'pure' historian, Stretton retorted that he had never been an historian: 'It would be more true to say that I never became one! I did think for five years of becoming one . . .'[37] There is some point to his jest in terms of the definition of history as a craft unto itself propounded by Crawford, under whom he studied as an undergraduate. But Stretton developed a definition of history which moved away from Crawford's. By about 1960 this marriage of history and sociology was fairly well formed in the younger man's mind. A growing sense of the limitations of history seems to have driven him towards a sociological approach, comparable in its essentials to that exemplified by Blainey and others. In an interview conducted in 1975, Stretton claimed that history 'is the discipline that ought to be doing all sorts of very general things':

But is the discipline as it presently stands capable of being that sort of
. . .?
If you described its function it could, but if you look at the blokes in it, it's very unlikely. Most of the types who select themselves into it are not likely to become genuinely alarmist about the state of the world, or the future. But a lot of history graduates are turned out with talents that can be very useful in other trades. They are used to keeping their balance and judgement in dealing with processes of great complexity (or the best of them are). So they can often be turned into good town planners, good sociologists, having escaped undergraduate studies in those disciplines which might have made them unduly narrow-minded.

Because they've escaped the peculiar delusions of those disciplines or
what?
. . . to take a roundabout route to your question: I can hardly think of a social scientist who is *justly* famous—who has made any kind of theoretical breakthrough and left his discipline with different

assumptions from which he found it—who got there by being brought up within the proper channels, doing an undergraduate course and graduate courses *in that discipline.* But on the other hand if you look at the valuable innovators, practically every one of them has been brought up in a different line or pursuit from the one in which he innovates . . . You're brought up inside a set of rules and a set of assumptions, a structured way of doing things . . . [Entering a new discipline] the first thing you notice is that its assumptions are different, perhaps stupid, and you start questioning them . . . Nowadays there is no way you could now be brought up in the way Marx was.[38]

Many of the issues Stretton raises here are echoes of *The Political Sciences,* which Stretton finally completed in 1969.[39] This was his first book, but the general argument had shaped itself at least as early as 1960, when he took sabbatical leave to teach at Smith College in Massachusetts. The book should have emerged then, but refused to come out, and the student essays continued to mount up on his desk. Stretton wrote at that time:

Apart from the cigarette burn through chapter two there is nothing wrong with my book except the trifle of five chapters not being written yet and a certain amount of child art from forgetting to keep it five feet from the ground at all times. Never mind now, here is this Junior supposed to be telling me The Causes of World War One and all she does is babble on objectivity. I should do something about her prose if I had the time. Objectivity, hell . . . The trouble with that girl, it costs too much to teach her. What ought to be done to that paper would cost a day would cost five pages would cost promotion would cost cash. Because nobody would see me do it and it would still be subjective if they did. I would be imparting literacy, and if anything is more subjective than teaching, literary is. Meanwhile I have a transmission job coming up at around a hundred and twenty five dollars and one summer left before some highly objective school fees set in.[40]

This provoked a seven page article in the *Massachusetts Review,* which was, in effect, a 'false start' for *The Political Sciences.* Stretton was not yet satisfied that his argument was ready for public display— and there was the task of building up the Adelaide history department throughout the late 1950s and 1960s. Asked if he thought the work had much impact when it was finally published, Stretton replied: 'I've no idea . . . There was one professor of economics who said he was converted by it . . . It would have been much more appropriate published ten years earlier . . . I was a hell of a long time writing it.

I mean it didn't take long to write—but getting around *to* write'.[41] Part of the difficulty was that his major argument could be buttressed with example after example in each and all of the social sciences—and Stretton felt this was necessary. As he puts it, *The Political Sciences* 'was a desperate effort to show that these things *are* true—the main line of the work—and can be illustrated with a number of examples'.

The argument of *The Political Sciences* is primarily oppositional: against the 'enemy', the 'objective Party', or, to use Manning Clark's fine turn of phrase, against the 'measurers'. It is, seen from this point of view, much less the manifesto of an ex-historian, as Encel implied in his review,[42] and rather more an attack on conventional social science by one schooled as an historian. Man as a valuing animal is Stretton's point of departure. Man is more than a mere repository of values, however, for he must create his own 'scaffolding of valuations'.[43] For the social scientist this means that the terrifying complexity of what it is to be human leads not to an attempt to shrug off responsibility by retreating into 'objectivity', but rather to a duty to work from structures of belief and stated purpose. As Stretton words it, '. . . almost every human event is conditioned by almost all of human history, so that any explanation has to be selective, and, according to its particular purpose, *ought* to have its selection rationally organized by that purpose'.[44]

> In social science it is tempting to look for purely technical principles of selection, and there are lots of trivial ones available... How do you decide whether you'll commit all your resources to finding out things that are generally true of the rich or generally true of the poor, or generally true of peace or war or true for much smaller sub-groups of these phenomena? How do you distinguish between those very useful purposes?[45]

In conversation, Stretton acknowledges that there is one difficulty with his formulation: that many social scientists pursue moral concerns simply to be in keeping with the research fashions of the day.[46] But his most severe criticism in *The Political Sciences* is reserved for those whom he calls 'non-interventionist'. It is *possible*, he agrees,

> to explain the whole process of knowledge-production as merely a function of the career-system of the profession . . . [But] such a model would have little relation to reality. If there is anywhere a 'pure' non-interventionist social scientist, he is unlikely to behave as in that model. He is more likely, if he does not want to manipulate society himself, to sell his discoveries to those who do. Not to those who would (contrary to his non-interventionist faith) engineer any fundamental

changes in society; rather to those who would manipulate themselves some profit out of society's existing arrangements.[47]

But perhaps the most significant aspect of Stretton's critique—so far as the manufacture of Australian history is concerned—was that it enabled him to transcend Crawford's moral conception of history. While his mentor had argued that an historian must suspend judgement until the data was gathered, by 1961 Stretton saw it as 'untrue' that 'the historian's bias arises after he has decided what to abstract and identify as facts'.[48]

Stretton's second major work, *Capitalism, Socialism and the Environment*, published in 1976, is a demonstration of the sort of social science advocated in *The Political Sciences:* 'I believe that people, including social scientists, should write 'good', 'bad', 'right' and 'wrong' when those are what they mean'.[49] After establishing that environmental issues are inextricably entwined with normal political concerns and should therefore be discussed in terms of alternative ideological possibilities, Stretton sketches out three optional futures for the liberal democracies (including Australia), which take three of these ideologies as their bases. In the first, 'the rich rob the poor' because the mainstream conservationist argument is taken to its logical conclusion and a small ruling class impose rationing on the majority once economic expansion is halted. This represents a return to the patterns of inequality characteristic of feudal régimes. In the second scenario, the democracies follow 'American commonsense leadership' and inequalities gently increase because the Left keep environmental and distributional demands separate: productivity declines, but the costs of left-wing reform are systematically if gradually distributed at the expense of the poorer sections of these societies. But Stretton announces his commitment to a third sort of future: a social-democrat scenario, where environmental issues are carefully used by the Left to engineer a reduction of inequality to a fourfold scale of incomes between the very rich and the very poor. The remaining two-thirds of the book examine the ideological and tactical considerations which underpin the achievement of this best possible future. *Capitalism, Socialism and the Environment* is a breathtakingly ambitious and remarkably coherent book which clearly marks Stretton off as one of Australia's few scholars of international standing: proof of the honesty of his convictions is to be found in the fact that he demoted himself to a readership in Adelaide University's history department, in 1968, on highly principled egalitarian grounds.

Stretton's harshest critics are the revolutionary socialists, who concede the purity of his convictions, and sometimes even describe him as the best of the 'bourgeois' scholars in Australia, but criticize *Capitalism, Socialism and the Environment* for its inadequate treatment of non-peaceful processes (war, revolution, police coercion), its assumption that households are relatively stable (thereby over-looking the importance of labour migration for capitalist economies) and its treatment of Marx:

> Stretton claims that Marx's fatal mistake was to identify 'ownership itself . . . as the root of evil'. Naturally, Stretton doesn't come straight out and say that we wicked Marxists are after his toothbrush, but such nonsense is the inescapable consequence of presenting Marx as opposed to property as such.[50]

McQueen is misrepresenting Stretton in order to make this joke. The quote he uses foreshadows a long discussion of the most probable 'single cause' of the socialist failure to build up electoral support in the liberal democracies, and it should be this sub-argument which receives attention:

> Besides the general distrust of ownership, socialists are prevented from understanding this [what the masses will *do* with what they *own*] chiefly by the Marxist theory of class. I believe that the least misleading way to understand modern inequalities is to see them as continuous from richest to poorest.

In other words, like other sociological historians, Stretton prefers a neo-Weberian model of social structure because the marxist model does not 'fit'.

> Parties of equality have the difficult task of persuading majorities of middle and poor to act together. The 'natural' working class, for which Marxists see a natural common interest and political role, is no longer distinguished by the fact of wage labor. It is distinguished in practice by low pay, blue collars and (very often) mean rental housing; and it has long been a minority class. Its 'lost' numbers—skilled or white collared or otherwise prosperous—are enjoying their possession of houses and gardens and cars and are unlikely to vote for anyone who wants them to trade all those for a standardized apartment near a jolly public park.[51]

This sub-argument is absolutely vital to the major argument of *Capitalism, Socialism and the Environment*, and is the key assumption in Stretton's search for a social-democratic future. The subject

of private home ownership is evident in every public lecture, article
or monograph Stretton has written since 1970.[52] It is therefore non-
sensical to argue that because he does not subsume the question of
'domestic economy' within a holistic analysis, such as that provided
by marxist theorists, this *in itself* vitiates his argument; rather, the
issue must first be debated within the limits of Stretton's problematic
itself. Assuming that the chief characteristic of the sociological school
is to proceed atomistically, by seeking connections between various
aspects of individual and social life within liberal democracies, the
pertinent criticisms are those which highlight the gaps in this
approach. It matters little if Stretton formally adopts a non-marxist
theory of social structure, if, in doing so, his model is able to satisfactorily explain historical processes. Following this reasoning, it
then becomes clear that Stretton's major omission is not the exploita-
tion of the housing industry for ruling-class interests (which, in fact,
it could be argued, he does explain very competently), nor the
capitalist use of migratory labour, nor the deeper causes of inflation,
nor other themes for which he has been upbraided by the revolutionary socialists. Instead the major omission in his writing is plain,
ordinary workforce participation. In at least two places, he shrugs his
shoulders and sighs, 'Work could often be made more interesting'.[53]
This signals his overemphasis on domestic as opposed to other work.
Stretton might reply that this was a deliberate choice, given the
tendency of most socialists to place too much weight on the role of
workers in the workplace 'itself', and neglect the importance of home
and hearth. This neglect does not mean that Stretton does not understand or ignores the marxist definition of capitalism, as tied
intimately to the means of production—as the revolutionary socialist
critics would tend to argue—but rather that his methodology leads
him closer and closer to an appreciation of the significance of the
workplace—and then draws him irresistibly away from it. One
example from his *Ideas for Australian Cities*, first published in 1970,
will highlight this problem. In chapter 7, he compares the South Australian experimental town, Elizabeth, with the outer Sydney suburb of
Green Valley—both of which are examples of public planning. Although he regards Elizabeth as the better of the two communities
('Green Valley is among this century's most deliberate, unnecessary,
concentrated and massive offences against Australian children'),
Stretton criticizes it also, especially in terms of its provisions for the
lives of its younger and female inhabitants.[54] But nowhere does he
discuss the effects on Elizabeth's workers of living in a town under the
shadow of General Motors-Holden: instead he merely states that 'it
is rarely a good idea to make [factory labour] families four-fifths of

a whole town's population', [55] which is consistent with his oft-expressed proposition that mixed neighbourhoods are preferable to segregated communities. Perhaps Stretton, true to his conviction about the necessity for innovative thinkers to question the assumptions of whichever field they take an active interest in, will go on to question the assumption held by town planners, that their business is merely to regulate and equalize the distributive effects of capitalism, leaving its productive base untouched. This task some New Left historians and theoreticians have already begun.[56]

The New Left

Although the New Left historians broadly share the fundamental assumption of the sociological historians, that it is possible to construct demonstrable laws of social change, their approach is much more holistic, and reflects the confidence of those oppositional groups within Australia from the late 1960s onwards, in seeking to transform the entire society. McQueen is the most interesting of the New Left historians, not only because he is the best known of their number but because his somewhat erratic social theory is indicative of the problems which beset the emergence of counter-hegemonic groups.

Born in Brisbane in 1942, Humphrey McQueen became active in politics at the young age of 15, when he joined the Labor Party. By 1960 he was President of the Young Labor Association, and had become enmeshed in a number of honorary positions in the Labor machinery. One of the strongest themes running through his later historical work is his conviction that the A.L.P. has acted in a manner contrary to the interests of those it claims to represent. A decade after he had left the Party, McQueen made this biting comment on the deradicalizing experience of being involved in the internal organization of the A.L.P.

> The young idealist who joins the A.L.P. to create a better world, perhaps to achieve socialism, will most likely find his enthusiasm burnt up in debates—not over issues like Vietnam or public ownership—but over how many election signs to erect, how many personal appeals to issue and how many how-to-vote cards to print. And the greatest of these is fund raising: silver-circle clubs, donation sheets and barbecues. The more a member has to offer the more the machine will take, for it has an insatiable appetite for volunteers—branch, State and Federal committees all demanding officers and organizers.[57]

This suggests a degree of alienation from the A.L.P., not evinced by other radical historians: R. W. Connell, for example, has been a member of the N.S.W. North Ryde branch since 1966.

After matriculating in 1959, McQueen worked in the Commonwealth Public Service for two years, before commencing full-time tertiary education. At the University of Queensland he edited the student newspaper and studied honours politics, graduating in 1965. His thesis was a study of Mao Tse-tung, but he was also reading widely, in the marxist tradition especially, and encountered the work of the Italian socialist Antonio Gramsci. Gramsci had developed a marxist approach to the problem of 'culture' and, amongst other things, emphasized the distinction between coercive control (*dominio*) and 'ruling culture' (*egemonia*). McQueen became interested in this concept of 'hegemony', and his break with the Old Left would turn principally on the Australian implications of Gramsci's theory. (Gramsci was also being read at this time by younger British historians who, in turn, especially E. P. Thompson, also influenced McQueen's thinking, and that of the Australian New Left.) In the meantime, McQueen had taken up a secondary school-teaching appointment in the middle-class Melbourne suburb of Glen Waverley, where he taught from 1966 to 1969. His interest in Australian history was rekindled when he was asked to take the matriculation class for Australian history.[58] At the same time he was actively involved in the burgeoning anti-war movement and, in 1968, became foundation chairman of the Revolutionary Socialists group, based in Melbourne.

It was not until late 1968, however, that McQueen attracted wide recognition: this came with the publication of his 'Convicts and rebels' article in *Labour History*. By enquiring into the extent to which the convicts in various penal settlements engaged in rebellious activities, and the degree to which these felonies could be regarded as political, McQueen began his task of demolishing the radical nationalist tradition erected by the Old Left school.

> Russel Ward claims that 'all we know about the convicts shows that egalitarian class solidarity was the one human trait which usually remained to all but the most brutalized'. From this we must conclude that Ward knows very little about the convicts and that he has a quaint notion of class. Ward uses class to mean nothing more than that group of people who came to the colony as convicts and ignores all social and national divisions within this category. It is misleading to clothe the convicts in the aura of class struggle since for its first fifty years Australia did not have a class structure, but only a deformed

stratification which had itself been vomited up by the maelstrom which was delineating class in Britain.[59]

McQueen's break from the Old Left is illustrated by this passage: he was dissatisfied with the imprecise manner in which Ward and the older socialist historians had employed class analysis, and was seeking to refine it as a tool of analysis. The ideological implications of this dissatisfaction emerge more clearly later in his writings. Another aspect of the emerging New Left programme for the re-writing of Australian history is implicit in this extract from the same article:

> If a class formula must be given to the majority of convicts it must be lumpen-proletarian or petty-bourgeois. The ideology of these is similar, and can be described as independent people 'who hate officiousness and authority, especially when these qualities are embodied in military officers and policemen'. Such an attitude is essentially bourgeois in origin and content and was well suited to the declasse small proprietors, dispossessed labourers and professional criminals who made up the bulk of the convicts. 'The greatest English criminals may have remained in England protected by birth and wealth', but those less fortunate who were deported also accepted the ideology of capitalism—individual acquisitiveness. The convicts lacked, albeit through no fault of their own, any feeling of class consciousness. Their interrelationship was based on the all too flimsy basis of the honour of thieves which will be shown to be no honour at all.[60]

This argument attests to the clear influence of Gramsci: the convict ideology is linked, not merely to their former economic position in England, but to the hegemony (dominant values and ideology) which was transplanted in the penal society. At this stage McQueen's concept of hegemony was not fully developed, a problem which was to recur in *A New Britannia*.

Russel Ward replied to McQueen's article by claiming that his argument in *The Australian Legend* had been precisely what McQueen had been demanding, and that he had been misinterpreted rather than challenged. Ward went one step further, and berated the younger man's iconoclastic tone:

> McQueen has written a stimulating article. Most historians, I think, will agree with its general drift while deploring its incidental displays of rudeness and hoping that he goes on to make the most of his gifts. Some sense of group solidarity with one's fellow historians should help us to disagree without rancour and to debate without sneering.[61]

If Ward seriously hoped that McQueen would obey the unspoken canons of Australian historiography and present his arguments in a 'gentlemanly' fashion, he was soon to be disappointed. For although of a consensual temperament in private, the public McQueen struts the stage with Bolshevik belligerence, and errs on the side of exaggeration to make his points. He did not respond publicly to Ward's criticisms for two years; rather he proceeded with the publication of *A New Britannia*. Late in 1969 McQueen had attempted unsuccessfully to gain entry into the Research School of Social Sciences at the A.N.U. as a postgraduate; he jumped at a senior tutorship in the School of General Studies, teaching under the aegis of Professor Manning Clark.

There are a number of ways in which *A New Britannia: An Argument Concerning the Social Origins of Australian Radicalism and Nationalism* could be read. Perhaps the most common reading was to understand it as an attack on the Australian 'Legend':

> The legend reached its fullest expressions towards the end of the nineteenth century when in a limited way it gave some direction to the life of those Australians who were moved by it. It produced certain famous phrases such as 'temper democratic, bias offensively Australian' and certain key words such as 'White Australia' and 'mateship', it was largely based on the bushman's egalitarian attitudes, it was expressed in some of Henry Lawson's poems and to a lesser extent to his stories, its main organ was J. F. Archibald's *Bulletin*, it was part of the ideology of the Labor Party. Whatever else it was, it was radical, populist, nationalist, racialist.62

The radical Humphrey McQueen writing in 1970? No, these words were penned by the conservative Peter Coleman in 1962. *A New Brittania* was, if nothing else, ideologically innocent.

The reviews of *A New Britannia* began with Noel McLachlan, writing in *Meanjin*. McLachlan made two important points: he argued that 'the most impressive thing in the end is not how different is the McQueen Version, but how profound is his debt to Ward and Gollan among others'. Secondly, McLachlan asked whether

> . . . 'racism' [can] really be used to discredit entirely the labour movement? McQueen apparently recognizes that it was endemic to Australian society as a whole at that stage (though it is often hard to tell whether he claims to be generalizing for Australian attitudes at large). And not only in Australia, but more or less universally. So it would have been extraordinary if Australian radicals had **not** been racists.63

Then, early in 1971, Ian Turner joined the growing list of reviewers of *A New Britannia;* like McLachlan, he had no complaints about McQueen's avowedly utilitarian motives for the study of history. Turner contended that McQueen had misread Ward and Gollan, but chose not to elaborate the point; rather the main thrust of his review was to show

> the argument about nationalism . . . to be simplistic and . . . to equate nationalism with 'sub-imperialism' is grossly to over-simpfly the ambivalence of Australian political and cultural attitudes towards the United Kingdom; while to equate it with 'racism' enables McQueen to slide too easily away from the basis of reality which underlay the ambiguous response of Australians towards their isolation, its simultaneous promise of security and threat of vulnerability.[64]

The final section of Turner's review was even more telling, for he attacked McQueen's methodology on two grounds: the way in which McQueen arbitrarily expelled facts from the 'club' of those facts which had already been admitted by historians, and McQueen's characteristic tendency of retrojection (notoriously in the case of his Lawson-as-fascist argument).[65]

A. A. Phillips concurred with Turner, in objecting 'to McQueen's ways of handling evidence', and argued that 'a professional historian' ought not 'to grab at any place of evidence which at first sight seems to support a desired conclusion'. Phillips tackled McQueen point by point on 'Waltzing Matilda', *Australia Felix,* Bernard O'Dowd and Henry Lawson.[66]

The angriest review was yet to come. In the autumn issue of *Overland,* Russel Ward denied that *A New Britannia* is 'as the author seems passionately to believe it is, an argument between himself and most previous Australian historians on whose work he has built, but an argument with himself occasioned by his misunderstanding or misinterpretation of their work'.[67] Ward agreed with other critics in describing McQueen's provocative arguments about Lawson and others as 'profoundly unhistorical and un-marxist', and took this line of criticism one step further by attacking McQueen's tendency to minimize change over time:

> History, from Cromwell to Mao tse-tung, amply demonstrates that revolutions tend to prosper in proportion as their protagonists show that *they,* and not the conservative, traditional leaders, are the guardians of the nation's *true* interests and honour. For example, could the Viet Cong resistance to American aggression have endured for a single month unless it had been, and *had seen itself to be,* the true heir of the Vietnamese national, including bourgeois-national,

resistance to foreign domination? Yet it is precisely this approach which McQueen, in common with all politically reactionary historians, denounces.[68]

However Ward concluded on a positive note by agreeing that most Australian historians, himself included, had 'tended to underplay' the racism of Australians prior to the First World War.

Significantly, virtually all the reviewers of *A New Britannia* were of a generally left-wing persuasion. In all, *A New Britannia* attracted thirty-three reviewers in various Australian newspapers and journals. McQueen took the unusual step of replying to thirteen of these, and in two cases provoked a rejoinder.[69] Probably the most significant of McQueen's rejoinders was his 'Reply to Russel Ward', which appeared in mid-1971. McQueen began by arguing that it is difficult to understand Ward's argument:

> Since the publication of *The Australian Legend* we have been confronted with a Dutch weather-clock: when someone says that Australia was not like the picture in Ward's book out pops a little man who tells, 'That's right, it's all a legend'; but when somebody praises Ward for capturing the essence of Australia's past out pops a little man who says, 'Thanks mate' . . . [It] is difficult to hit a moving target—especially one that slips and slides.[70]

McQueen was right to highlight the rather sloppy way in which Ward treated the ideological functioning of ideas in Australian history, and he also answered Ward's specific criticisms—'his middlebrow and largely fallacious pedantry'—one by one, refusing to give ground on the issue of Lawson-as-fascist, and the piano argument. However Ward's central criticism, that McQueen's approach blinded him to a sense of the dynamics of Australian history—the issue of change over time—was left unanswered by McQueen; in fact, he sidestepped it.

How much support is there for Ward's criticism? *A New Britannia* can, in fact, be regarded as a circular argument in at least three important aspects: at the level of the social theory underpinning it, in McQueen's use of data, and in terms of its ideological implications. Its social theory is difficult to understand, but he certainly seems to assume that consciousness is the critical criterion of class,[71] and yet does not locate the origins of this consciousness in class relations, since no dominant class is systematically referred to in the book.[72] In 1972 McQueen defended himself against this line of criticism, by arguing that some sections of *A New Britannia* do, in fact, provide a 'base', for explaining 'petit-bourgeois' consciousness:

the 'base' is there right enough in the materially uplifting experiences of 'convicts', 'diggers', 'unionists' and to a lesser extent 'selectors'. The 'selectors' chapter introduces the 'base' in a different form by making the developing industrial relations of production something from which labourers wished to escape. Thus it is present as an integral part of their lives and not as a reified category. More importantly still it is present in the account I give of Australia's privileged position in the British imperial systems.[73]

This rejoinder is something of a sleight-of-hand, since McQueen had previously implied that what other marxists call the 'base' was not so significant, after all, in determining the nature of colonial society. And when the chapters he mentions are examined, there is hardly any mention of anything which could even vaguely be construed as a 'base'. Other modes of production—besides the incipient capitalist one—are not analysed, nor is there any substantial discussion of the labour market, occupational mobility, wage differentiation, the role of any 'labour aristocracy' or other traditional foci of marxist concern.[74] Nineteen-twentieths of these chapters concentrate on ideological consequences: is this justifiable, even for someone who (probably correctly) wants to posit a less economically reductionist marxism? The near-absence of a 'base' threatens to render McQueen's argument circular, for he only accepts as 'genuinely' proletarian those cultural breaks which match up to a predetermined set of 'counter-hegemonic' criteria: as one New Left historian has commented, 'McQueen's conception of class is at once ahistorical and teleological'.[75] This tendency towards an organicist social theory affects McQueen's use of data. A recent commentator has contended that '*A New Britannia* relies largely on the Old Left historians for its data'.[76] It is more accurate to say that when McQueen is dealing with something resembling the 'base' of nineteenth-century society, he is forced by the logic of his implicit theory to refer back to the evidence proferred by conservative and liberal (rather than radical) historians. So he cites Robson on the previous convictions of convicts, Bolton on miners' wages, Nairn on W. G. Spence, Blainey on gold-stealing and so on. His use of Blainey is particularly fascinating: *The Rush that Never Ended* is occasionally so 'deadly accurate' that McQueen draws on it for his 'diggers' chapter; but when arguing that the coalminers were exceptional 'unionists' (that is, they displayed 'correct' proletarian attitudes), Blainey drops out of the picture, for his history of mining omits coalmining (because, euphemistically, 'its industrial tensions differed'!)[77] In other words, McQueen often lifts data from these less-than-radical historians without any consideration of the very real differences that exist between the theoretical context of this data and his own (espoused) social theory. McQueen is also epistemologically compelled to use some evidence in a highly undifferentiated manner: so he totally neglects regional differences by using such data as North Queensland wage-levels and the setting up of the Agricultural Bank of Western Australia. Finally, the ideological implication of *A New Britannia* is, at best, ambiguous, as McQueen has subsequently admitted: 'There has been some attempt to foist 'responsibility' for racism onto the labouring classes and *A New Britannia* has undoubtedly been employed to this end'.[78] It goes much deeper than this. Despite the protestations of its author that *A New Britannia* sought to contribute to a radical transformation of Australian society, the argument comes so perilously close to a denial of any revolutionary possibility that the majority of its readers might have been justified in assuming an anarchist or conservative implication from it.

There is evidence that McQueen has begun to modify his social theory progressively, since 1970; but in 1971 he was still pursuing the agenda he had set himself at that time. In April he had completed his 'Living off Asia' article, which was eventually published in *Arena*.[79] Here, he argued that the foreign policies of the A.L.P. during the 1960s, were counter-revolutionary: to do this he implied that the differences between men like Jim Cairns and Gough Whitlam were minimal. But one of his main interests was to develop his study of Australian racism.[80] McQueen's argument was that, although White Australian novelists, film-makers and short-story writers had paid more attention to Aborigines than had historians (except for Manning Clark), they had essentially misunderstood and misrepresented them. The one exception he conceded was Robert Tudawalli's portrayal of the wild fella in the 1955 film *Jedda*; he is 'the only genuine Aboriginal human being in the entire artistic output of Australia'.[81] McQueen also began at this stage to substantiate further his proposition 'that the A.L.P. is organizationally and ideologically fog-bound within capitalism', by examining certain key aspects of the way in which the A.L.P. has served 'as an agent for integrating the workforce within capitalism' during the twentieth century.[82] This particular essay was significant for a number of reasons. It was much more lucidly written and lacked many of the obvious over-simplifications of *A New Britannia*. It had a stronger sense of the dynamics of specific historical periods than anything McQueen had previously written: he was able to demonstrate the force of some of his blanket generalizations (which are supposed to continue over very long periods of time), by reference to critical points, such as the depression:

> The point is this: in the midst of the gravest internal crisis that Australian capitalism has encountered, the A.L.P. was organically incapable of understanding what was happening, and of making any moves to build socialism. Instead it retreated into its populist nationalism and strove to keep its erstwhile and remaining supporters safely within this tradition. Its entire experience had conditioned it for this role and it in turn assisted in conditioning workers to expectations consistent with its capacity and intent.[83]

An obvious criticism is that McQueen was not yet able to integrate satisfactorily the various aspect of A.L.P. policy he regarded as important, to construct them into a coherent whole and relate them to the anguish of being enmeshed in the Party machinery—an anguish which he had felt acutely as an adolescent. The reason for this, of course, is that he had yet to consider the social base of the A.L.P. in the twentieth century (the 'petit-bourgeoisie') in any detail. But one significant aspect of this essay is that McQueen was able, for the first time in public, to set out clearly and explicitly what he had been attempting to achieve in his first monograph. Now, two years separated him from his first full-length historical study, and its aims were at last obvious:

> In *A New Britannia* an attempt was made to fulfil Antonio Gramsci's demand that the history of a political party should be the history of an entire society, from a monographic point of view. Thus it traced out the social forces which combined to form the Australian Labor Party and which so effectively integrated the party into capitalism. In order to demonstrate this integration the narrative went up to the period around the First World War. On questions such as racism, defence and state activity it became clear that the Labor Party was not a passive receptable but was the active advocate.[84]

A New Britannia was still provoking debate. In mid-1972, McQueen apologised for not making the argument more explicit, and suggested that a more appropriate subtitle would have been 'An argument concerning the origins and nature of the Labor Party'.[85] McQueen also implied that his attitudes had already changed since 1970,[86] and, from 1972, he has continued the task of filling out his conception of twentieth-century Australian history.[87] It is clear from the main thrust of this body of material, that McQueen had been fundamentally concerned with understanding the components of bourgeois hegemony in contemporary and recent history. In 1971 he had accepted an invitation to contribute a chapter on 'Taking a strong stand' to an anthology on the practice of history-writing in Australia.[88] Clearly McQueen's reputation had by then extended widely: as he implied in the opening lines of his chapter, he was the token deviant historian amongst the contributors. He used the opportunity to demonstrate that his variety of history was no more 'biased' than that style practised by more 'conventional' historians. Significantly, the chapter was preceded by a photograph of McQueen being arrested in Canberra in 1972, for distributing anti-conscription leaflets. This is a striking pictorial representation of McQueen's public self-image: he wears striped trousers, an ill-fitting suit coat, hands in his pockets, goatee, darkened glasses, unkempt hair and a smile for the readers of the *Canberra Times*. Photographers in front of him, plain-clothes police behind him dwarfed by his stature, McQueen strides confidently on to whatever fate the court system has in store for him. Another indication of McQueen's obvious notoriety was his inclusion in the 1973 A.B.C. series, *Heresies,* a forum intended for unorthodox views about Australian society. McQueen proved himself witty and often wise in discussing the politics of pollution, inequality, Whitlam's foreign policy and European attitudes to the Aborigines. For example, he succinctly demonstrated how Australian capitalism would make money from one of its most glaring problems, that of pollution:

> Planned obsolescence is to be supplemented by planned sustenance. Survival kits will be marketed each year with new and bigger attachments. Colour preferences will be altered and the whole thing streamlined. The economy will function on two levels: it will sell pollution producers and will sell the means to diminish or evacuate the pollution produced.[89]

Interestingly, in his talk on Aborigines, McQueen implied that the degree of racism within Australian society had only partially diminished since *A New Britannia:*

> Attitudes will persist for years but institutions can and must be changed at once. Eventually prejudice attitudes will disappear, but they will not disappear entirely until the present position of Aborigines has changed.[90]

This comment is significant in that it demonstrates clearly McQueen's position in the idealist-materialist debate. Attitudes have their origins in institutional arrangements, and cannot easily be changed in the long-term unless there is a concomitant change in the social structures which support them, presumably for fear that if attacks on the hegemony diminish in the near future, the attitudes frozen in the institutional matrix will re-assert themselves. Campaigners against racism, such as Al Grassby, may not be thrown up by the conditions of Australian society in the late 1970s.

By the middle of 1974 it was clear that McQueen was not yet able to deal with the history of twentieth-century Australia in a single monograph. Although he was gaining immensely from the ideas thrown up by some of his best students at the A.N.U., where he was still teaching, it seemed time for a change of environment, so he applied for a Literature Board fellowship to enable him to devote all his time to writing, and took this up at the beginning of 1975. In an article in *Arena*, in the same year, he commented in a fairly sarcastic tone on the dilemma he faced as a full-time writer:

> During the past three years I have recognized two themes in twentieth century Australia about which I would like to write books. One book would deal with the interplay of class and nation this century and has the best selling title of *Gallipoli to Petrov*. The other would establish the ways in which Australian intellectuals perceived the 'crisis in civilization' and has the rich but non-money-making title of *The Black Swan of Trespass*. When I am most tempted to be a marxologist I want to write the second of these and display the wealth of my learning, the elegance of my prose, the range of my theoretical reading—in a word, what a good professional I am even though a marxist. When I am most tempted to be a revolutionary I want to write about the ways in which various classes have employed nationalism and thus assist the struggle for national independence and socialism. The dilemma was resolved by beginning to write both.[91]

An indication of the personal intellectual progress McQueen was making, partly because of the conflict he perceived in being both a professional scholar and a marxist polemicist, can be gleaned from his review of John Docker's *Australian Cultural Elites*.[92] McQueen took Docker to task for largely ignoring the milieux in which those aspects of intellectual history he was examining took place, and showed himself well-read in the neo-marxist sociology of literature. Even more interesting was the fact that McQueen criticized Docker's retrojection of some of the evidence underpinning his work—precisely the same failing that A. A. Philips had detected in McQueen himself in 1971! In June 1971 he had written a paper on the origins of the

A.L.P. in Victoria which, when finally published four years later, won professional acceptance.[93] McQueen also impressed many of his 'bourgeois' colleagues in the history profession, with a paper at the 1973 ANZAAS conference in Perth.[94] Finally, on 30 June 1975 McQueen rewrote the introduction to *A New Britannia* for its third reprinting, and conceded the importance of 'questions about modes of productions and of class struggles'. Yet he still insisted that much of the book was concerned with the 'economic' environment 'from which the Labor Party was formed'.[95] But at least he had stated his shift of ground publicly.

In May 1976 McQueen also publicly admitted that he had made a 'theoretical error . . . in describing Henry Lawson as a fascist' in that early work.[96] And, in an amazing turn-about, McQueen propounded in mid-1977 that 'for a class analysis to be valid it needs two inter-locking characteristics. First, classes must be seen as relationships; second, all subjective criteria must be rejected'.[97] He also insisted on the importance of modes of production, for 'other modes of produc-tion—slavery with the convicts, primitive communism with the Aborigines—have existed alongside the capitalist mode in Aus-tralia . . .'[98] These two statements are in direct conflict with the social theory underpinning *A New Britannia,* and suggest the dramatic degree of re-thinking which has taken place among New Left historians during the 1970s. It is not yet altogether clear whether, in the task of breaking free of more deeply-ingrained varieties of the manufacture of Australian history, McQueen still finds himself in the position of Brer Rabbit and Tar Boy: each punch and kick, no matter how well delivered, getting stuck in the messy opponent.

McQueen's vigorous, often 'bad-mannered' book reviews and journal articles have continued to issue forth from his typewriter for a decade. The angry McQueen writes organicist history. His book-length history of the media, *Australia's Media Monopolies,* is full of such virulent polemic against the press monopolists that, except for a sympathetic section on the alcoholic cynicism of journalists, the logic of the argument forcibly excludes any positive remark which might be made about the media industry.[99] Yet much of the spectacular evidence which McQueen brings forward to flesh out his argument, comes from journalists working within this industry. His other books are much more persuasive. His school-teaching experience makes him an able writer of school textbooks. *Aborigines, Race and Racism* was published in 1974, and, in 1978, his *Social Sketches of Australia, 1888-1975. Social Sketches* is McQueen at his angry best: he does not compromise his ideological position, and his adroit selection of evidence yields a compassionate understanding of ordinary Aus-

tralians, living in a society they do not control. The mechanisms of
class power which govern the lives of twentieth-century Australians,
are exposed on every page and in every illustration of this textbook.
Yet McQueen is able to rejoice at times: in the 1940s, for example,
the Presbyterian mission at Ernabella, South Australia, had an unorthodox attitude to Aborigines. There

> children were taught in Pitjantjata-jara, could come to school naked and
> live with their parents. Within six years, fifty of them could read and
> write in their own language. Church-going was not enforced and all the
> Aborigines were free to come and go.[100]

In September 1977 McQueen took up a senior lectureship in art
history at the Canberra School of Art. His study of modernist painting,
The Black Swan of Trespass, and numerous articles on Australian
literature, reflect his continuing interest in questions of cultural
hegemony. The more sophisticated work on patterns of class formation has been largely left to two other New Left historians:
R. W. Connell and T. H. Irving.

In the work of Connell and Irving the manufacture of Australian
history moves in a new direction, for, although neither would claim
to be 'pure' historians, their work has important implications for the
study of social history. In important respects, their so-called 'class
analysis' is similar to McQueen's, and in terms of the more
generalized features of social theorizing there are obvious affinities
between their approach and that of the sociological historians.

R. W. Connell was born in 1944, in Lindfield, Sydney, the son of
educational historian W. F. Connell. He was educated in England, the
United States and Australia—as his father moved from one post to
the next. Connell gained an honours degree in history from Melbourne, his Ph.D. from Sydney, and was a post-doctoral Fellow in
the department of sociology at Chicago in 1970. A lectureship in
government at Sydney followed, then a senior lectureship at Flinders
University, S.A.[101] In 1976 he was appointed founding professor of
sociology at Macquarie University, N.S.W.

As an undergraduate, Connell had been involved in 'fairly orthodox
academic student activity' until about 1965. He 'had been crapped off
by it, but didn't know what good alternatives there [were] . . .' The
four years he spent in Sydney, as a PhD. student, seem to have been
crucial for his intellectual and political development. Connell had
graduated from Melbourne with a hunger for politically relevant
social analysis, which he sought in the newly emerging discipline of
sociology.[102] His Ph.D. research, which was published in 1971 as

The Child's Construction of Politics, provided the material for a number of papers, the interview technique experience for later studies and, ultimately, his professional reputation among fellow sociologists.[103] In intellectual terms, Connell would undoubtedly find a coherence between this early work and his later publications. It behoves anyone reviewing his work to ask whether he has successfully integrated his research interests in psychology and sociology; but, before that, it is essential to examine one of his early papers in detail. 'Images of Australia' is arguably Connell's best early writing, first published in *Quadrant,* and then reprinted in a later anthology of sociological writings.[104] In this paper Connell pointed out that 'the themes developed or crystallized by Hancock have been taken over by his successors with only minor modifications, though with many new illustrations. The result has been a homogeneous tradition of social comment and criticism'.[105] This clear statement of the rigidifying dominance of Hancock's *Australia*—and the implications for the study of history and sociology in this country—should have sounded like a rifle-shot through the ranks of Australian academics. Instead, as Connell noted seven years later, 'I don't know how many of them even read it'. Surprisingly, although he concedes that the article didn't make much of a dent at all on the history profession, Connell is still hard put to explain the dominance of the Hancock thesis:

> I wouldn't think on the whole it's a matter of a set of rules and procedure among historians, because I think the rules and procedures there are essentially very low-level ones . . . I think it's more to do with the lack of any limited theory at a higher level. Any historians— academic historians, or for that matter, political scientists—are practically trained to be untheoretical, by going through various exercises as undergraduates where they refute Marx and so forth . . . Hence almost all Australian historians count it almost a positive virtue to be untheoretical. And given that, I guess any persuasive set of formulations like Hancock's would have a much more powerful influence than its content would.

But, pressed to account for the almost total absence of high-level theorizing amongst academics, Connell was asked if it had something to do with larger cultural considerations:

> I think it probably does, and this is something I just don't know. By and large, [there has been a] lack of connection with academics and the labor market: so you never get a phenomenon here like the Fabians, I guess. Or the socialists with a chair in Germany.[106]

Perhaps Connell has pigeon-holed this vexing problem for a later date; he had not bothered to read the examples of 'pop sociology', such as Ronald Conway's *The Great Australian Stupor*, which have come out in the meantime. The sudden theoretical cul-de-sac in which Connell finds himself on this issue is suggestive of a more general problem within his social theory which recurs toward the end of his most recent monograph, *Ruling Class, Ruling Culture*, which will be discussed later.

In the meantime Connell's Ph.D. thesis, *The Child's Construction of Politics*, was published. In what was rightly acclaimed as a masterly and perceptive work, he attempted to use the interviews he had conducted with his sample of 151 children as a means of understanding the processes of political socialization.[107] At various points, he discerned relationships between these children's views, on various topics related to parliamentary politics, and the broader themes of Australian history. Some of these connections were out-lined in chapter 5, 'The fears of their fathers', where Connell analysed the children's ideas about Vietnam in terms of 'the threat tradition'.[108] After alluding to the defence fears of the nineteenth century, Connell showed how the idea of external threat was modified earlier this century:

> Threats of internal subversion, as protean as those of external attack, crystallized after the Russian Revolution into a fear of communism, which by reason of the international character of the communist movement has linked up with the idea of external threat. The threat in Vietnam manages to combine this historic fear of communism with the even older fear of Asia.[109]

Connell noted that research conducted by Oeser and Emery in a Victorian country town, in the 1940s, had revealed the same percep-tion of external aggression, and surmised that those children, now the parents of his sample of children, provided a link in the generational transmission of the threat tradition. But there were also children in Connell's study who were sceptical of this set of beliefs, and he ascribed this to a 'working class—labor tradition', an alternative minority structure of beliefs which runs counter to the 'mainstream nationalist tradition'. Connell speculated that the nature of the tradition, which the child assimilated from adults, was due partly to a 'hook-up' between political tradition and some political emotion already present in the child's life, and partly to a consciousness of politics as 'an autonomous sphere of activity'.[110] The two traditions which Connell was able to disentangle are not, however, frozen and static, for 'it is possible for current developments to provide some of the basic structure, and thus be a force which will eventually remould the traditions themselves'.[111] Connell argued, later in the book, that this analysis of the children's political socialization shows the inapplicability of 'the consensual systems-theory, or production-line approach'; and that 'the development of political belief is to be regarded, not as a mechanical function or input of a system, but as a contingent, historical process'.[112]

> We may characterize the historical context in which the child is growing up by describing the set of traditions with which he is in contact and the social relations through which their elements are communicated. Not all, it is obvious, have the regular services of a specialized group of catechists. The military—conservative tradition has to rub along with only occasional access to the services of the school, and the working—class—Labor tradition without any access at all. Both of these, however, are institutionalized in the adult world (notably in the Returned Services League and the industrial unions), and this provides a basic continuity while the transmission between generations occurs, informally, within families and neighbourhoods.[113]

Connell nowhere systematized the various 'traditions' he alluded to, but seemed rather to proffer them as constructs which the reader would readily accept: working class—Labor, military—conservative, 'mainstream nationalist' and Imperial (now almost defunct) are the four that he mentioned. It is at this point that his theory runs into difficulties, for it would be extraordinarily difficult to tease out such traditions, demarcate them one for the other and suggest their relative strengths at any given historical juncture.

Precisely what is lacking in Connell's schema? He accepts Piaget's notion of belief systems as *structuring,* as well as *structured;* but perhaps doesn't follow this through. To put it another way: Connell's analysis demonstrates that the various attitudes which adult agents gradually instil into his sample of youngsters do not so much affect the content of their acquired beliefs, as the *form* in which their political reasoning will take place. Connell himself seems aware of the same problems in this analysis, and there are important differences between this 1971 formulation and the concluding chapter of *Ruling Class, Ruling Culture.* In 1971 he discussed how political socialization relates to children's access to formal adult agencies, such as education and the media, and also, secondarily, to the family and neighbourhood. But the tendency in the later work is to emphasize the formal adult agencies at the expense of family and kinship structures. Of course, he concedes the point that

> partly under the influence of the women's movement, [theoretical] arguments have established processes such as personal socialization and sexual interaction, and structures such as the household and family, as central rather than marginal features of an analysis of oppressive social structures.[114]

But twenty pages earlier he had contended that 'a structure can persist despite the circulation of families from generation to generation within it, or indeed the rise of 'new men' within a lifetime'.[115] It would be unfair to exaggerate the degree of this shift, since Connell's work is explicitly exploratory at this stage, but it is illustrative of the importance Connell attaches to historical specifity.

Underlying all of Connell's theorizing is the proposition that many theoretical issues cannot be settled by aprioristic thinking, but are only discoverable through empirical means. When asked in mid-1975 to demonstrate the importance of sexism within the overall structure of his social theorizing, and to suggest how power within a society is ranked, he replied that it was impossible to specify the relativities between various sorts of power at the level of theory. This was a

> view which I would very strongly hold, that we can't in fact demonstrate a position on that point by abstract argument, that you can perhaps set up a system of definitions which will make, say, economic power more important than sexual power. But that's not a very interesting exercise. The only way that you can establish a case on that point, it seems to me, is to exhibit an analysis of society which will be persuasive and which has within it some claims about what factors in this society at this point of time are the leading forms of organized power.[116]

Despite this tension between the idiographic and the nomothetic polarities, reflected in his twin interests in sociology and history, Connell stated fairly explicitly at the beginning of *Ruling Class, Ruling Culture* that the 'basic hypothesis' upon which he works is the traditional socialist one of the importance of private ownership and the labour market, from which he sees the class structure as 'generated'.[117] He differs from Marx in a number of ways, especially in his rejection of the marxist theory of the declining rate of profit, but he is not so much eclectic as imaginative and inventive within the boundaries of the socialist tradition.

Connell's great strength as a theorist ultimately rests on his ability to grapple with the way theoretical constructs both marshal data and are informed by evidence of a particular historical kind. Thus he disposes, for example, of the view sometimes found in New Left writing, that home ownership is in itself a criterion of the class of property owners.[118] Connell's theoretical agility is also reflected in his ability to proceed from larger theoretical statements to particular ones, and to discard concepts used by other theorists as trivial and unimportant or unnecessary. For example, he attacks the view that the central attribute which bureaucrats have in common is their set of attitudes.[119]

The essential difference between the New Left and the sociological historians, as already noted, is that the former tend to ground their search for laws of historical process within a totality. What, then, are the outer limits to Connell's theorizing? To begin with, he is much more concerned with the internal workings of capitalism in Australia than with their links to the world economy. So, although he has a great deal of admiration for Brian Fitzpatrick, he does not place much emphasis on the connections between Australia and the general pattern of imperialism. That is not to say, however, that he ignores the larger global forces completely, but these are introduced as relatively epiphenomenal aspects of his theory. Regarding Australia itself, the boundaries of his theorizing are primarily the nature of the capitalist economy, from which a number of consequences flow. This emphasis on the capitalist mode of production generally leads him to underemphasize the importance of other modes of production, especially the domestic mode. For example, in his analysis of the major companies operating in Australia, he defines them partly in terms of their control over 'total output'. By this he must mean Gross National Product, as ordinarily derived by conventional economists. A number of contemporary theorists have noted that this figure only represents perhaps three-quarters of the real output of an advanced liberal democracy and ignores the productivity generated by housework. Connell's rejoinder would presumably be that the capitalist mode exercises disproportionate power over other modes, regardless of how the overall economy is to be constituted theoretically.

Another important aspect of New Left thinking, is their emphasis on the 'ruling culture' as well as the ruling class. As Connell puts it:

> Simply being a member of a class may have important consequences for action and experience; but it is only the shared consciousness of membership that can transform a class into a transforming political force. That idea has been the basis of socialist strategy ever since

modern class structures began to emerge. The troubles of western socialism in the last generation have naturally led to a search for changes in the conditions of class consciousness.[120]

The final third of *Ruling Class, Ruling Culture,* is taken up with a summary of his own work on class and personal socialization, the media and middle-class culture, and the pattern of hegemony. Connell adroitly demonstrates the class bias built into the education system, the media and, to a lesser extent, the family. He is impressed not only with the generalized way in which a ruling class imposes the legitimacy of central tenets, such as the idea of private property, but with the way adolescents (whom he never regards as simple victims of the historical process) are 'cool' in their responses to external pressures. It is partly this impatience with blanket generalizations about the effects of formal adult agencies on children which raises the quality of Connell's theoretical speculations. But although Connell emphasizes the relative autonomy of children as learners, they are sometimes presented in his account as somewhat passive receptacles of the given order:

> The whole pattern of social relationships constituting the class structure confronts growing children as facts, which they duly learn, much as they learn about the weather or school bus schedules. Their own inescapable participation in the network of class relationships is their educator, and this real experience, I am convinced, is far more powerful in shaping them than any second-hand experience of class that may be passed on by familiar adults.[121]

There is a tone of despair to this passage, for it implies an almost complete absorption of the 'ruling culture' by children, and Connell is similarly despondent on the next page—in contrast to theorists such as Marcuse—where he is cynical about the counter-cultural movement, which he finds 'anti-bourgeois in intention but still contained within the boundaries of the dominant ideology'.[122]

Connell's chapter on the media is very good, for he debunks the common left-wing view that the press shows 'bias': the operations of the press, rather, are 'an outcome of the normal, regular processes by which commercial mass communications work in a capitalist system, producing and reproducing an ideological interpretation of the world'.[123] Connell gives one example of these processes, through the category of 'progress', but this analysis is not carried through to its logical conclusion, and the final chapter of *Ruling Class, Ruling Culture,* 'The Pattern of Hegemony', is an unusual mixture of different theories of ideology, consciousness and cultural control. To be fair, Connell is often merely summarizing these theories, seeking out the evidence underpinning them, but only one consistent thread runs through this final, speculative chapter. This is Connell's realization that to be effective, propaganda must to a large extent 'explain' the world: that is to say, any set of ideological constructs must, at some level, be consonant with the perceived reality. So, for example, in the post-war period, 'the economic changes . . . made the positive side of conservative propaganda plausible'.[124] Connell looks at three important aspects of this post-war hegemonic situation: the threat tradition (which he had already discovered among the children surveyed in his study of *The Child's Construction of Politics*), the question of sexuality, and the 'routine patterns of interaction' in suburban life. These three aspects of the 'ruling culture' are principally unconscious, that is, they derive from an 'inculcational' theory of the mechanisms by which the hegemony is imposed. Yet thirty pages earlier, Connell had stated:

> The crucial feature of the cultural defence of capitalism is not so much the inculcation of middle-class values through the whole society (though that would do the trick), as the prevention of the formation of an oppositional working-class culture.[125]

This suggests a basic and unresolved contradiction in Connell's theorizing, between 'inculcational' and 'institutional' mechanisms of hegemony.[126] On the one hand, Connell talks about the institutions through which a ruling culture is maintained, and on the other he talks about the *content* of the ruling culture, as if it were a body of ideas which are somehow permeated throughout the entire society. Occasionally he suggests that the institutions are more important than the ideas which are inculcated through them, and at other points he seems to be arguing the opposite. Despite these criticisms, Connell has emerged as the most systematic and wide-ranging New Left theorist in Australia, and has brought whole new areas within the ambit of the social historian. He also shows a considerable advance over the past decade.[127] Since 1970 Connell has been working with T. H. Irving on their planned *Class Structure in Australian History,* a general history of Australia, which takes as its organizing principle the idea of class analysis. This is likely to be a work which will profoundly affect interpretations of Australian history. Connell and Irving's association dates from their involvement with the Free University in the late 1960s. The Free University was an adventurous attempt to set up an alternative to the academic orthodoxy, and, although short-lived, it brought together some of the more versatile members of the Sydney student movement.[128] It was at this time that Connell and Irving came together in an intellectual partnership which holds the promise of a major New Left restatement of Australian history.

T. H. Irving entered the University of Sydney as an undergraduate in 1956, and did his higher research under J. M. Ward. As Irving remembered in mid-1975:

> I think he wanted me to write a much more standard account of political history in the colony, particularly in the context of British imperial administration. But I felt that they paid no attention to the development of indigenous forces in the colony, the patterns of class society that were emerging in this period.[129]

Irving therefore concentrated on two main areas in his early work: the relationship between social processes and political practice in New South Wales in the mid-nineteenth century, and an historiographical attack on conventional 'categorical' theories of class.[130]

Connell and Irving have already collaborated on a short paper setting out their basic argument for the existence of a ruling class in Australia, under the ironic title of 'Yes, Virginia, there is a ruling class'.[131] But the main focus of their collaboration is *Class Structure in Australian History*. The authors have distributed freely their manuscript draft of this book, as each section is written.[132] Chapter 3—which at least one historian has already drawn upon in her work [133] —deals with the 'convict settlements and the origins of colonial capitalism, 1788-1840'. Of the two, Connell provides the theoretical consistency to their work, and the social theory underpinning this third chapter is remarkably consonant with the major theoretical propositions put forward in *Ruling Class, Ruling Culture*. The chapter begins with an examination of the 'transplantation of the state' from England to Port Jackson, shows the incipient elite of the early colonial period manoeuvring to use the institution of private property and the labour market (both bond and free) to establish a capitalist mode of production. The operations of the labour market generate a mobilization of the convicts, whose actions are explained dynamically mainly in terms of the labour market. Adroit use of the historical evidence demonstrates the degree to which the convicts were able to raise demands within the system and the 'processes of class formation' operative in the period up until 1840. Connell and Irving show very clearly the factions within the emerging ruling class, and conclude the chapter with a discussion of the significance of religion, education and family structures. These cultural institutions feed back into the earlier analysis, but, once again, the discussion of 'culture and social control' is a mixture of 'ideational' and 'institutional' forces, which suggests that the elusive problem of hegemony has yet to be resolved satisfactorily at the level of theory by the authors. However the emphasis placed on class formation in this period is arguably the most convincing demonstration of the changes in the colonies during this period that has yet been proffered in Australian historiography, and augurs well for the eventual argument of *Class Structure in Australian History*. But, like earlier radical historians in Australia, Connell and Irving may find themselves labelled as hard-headed propagandists whose view of the past is rather too unsettling.

6 The manufacture of Australian history

6 The manufacture of Australian history

The boot of the European has left a lasting imprint on the Australian landscape. White Australia is one of the most heavily documented societies ever to have existed. The Europeans came armed not only with advanced techniques of warfare and material technology but with complicated methods of information collection and storage. From its first white occupation, most details of Australia's physical environment, its original inhabitants and its new population were recorded for posterity. There were gaps and omissions in this process, of course, but these pale into relative insignificance alongside, for example, the meagre historical record bequeathed by the barbarian tribes which stormed across Western Europe in the fifth century. No one should ever doubt that a European civilization once flourished on the Australian continent.

But the twentieth-century historians of this civilization disagreed about how their origins should be explained. They were divided among themselves, and wrote different accounts of their history. There were some obvious differences in the types of evidence they drew upon, in order to construct their views of the past; this was not surprising given the wide variety of raw materials out of which their histories might have been manufactured. Liberal patriotic historians, like Hancock, had an eye for the environmental changes wrought by European settlement; others relied upon legislative records, the despatches of colonial governors and Downing Street administrators, or the newspaper reports of public meetings in Sydney or Melbourne. The Old Left strove to resurrect long-forgotten bush ballads, pamphlets produced by agitators, or official minutes of labour organizations. Manning Clark used private letters, personal diaries and even paintings to evoke people and ideas. Later historians drew upon opinion polls, electoral results, demographic records, court proceedings, streetscape photographs and many other fragmentary glimpses of the past.

Some pattern began to emerge between approaches to these raw materials. The empiricists believed that it was possible to extract 'facts' from the available evidence; such 'facts' were harder, more reliable when taken from non-literary sources, such as newspapers, court records or statistical surveys. Manning Clark agreed with them that there were such facts, which could be used as the basis for an evocation of people, places and periods, but inferred from them much more than the empiricists could allow. The syncretic conservatives and the feminists saw little autonomy in these facts; they were elements of a larger process which ran through the Australian past and meant little outside the larger framework. The naked nymphs painted by Norman Lindsay, for example, meant little to A. G. L. Shaw, since they failed to penetrate the philistine culture of Lindsay's period. For historians as different as Hancock and Turner, the evidence of the past reflected the broader context which produced it and also, to some extent, confirmed it. A song celebrating the life of a bushranger, for example, both mirrored popular feeling and helped give shape to sentiment. But for historians of a sociological or New Left persuasion, the difficulty arose that the evidence was not only illustrative of the past but was also created by it. They therefore sought to overcome this difficulty by postulating theories which would enable them to order the evidence outside the processes by which it had become available to the historian in the first place.

In this analysis of the manufacturing process, the four-fold typology of Stephen C. Pepper has been used as a heuristic device. Pepper argues that four basic 'world hypotheses', contextualism, formism, organicism and mechanism, underpin the strategies employed by intellectuals to explain reality. At least one Australian historian, Hugh Stretton, had recognized that there was a pattern underlying the attempts of social scientists to construct an order out of the disparate factors which confronted them in their everyday work: Stretton argued that town planners use the metaphor of an arena, an organism, a system or a market-place to conceptualize the city.[1] He did not clearly demonstrate the differences between these metaphors, and Pepper's typology is arguably a more accurate representation of the different perceptions of social process imagined by historians. The best test for Pepper's schema is that it actually corresponds with the history produced by these Australian historians.

Contextualism, as defined by Pepper, accurately describes the scholarship of two schools of Australian historians, the liberal patriots and the Old Left. During the interwar period, and even into the

1950s, their view of how Australian history should be manufactured remained dominant. The liberal patriots were concerned to understand how English practices were transplanted into a new environment so that a genuinely Australian civilization was created: this was the broad context of events and ideas. Historians such as Hancock, Crawford and J. M. Ward, though taking up a diverse range of themes, also agreed that it was wrong to judge the follies and errors of the historical actors without understanding the specific options available to them within this broad context. The Old Left bypassed this moral conception of history in their efforts to construct a scientific, marxist understanding of the Australian past. But their view of Australian history did not amount to a thorough-going break with the essential paradigm implicit in liberal patriotic historiography. They were also beguiled by the effects of an ill-defined environment upon an Australian 'character'; they also accepted at face value the 'Legend of the Nineties', and they were also cautious about establishing general laws of history, in order to make sense of patterns, especially of class formation, which were not readily discernible by empirical observation.

Formism represented a cleaner break with the orthodoxies of the Crawford department at Melbourne University, and was first evident in the work of Manning Clark, from the mid-1950s. Clark sought to concentrate on the unique and particular aspects of the Australian past. He did this not by sketching out the general context of events; and then relating them one to the other, as the contextualists had done. Instead he treated individuals, their beliefs, personalities and actions as discrete elements, organized ostensibly only by the structure of narrative. Clark's characters personified the worldviews of their age, and the narrative of his history was tightly structured, so that the empiricism evident in normal formism was not a feature of his historiographical style. Empiricism proper also emerged in Australian history-writing from the late 1950s—partly as a result of Clark's influence—and the representatives of this style were agreed upon the epistemological foundations of their history to the extent that they can usefully be categorized together.

Organicism appeared as the overall quality of two separate groups of Australian historians. As has already been outlined, an historiographical approach may be said to be organicist when all individual phenomena are assumed by the historian to be indicative of a single theme running through the past, a unilinear teleology to the pattern of events. This approach was first evident in the work of the syncretic conservatives, who fused together disparate themes—especially an equilibrium between capital and labour, the Australian passion for sport, a collective disregard for high culture, and the dominance of political elites. These trends were all evident as early as the 1880s, argued the syncretics, and nothing had shaken this merry-go-round subsequently. For the feminists, the fundamental mechanisms governing the lives of Australian women were also in force late last century, and women to-day are oppressed in essentially the same way as their great-grandmothers were. The stereotypes of 'damned whore' and 'God's police', linked by a notion of the ideal family, were moulded out of the patriarchal conditions of late colonial society, and have persisted unchanged in their broad dimensions.

Mechanism, finally, was an approach favoured by the sociological historians and the New Left. Both these groups of historians sought to underpin their interpretations of the Australian past with abstract conceptions of cause and effect which would generate an invariant and regular pattern of explanation. These laws of history, for the sociological historians, did not link up in any overarching way to provide a uniform explanation of the entire past. Blainey, for example, postulated a theory of mineral discovery which would explain precisely what it set out to, but which was not invariantly linked with other theories, such as a model of the industrial relations that existed on the goldfields. The New Left, in sharp distinction, advanced hypotheses which sought not only to explain individual phenomena, but which were also holistically interrelated. Connell's ruling class, for example, derived its power from an identifiable set of property relations, exercised its class power in predictable ways and maintained itself through hegemonic processes which were tightly interrelated with the existence of the ruling class.

None of these schools developed in a vacuum, of course, and they not only acted upon each other in mutual self-definition, but were also part of broader intellectual traditions both in Australia and overseas. Passing reference was made to this larger context as a source both of theoretical and ideological influences, although in this study the ideological trends have received more attention because the partisanship of each group was seen as one of its defining qualities. Each group adopted a characteristic way of manufacturing out of the raw materials of the past a view of Australian history, and implicit in these views were different ideological standpoints, which they communicated to their readers. The final products of each school—the books, articles and lectures, written and published by historians—are thus in part interpretations of the past, and in part ideological artefacts. Following a conventional classification of ideological types, the schools were defined as liberal, radical, conservative or anarchist in their ideological implication.

The liberal tradition in Australian historiography has clearly been the strongest. Liberal history has been part of a broader intellectual continuity in Australian culture, as documented and explained by Tim Rowse. His book, *Australian Liberalism and National Character*, shows how dominant and resilient this tradition of ideological thinking has been in Australia. Rowse devoted an entire chapter to Hancock's *Australia* and argued that it was an important statement of local liberalism.[2] The school of historians clustered around Hancock—the liberal patriots—were succeeded by the sociological historians as the liberal interpreters of the Australian past. These younger historians differed from the Hancockians in embracing sociological methods to understand Australian history, but enunciated an ideological standpoint which was not fundamentally different.

A similar process took place in the Australian radical tradition, so that a comparable continuity of radical historiography can be traced back from the New Left, through Turner, Russel Ward and other Old Left historians, to Fitzpatrick and possibly Childe. Radical history has not been as influential as the liberal view of the Australian past, but each generation since the First World War has produced a number of historians writing in this left-wing tradition. And, just as the liberal historians developed from a contextualist mode to mechanist one, so the Old and New Left schools were distinguished by the change from one style to the next.

A conservative tradition was also present but not as continuous. Historians such as the syncretics—A. G. L. Shaw, F. K. Crowley and N. B. Nairn—developed as a tendency in the late 1950s, at roughly the same time as the empiricists. But conservative intellectuals—men such as James McAuley, Frank Knopfelmacher or Patrick O'Brien—have not been prominent or numerous, and it would have been remarkable had a different pattern emerged in history-writing. Apart from these comparatively recent articulators of conservative historiography, one would probably need to go back to E. O. G. Shann before encountering a like-minded historian.

Anarchism has been weaker still in Australian historiography. There has been nothing approaching, for example, the Andersonian school in philosophy. Manning Clark, and the feminists also, have written history which shakes off the traditional ideologies, and might therefore be best described as anarchistic. But their anarchism, if it may be called that, is certainly not immediately familiar. It is the anarchism of those who would strive, by means of individual or small group action, to be free either of the dogmatic mind-dimmers, or of the shackles of patriarchy.

All of these historians—whatever their ideological hue or mode of social theorizing—had and have a perception of the Australian future. Historians cannot avoid being soothsayers, and, paradoxically, it may be in their ability to prognosticate that one might ultimately judge the worth of their views of the past. Some are pessimists: Clark, the prophet of despair, sincerely fears for the future of Australia; feminists such as Anne Summers believe that the merry-go-round of female oppression will continue turning; empiricists, such as Robson, and syncretics, such as Cannon, cannot envisage a future which will be less bleak than the past. But others take a different view: Hancock's optimism in *Australia* was shared by his contemporaries, both the liberal patriots and the Old Left—that 'fine dreamer', Brian Fitzpatrick, never swerved from his faith in the goodness of the Australian people. Similarly the New Left imagine a future less grim than the past: McQueen, for example, can conjure up a 'people's media' which will dispense with the monopolists. The sociological historians—especially Blainey and Stretton—have used 'realistic mechanisms of historical change' to declare that a better future is possible.[3] The optimists appear to have put up better arguments.

Notes

1 The ground rules of criticism

1 Stephen C. Pepper, *World Hypotheses: A Study in Evidence,* Berkeley and Los Angeles, 1942. Pepper's typology has been used for historiographical purposes before, in Hayden White's *Metahistory: The Historical Imagination in Nineteenth Century Europe,* Baltimore, 1973. White's summary of the four types of 'world hypotheses' (pp. 13-18) is particularly lucid.

2 An almost complete list of articles published in Australian historiography until the end of 1973 may be found in Terry Hogan, *Index to Journal Articles on Australian History,* Armidale, 1976, p. 44. Only one book has hitherto been published in the area: David Dufty et alia (eds), *Historians at Work: Investigating and Recreating the Past,* Sydney, 1973. Monographic studies of Bean and Wood, and occasional chapters or sections of particular intellectual histories pertaining to Australian historiography have also appeared. Most of these have been cited in the notes which follow. For the distinction between 'the rough' and 'the smooth', see Donald Horne, 'The rough and the smooth', *Times Literary Supplement,* 9 April 1976, pp. 410-411; for 'whig' and 'anti-whig' see Michael Roe, 'Challenges to Australian identity', *Quadrant* 22 (April 1978), pp. 34-40; and for 'bourgeois' and 'radical', see Stuart Macintyre, 'Radical history and bourgeois hegemony', *Intervention* 2 (October 1972), pp. 47-73.

2 From the general to the particular

1 C. E. W. Bean, *On the Wool Track,* Sydney, 1945, p. vii.
2 *ibid.,* p. ix.
3 *ibid.,* p. vi.
4 *ibid.,* p. vi.
5 *ibid.,* p. 109.
6 *ibid.,* p. 34.
7 *ibid.,* p. 152.
8 H. M. Green, *A History of Australian Literature Pure and Applied: A Critical Review of All Forms of Literature Produced in Australia From the First Books Published After the Arrival of the First Fleet Until 1950, with Short Accounts of*

Later Publications up to 1960, 2 vols, Sydney, 1961; reprinted 1962, p. 795, footnote 84.

9   K. S. Inglis, *C. E. W. Bean: Australian Historian,* St. Lucia (Qld), 1970; A. W. Bazley, 'Obituary: C. E. W. Bean', *Historical Studies* 14, 53 (October 1969) pp. 147-154; H. M. Green, *op. cit.,* ch. XVI.

10 R. M. Crawford, *A Bit of a Rebel: The Life and Work of George Arnold Wood,* Sydney, 1976.

11 J. A. La Nauze, 'The study of Australian history, 1929-1959', *Historical Studies* 9, 33 (November 1959), p. 2.

12 Ernest Scott, *Australia During the War,* vol. XI, *The Official History of Australia in the War of 1914-1918,* Sydney, 1936.

13 Stuart Macintyre, 'Radical history and bourgeois hegemony', *Intervention* 2 (October 1972), p. 49.

14 Robin Gollan, 'John Docker and his critics', *Overland* 62 (1975), p. 63.

15 R. B. Joyce (ed. & introd.), A. C. V. Melbourne, *Early Constitutional Development in Australia: New South Wales, 1788-1856; Queensland, 1859-1922,* St Lucia (Qld), second edition 1963, esp. pp. v-vi. The original text was published first in 1934.

16 G. V. Portus, *Australia Since 1606: A History for Young Australians,* Melbourne, 1932, second edition 1948: 'A foreword for grown-ups'. On Portus, see also his autobiography, *Happy Highways,* Melbourne, 1953, and the comments by Crauturd D. W. Goodwin, *Economic Enquiry in Australia,* Durham, N. C., 1966, pp. 559-563.

17 Portus, *Australia Since 1606,* p. 1

18 *ibid.,* pp. 21-22.

19 *ibid.,* p. 37.

20 *ibid.,* p. 229, cf. p. 97.

21 *ibid.,* p. 83.

22 *ibid.,* pp. 196-199.

23 *ibid.,* p. 211.

24 *ibid.,* p. 231.

25 R. M. Crawford, *Ourselves and the Pacific,* Melbourne, third edition, 1952, p. 273.

26 The 'essay' is W. K. Hancock's *Australia,* London, 1930, repr. Brisbane, 1961 One of A. G. L. Shaw's references in *The Story of Australia,* London, 1955, is to *Survey of British Commonwealth Relations* (sic), p. 235.

27 G. Greenwood (ed.), *Australia: A Social and Political History,* Sydney, 1955.

28 R. A. Gollan, *Radical and Working Class Politics: A Study of Eastern Australia 1850-1910,* Melbourne, 1960, pp. 114-5; Russel Ward, *The Australian Legend,* Melbourne, second edition, 1966, pp. 165, 228.

29 R. W. Connell, 'Images of Australia', originally published in *Quadrant* 12 (March-April 1968), pp. 9-19, republished in D. E. Edgar (ed.), *Social Change in Australia: Readings in Sociology,* Melbourne, 1974, p. 30.

30 The commentators have been H. M. Green, *op. cit.,* pp. 1333, 1339-41; Connell, *loc. cit.;* G. C. Bolton, 'Australian historians in quest of a theme', *Teaching History* 3, 2 (September 1969), pp. 8-10; C. M. H. Clark, 'Hancock's *Australia* and Australian historiography: a note', *Historical Studies* 13, 51 (October 1968), pp. 329-332; and Anne Summers, *Damned Whores and God's*

Police: The Colonization of Women in Australia, Ringwood (Vic.), 1975, pp. 57-64.

31 W. K. Hancock, *Country and Calling,* London, 1954, p. 65.

32 C. E. W. Bean, *On the Wool Track,* p. xi.

33 W. K. Hancock, *Attempting History: The University Lectures 1968,* Canberra, 1969.

34 W. K. Hancock, 'Mezzadria in modern Tuscany', *Report of the Eighteenth Meeting of the Australasian Association for the Advancement of Science,* Perth, 1928, pp. 417-418.

35 Q. Hoare and G. N. Smith (tr., ed.), *Selections from the Prison Notebooks of Antonio Gramsci,* London, 1971, p. 283.

36 Hancock, *Australia,* Brisbane, 1961, p. 232.

37 Both quotes come from an interview (21 September 1974, Claremont, W.A.). Further evidence that Hancock did not wish to become involved in the problems of the urban environment is his disparaging reference to Adelaide 'flattened by a giant's saucepan' in *Country and Calling,* p. 115. There is a similar distaste for 'suburbanism' in *Australia* (1961), pp. 160, 245-6, and elsewhere, though at the time he wrote these remarks Hancock had not lived in Birmingham or London, of course. *Discovering Monaro: A Study of Man's Impact on his Environment* was published in 1972.

38 *English Historical Review* 51 (April 1936), p. 372.

39 Hancock, *Australia* (1961), p. vii; much the same point is made in *Country and Calling,* p. 122.

40 H. Radi, '1920-29', in F. K. Crowley (ed.), *A New History of Australia,* Melbourne, 1974, p. 387; cf. p. 394.

41 Sir Keith Hancock, interview, 21 April 1974, Claremont, W.A.

42 Tim Rowse, 'Liberalism and Hancock's *Australia*', *Arena* 44/45 (1976), pp. 60-93, has now taken this line of inquiry to its logical endpoint, and attempts to situate the book's argument in the economic crisis of the period. Rowse connects Hancock's *Australia* to the economic conflicts of 1926-1933 through various mediations (such as the role of other intellectuals). The article is reprinted in Tim Rowse, *Australian Liberalism and National Character,* Malmsbury (Vic.), 1978, ch. 3.

43 Hancock, *Australia* (1961), p. 57.

44 C. M. H. Clark, *loc. cit.*

45 Hancock's self-recriminations are to be found in *Country and Calling,* pp. 121-122, *Australia* (1961), p. vii and in an interview (21 September 1974, Claremont, W.A.).

46 Hancock, *Australia* (1961), p. 225.

47 *ibid.,* p. 66.

48 *ibid.,* p. 13.

49 *ibid.,* pp. 26-27.

50 *ibid.,* p. 2.

51 Letter from W. K. Hancock to Mrs Palmer, 12 June 1929, National Library of Australia, MS 1174/1/3364.

52 Hancock, *Australia* (1961), p. 236.

53 *ibid.,* pp. 22-23.

54 See the following section on Crawford, and ch. 5 for Stretton.

55 Hancock, *Australia* (1930), p. vii.

56 Hancock, *Attempting History*, p. 43.

57 W. K. Hancock, *Two Centuries of Change: An Elementary History for Young Australians*, Melbourne, 1934, p. 152.

58 *ibid.*, pp. 92-93.

59 *ibid.*, p. 135.

60 *ibid.*, p. 158.

61 W. K. Hancock, *Survey of British Commonwealth Affairs, Vol. 2: Problems of Economic Policy, 1918-1939*, Part 2, London, 1940, pp. 301-302.

62 Hancock, *Country and Calling*, p. 20.

63 *ibid.*, p. 214.

64 *ibid.*, p. 215.

65 Interview, 21 September 1974, Claremont, W.A.

66 W. K. Hancock, *Politics in Pitcairn and other Essays*, London, 1947: 'A note on Mary Kingsley'.

67 W. K. Hancock, *The Battle for Black Mountain*, Canberra, 1974.

68 D. A. Low, 'The Buganda mission, 1954', *Historical Studies* 13, 51, (October 1968), pp. 353-380; W. K. Hancock, *Professing History*, Sydney, 1976, pp. 90-109.

69 Hancock, *Professing History*, pp. 88-89.

70 W. K. Hancock, 'History: the manner and the matter', *Quadrant* 19 (December 1975), p. 30.

71 G. C. Bolton, *loc. cit.*, p. 10.

72 e.g., J. A La Nauze, *loc. cit.*, p. 6.

73 J. R. Poynter, *Historical Studies* 15, 57 (October 1971), p. 3.

74 G. C. Bolton, *loc. cit.*, p. 12.

75 C. M. H. Clark, 'R. M. Crawford: some reminiscences', *Historical Studies* 15, 57 (October 1971), p. 5.

76 Stuart Macintyre, *loc. cit.*, p. 55.

77 Brian Fitzpatrick, 'The origins of the people are not in the library', *Meanjin* 14 (1955), p. 352.

78 *Historical Studies* 3 (November 1947), pp. 153-175.

79 Stuart Macintyre, *loc. cit.*, p. 53.

80 *ibid.*, p. 52.

81 *ibid.*, p. 54, quoting R. M. Crawford, 'Historical aspects of the problem of recurrent wars', in V. H. Wallace (ed.), *Paths to Peace: A Study of War, Its Causes and Prevention*, Melbourne, 1957, p. 14.

82 A. L. Burns, 'R. M. Crawford: some reminiscences', *Historical Studies* 15, 57 (October 1971), p. 7.

83 *ibid.*, pp. 8-9.

84 Stuart Macintyre, *loc. cit.*, p. 57.

85 C. M. H. Clark, 'Re-writing Australian history', in T. A. G. Hungerford (ed.), *Australian Signpost: An Anthology*, Melbourne, 1956, pp. 130-143.

86 A. L. Burns, *loc. cit.*, p. 10; cf. Geoffrey Serle, 'A survey of honours graduates of the University of Melbourne School of History, 1937-1966', *Historical Studies* 15, 57 (October 1971), pp. 43-58.

87 R. M. Crawford, *Ourselves and the Pacific*, Melbourne, third edition, 1952, pp. 146-149.

88 *ibid.*, p. v.

89 *ibid.*, p. 26.

90 *ibid.*, pp. 270-271.

91 W. K. Hancock, 'R. M. Crawford—some reminiscences', *Historical Studies* 15, 57 (October 1971), p. 20.

92 A. L. Burns, *loc. cit.*

93 Hugh Stretton, 'R. M. Crawford: some reminiscences', *Historical Studies* 15, 57 (October 1971), p. 12; cf. ch. 5 for details of this process.

94 J. S. Gregory, 'R. M. Crawford: some reminiscences', *Historical Studies* 15, 57 (October 1971), pp. 15-19.

95 J. M. Ward, 'An historian's view of "national objectives—social, economic and political goals" ' (unrevised notes of an address delivered to the 46th ANZAAS Congress, Canberra, 22 January 1975, kindly supplied by the author), p. 2.

96 J. M. Ward, 'An Australian historian', *Royal Australian Historical Society Journal* 41 (1955), p. 55.

97 J. M. Ward, 'Some recollections of a student's view of the 1930s', *Teaching History* 9, 1 (March 1975), p. 28.

98 *ibid.*, p. 24.

99 *ibid.*, p. 22.

100 *ibid.*, p. 23-24.

101 *ibid.*, p. 27.

102 Conversation, 25 June 1975, Sydney University.

103 J. M. Ward, 'Some recollections', p. 27, and ibid.

104 J. M. Ward, *Earl Grey and the Australian Colonies, 1846-1857: A Study of Self-Government and Self-Interest*, Melbourne, 1958, pp. 24-34, 37, 44.

105 J. M. Ward, 'National objectives', p. 10.

106 J. M. Ward, 'Reflections on Australian history and historians', in D. Dufty et alia (eds), *Historians at Work: Investigating and Recreating the Past*, Sydney, 1973, p. 281.

107 See ch. 5.

108 Cf. W. A. Sinclair, *The Process of Economic Development in Australia*, Melbourne, 1976, esp. pp. 15-18, 35-37, 68-70, 117-119, 158-159, for historiographical details of this debate; J. A. La Nauze, *loc. cit.*, p. 6 supports this interpretation.

109 Percival Serle, 'History and the search for truth', *Meanjin* 6 (1947), p. 254.

110 Humphrey McQueen, *A New Britannia: An Argument Concerning the Social Origins of Australian Radicalism and Nationalism*, Ringwood (Vic.), 1970, p. 15.

111 Stuart Macintyre, *op. cit.*, esp. pp. 58-65; Helen Bourke, 'A reading of Brian Fitzpatrick', *Labour History* 27 (November 1974), pp. 1-11; D. L. Clark, 'Marx versus Butlin: Some comments on the Snooks-Rowse debate', *Labour History* 30 (May 1976), pp. 58-65; Don Watson, 'Brian Fitzpatrick: The pragmatic utopian', *Meanjin* 35 (1976), pp. 383-393; R. W. Connell, *Ruling Class, Ruling Culture: Studies of Conflict, Power and Hegemony in Australian Life*, Cambridge, 1977, pp. 8-12.

112 Derek Whitelock, *The Great Tradition: A History of Adult Education in Australia,* St Lucia (Qld), 1974.

113 Geoffrey Blainey, 'Brian Fitzpatrick (1906-1965) and his works', *Business Archives and History* 6 (February 1966), p. 77. Fitzpatrick was actually born in 1905.

114 Percival Serle, *loc. cit.,* p. 258.

115 Details of Fitzpatrick's biography may be found in Ian Turner, 'Introduction' to Brian Fitzpatrick, *A Short History of the Australian Labour Movement,* Melbourne, 1940, repr. South Melbourne, 1968, pp. 1-59; and in Don Watson, *Brian Fitzpatrick: A Radical Life,* Neutral Bay (N.S.W.), 1978.

116 Brian Fitzpatrick, *The British Empire in Australia: An Economic History, 1834-1939,* Melbourne, 1941, reprinted, South Melbourne, 1969, pp. 280-282. A venerable legend insists that this entire book was written in only seven weeks.

117 *ibid.,* pp. 279-280.

118 *ibid.,* p. 281.

119 *ibid.,* Geoffrey Blainey, 'Foreword', p. ix.

120 *ibid.,* pp. 56-70.

121 *ibid.,* p. 124.

122 Brian Fitzpatrick, *The Australian People, 1788-1945,* Carlton (Vic.), 1946, pp. 56, 60, 61.

123 Fitzpatrick, *The British Empire in Australia* (1969), p. 35.

124 N. G. Butlin, *Investment in Australian Economic Development, 1861-1900,* Cambridge, 1964.

125 C. M. H. Clark, 'Foreword' to Humphrey McQueen, *op. cit.,* p. 7.

126 Helen Bourke, *loc. cit.,* p. 9.

127 Ian Turner, *loc. cit.,* p. 33.

128 Humphrey McQueen, *loc. cit.*

129 Stuart Macintyre, *loc. cit.,* pp. 65-71.

130 Neil McInnes, 'Dangerous corners', *Times Literary Supplement,* 9 April 1976, p. 442.

131 As Geoffrey Serle himself notes, *From Deserts the Prophets Come: The Creative Spirit in Australia 1788-1972,* Melbourne, 1973, p. 78.

132 Russel Ward, *Man Makes History: World History from the Earliest Times to the Renaissance—for boys and girls in the First Year of Secondary School Courses,* Sydney, 1952, p. 6.

133 *ibid.,* p. 118.

134 Interview, 19 June 1975, Armidale, N.S.W.

135 Russell [sic] Ward, *The Australian Legend,* Melbourne, 1958, second edition, 1966, pp. vi-vii.

136 Hancock, *Professing History,* pp. 32-33.

137 See ch. 4.

138 Gollan, *Radical and Working Class Politics;* interview 17 June 1975, ANU, Canberra.

139 R. W. Connell, *op. cit.,* pp. 13-14.

140 *National Times* 15-20 June 1974, p. 3. See also Turner's autobiographical article, 'My Long March', *Overland* 59 (1974), pp. 23-40.

141 Ian Turner, *Industrial Labour and Politics: The Dynamics of the Labour Movement in Eastern Australia, 1900-1921*, Canberra, 1965. (The article was entitled 'Socialist political tactics, 1900-1920', *Labour History* 2 (May 1962), pp. 5-25.)

142 *ibid*., p. xx.

143 Henry Mayer, 'Some conceptions of the Australian party system, 1910-1950', *Historical Studies* 7, 27 (1956), pp. 253-270.

144 Ian Turner, *op. cit*., pp. xvii-xviii.

145 Ian Turner, *loc. cit*.

146 'An evening with Ian Turner', ABC TV, 2 February 1976 (Ceduna, S.A.).

147 Ian Turner (ed.), *The Australian Dream: A Collection of Anticipations about Australia from Captain Cook to the Present Day*, Melbourne, 1968.

148 *ibid*., pp. 345-347.

149 C. M. H. Clark, 'The end of the ideologies' (*ibid*., pp. 348-351), which was originally published in 1963.

150 Turner, *op. cit*., p. xix.

151 Ian Turner, 'Manning Clark: history and the voice of prophecy', *Overland* 44 (Winter 1970), pp. 12-20.

152 Ian Turner, 'Prisoners in petticoats: a shocking history of female emancipation in Australia', in Julie Rigg (ed.), *In Her Own Right: Women of Australia*, Melbourne, 1969, p. 3-23. (Turner did not choose the title of this article.) cf. *Industrial Labour and Politics*, p. 9. The latter point was noted wryly by R. W. Connell, *op. cit*., p. 13.

153 Ian Turner, 'The significance of the Russian Revolution', in Eugene Kamenka (ed.), *A World in Revolution? The University Lectures 1970*, Canberra, 1970, p. 37.

154 Ian Turner, '1914-19', in F. K. Crowley (ed.), *op. cit*., pp. 312-356.

155 Phillip Adams, 'The literature of graffiti', *Age*, 25 October 1975, p. 16.

156 Ian Turner, 'High Noon at Yarralumla: some causes and some consequences', *Overland* 65 (1976), pp. 13, 21.

157 Geoffrey Serle, 'Recreating an era: Victoria in the 50s and 80s', in David Dufty et alia, *op. cit*., p. 59.

158 *Shop* 2, 2 (1946), p. 8. P. Serle to N. Palmer, 25 May 1946, N.L.A. MS 1174/I/6990.

159 Geoffrey Serle, 'The Victorian Legislative Council, 1856-1950', *Historical Studies* 22 (May 1954), and, with J. Grant, *The Melbourne Scene, 1803-1956*, Melbourne, 1957. This latter work was one of the first uses of photographs as source-material.

160 Geoffrey Serle, 'God-Professors and their juniors', *Vestes* 6 (1963), pp. 11-17; *The Golden Age: A History of the Colony of Victoria, 1851-1861* Melbourne, 1963, corrected reprint, 1963. This book has a brown and yellow cover, allegedly because they are the colours of Serle's football team, Hawthorn.

161 Geoffrey Serle, 'The causes of Eureka', *Historical Studies* (Eureka Supplemen, 1954), pp. 15-24.

162 Serle, *The Golden Age*, pp. 182-183.

163 Geoffrey Serle, *The Rush to be Rich: A History of the Colony of Victoria, 1883-1889*, Carlton (Vic.), 1971.

164 Serle, 'Recreating an era', p. 59.
165 Serle, *The Golden Age*, p. 92
166 *ibid.*, p. 376.
167 As R. W. Connell does, in *op. cit.*, ch. 2.
168 Serle, *The Golden Age*, pp. 16-17.
169 *ibid.*, pp. 318, 379.
170 As suggested by his 'Victorian history 1850-1900: A guide for research workers and book collectors', *La Trobe Library Journal*, 1, 1 (April 1968), pp. 1-5; 1, 2 (October 1968), pp. 36-40.
171 Serle, *The Golden Age*, p. 377.
172 *ibid.*, p. 212.
173 Serle, *The Rush to be Rich*, pp. 336-337; pp. 100-105.
174 *ibid.*, p. v.
175 Serle, *The Golden Age*, p. 375.
176 Serle, *The Rush to be Rich*, p. 86-90.
177 *ibid.*, p. 225, see footnote.
178 *ibid.*, p. 339.
179 *ibid.*, p. 271.
180 Serle, 'Recreating an era', p. 55.
181 Michael Cannon, 'Dipping in the Victorian bucket', *Nation*, 21 August 1971, p. 21.
182 See ch. 4.
183 Serle, *The Rush to be Rich*, pp. 167-172.
184 *ibid.*, pp. 83-84, 167.
185 Serle's concern for the profession is demonstrated in his 'A survey of honours graduates . . .', *loc. cit.*; 'The state of the profession in Australia', *Historical Studies* 15, 61 (October 1973), pp. 686-702; and in various public addresses he has given.
186 Ian Turner, 'New fashions in Australian history', *Overland* 11 (1958), p. 25.
187 R. A. Gollan, 'Labour history', *The Bulletin of the Australian Society for the Study of Labour History* 1 (January 1962), pp. 3-5.
188 J. A. La Nauze, 'Symposium: what is labour history?', *Labour History* 12 (May 1967), p. 66.
189 N. B. Nairn, *ibid.*, p. 72.
190 T. H. Irving, *ibid.*, p. 80.
191 J. W. McCarty, 'Australian capital cities in the nineteenth century', in C. B. Schedvin & J. W. McCarty (eds), *Urbanization in Australia: The Nineteenth Century*, Sydney, 1974, pp. 20-21.

3 Evoking a person, a period, a place

1 Peter Coleman (ed.), *Australian Civilization*, Melbourne, 1962, esp. pp. 7-9.
2 See, e.g., the diversity of anti-Whig historians cited by Michael Roe, 'Challenges to Australian identity', *Quadrant* 22 (April 1978), pp. 34-40.
3 A. W. Martin, 'The Whig view of Australian history' (mimeo, n.d. [1962]), pp. 1-15; and A. W. Martin, interview, 28 May 1975, Murdoch University, W.A.

4 W. K. Hancock, *Country and Calling*, London, 1954, 'Prologue'.
5 These details are based largely on C. M. H. Clark, *Disquiet and Other Stories*, Sydney, 1969, an anthology of thinly disguised autobiographical short stories Clark wrote during the late 1950s and 1960s.
6 C. M. H. Clark, 'Themes in *A History of Australia*' (mimeo, March 1978), p. 5.
7 *ibid.*, pp. 6-7.
8 C. M. H. Clark, 'Letter to Tom Collins', *Meanjin* 2, 3 (Spring 1943), pp. 40-41; repr. in Ian Turner (ed.), *The Australian Dream*, Melbourne, 1968, pp. 345-347.
9 C. M. H. Clark, *Sources of Australian History*, London, 1957, p. 392.
10 Clark, 'Themes', pp. 2-3.
11 Roe, 'Challenges', p. 37.
12 C. M. H. Clark, *Meeting Soviet Man*, Sydney, 1960.
13 C. M. H. Clark, *A History of Australia, I: From the Earliest Times to the Age of Macquarie*, Carlton (Vic.), 1962; repr., with corrections, November 1962, repr., with alterations, 1963, p. 160.
14 As Humphrey McQueen pointed out: 'Australia's finest bourgeois historian', *Nation Review* 11 − 17 January 1974, p. 409.
15 C. M. H. Clark, *A History of Australia, III: The Beginning of an Australian Civilization, 1824-1851*, Carlton (Vic.), 1973, p. 12.
16 M. H. Ellis, 'History without facts', *Bulletin*, 22 September 1962, p. 36.
17 Peter Grant, 'Manning Clark debated, 2', *Dissent* 23 (Spring 1968), p. 49.
18 C. M. H. Clark, 'The colonisation of women', *Australian*, 8 November 1975, p. 27.
19 Clark, *A History, III*, ch. 11.
20 See Paul F. Bourke, 'Some recent essays in Australian intellectual history', *Historical Studies* 13, 49 (October 1967), pp. 97-105, for a discussion of the work of this group (especially Roe, Suttor and Barrett).
21 P. J. O'Farrell, 'Historians and religious convictions' (mimeo, n.d.; kindly supplied by the author, 6 January 1977), pp. 27, 26; this article has subsequently been published in *Historical Studies*, 17, 68 (April 1977), pp. 279-298.
22 See, esp., Colin Roderick, 'Can this be Henry Lawson?', *Sydney Morning Herald*, 12 May 1978, pp. 7-8; *Australian*, 18 May 1978, p. 9; *Australian* 22 May 1978, p. 6 (cartoon, letters to editor); 22 May 1978 (editorial); *Australian* 25 May 1978, pp. 6-7.
23 Alistair Davidson, 'Manning Clark debated, 1', *Dissent* 23 (Spring 1968), p. 47.
24 A. T. Yarwood, 'Pursuing a theme: The 'White Australia' policy', in David Dufty et alia (eds), *Historians at Work*, Sydney, 1973, p. 65.
25 *ibid.*, p. 71.
26 A. T. Yarwood, 'Writing an ecclesiastical biography', *Armidale and District Historical Society J & P* 16 (January 1973), p. 32.
27 *ibid.*, p. 36.
28 Yarwood, 'Pursuing a theme', p. 63.
29 L. L. Robson, *The Convict Settlers of Australia: An Enquiry into the Origin*

and Character of the Convicts Transported to New South Wales and Van Diemen's Land 1787-1852, Melbourne, 1965; B. K. de Garis, lecture, 4 October 1976, University of Western Australia.

30 Hugh Stretton, *The Political Sciences*, London, 1969, pp. 405-406.

31 Interview, 25 March 1974, Melbourne University.

32 Robson, *The Convict Settlers*, p. 146.

33 *ibid.*, p. 149.

34 Yarwood, 'Writing an ecclesiastical biography', p. 30.

35 See ch. 5 for a discussion of Stretton.

36 Yarwood, *loc. cit.*, p. 32.

37 Lectures, 31 July 1972, 2 August 1972, Melbourne University.

38 B. K. de Garis, 'An incident at Fremantle', *Labour History* 10 (May 1966), pp. 32-37.

39 Robson, *The Convict Settlers*, p. 150.

40 Gareth Stedman Jones, 'History: the poverty of empiricism', in Robin Blackburn (ed.), *Ideology in Social Science: Readings in Critical Social Theory*, Great Britain, 1972, p. 96 (abstract).

41 Frederic Jameson, 'Figural relativism, or the poetics of historiography', *Diacritics* 7, 2 (Spring 1976), p. 2.

42 Gary Nicholls, 'So vacuous', *Australian*, 25 May 1978, p. 6.

43 W. F. Mandle, *Going It Alone: Australia's National Identity in the Twentieth Century*, Ringwood (Vic.), 1978, p. 2.

44 *ibid.*, ch. 2.

45 Peter Spearritt, 'Why the Australian Legend won't die' *National Times* 10–15 April 1978, p. 28.

4 History as a circular argument

1 Douglas Pike, *Australia: The Quiet Continent*, London, 1962, p. 222.

2 *ibid.*, 'Destiny', pp. 222-232.

3 Michael Cannon, *Who's Master? Who's Man?*, vol. 1 of *Australia in the Victorian Age*, West Melbourne, 1971, p. 7.

4 W. F. Mandle, *Going It Alone: Australia's National Identity in the Twentieth Century*, Ringwood (Vic.), 1978.

5 N. B. Nairn, *Civilising Capitalism: The Labor Movement in New South Wales, 1870-1890*, Canberra, 1973.

6 *ibid.*

7 Michael Cannon, *Australia in the Victorian Age*, 3 vols, West Melbourne, 1971, 1973, 1975. For Serle, see ch. 2.

8 Bruce Mitchell, *The Australian Story and Its Background*, Melbourne, 1965, pp. 271-273.

9 *ibid.*, pp. 246-259.

10 *ibid.*, pp. 220-221.

11 A. G. L. Shaw and H. D. Nicolson, *Australia in the Twentieth Century: An Introduction to Modern Society*, Sydney, 1967, pp. 31-32. These authors had previously published *Growth and Development in Australia*, a study of the pre-Federation period.

12 *ibid.*, p. 259.
13 *ibid.*, p. 95.
14 *ibid.*, p. 103.
15 *ibid.*, p. 117.
16 *ibid.*, p. 151.
17 *ibid.*, p. 232.
18 *ibid.*, p. 6.
19 *ibid.*, pp. 88-91.
20 *ibid.*, p. 59.
21 *ibid.*, p. 247.
22 F. K. Crowley, *State Election: The Fall of the Hawke Government,* Perth, 1959. 'Acknowledgements'.
23 *ibid.*, p. 77.
24 Humphrey McQueen, *Canberra Times,* 26 June 1971, p. 15.
25 F. K. Crowley and Lorna Cartwright, *A Citizen's Guide to Marihuana in Australia,* Sydney, 1977.
26 *Sunday Telegraph,* 22 September 1974, p. 1.
27 F. K. Crowley, '1901-1914', in F. K. Crowley (ed.), *A New History of Australia,* Melbourne, 1974, p. 311.
28 Interview, 27 June 1975, University of New South Wales.
29 F. K. Crowley (ed.), *Modern Australia in Documents,* 2 vols, Melbourne, 1973.
30 C. M. H. Clark, 'Report from the kingdom of nothingness', *Australian,* 1 February 1975, p. 21.
31 F. K. Crowley and B. K. de Garis, *A Short History of Western Australia,* second edition, South Melbourne, 1969.
32 *ibid.*, p. 21.
33 *ibid.*, p. 53.
34 A. G. L. Shaw, *Nation,* 27 August 1960, p. 21.
35 Russel Ward, 'The other half of Australian history', *Age,* 12 August 1978, p. 22.
36 See, for example, the influential article by Ann Curthoys, 'Historiography and women's liberation', *Arena* 22 (1970), pp. 35-40.
37 Interview, 25 June 1975, Sydney University.
38 Anne Summers, *Damned Whores and God's Police: The Colonization of Women in Australia,* Ringwood (Vic.), 1975, pp. 201-218 and pp. 160-163.
39 *ibid.*, ch. 14, pp. 459-473.
40 *ibid.*, p. 21.
41 Interview, 20 May 1975, Armidale, N.S.W.
42 Miriam Dixson, *The Real Matilda: Woman and Identity in Australia, 1788 to 1975,* Ringwood (Vic.), 1976, pp. 135-140.
43 *ibid.*, p. 119.
44 *ibid.*, esp. pp. 22, 106-107.
45 *ibid.*, p. 227.
46 Julie Marginson, 'Women: reappraisals', *Overland* 63 (1976), p. 65. Marginson, however, argues that the analogy of colonization is the basis of the argument in *Damned Whores.*
47 Summers, *Damned Whores,* p. 20.

48 *ibid.*, pp. 201-218; see also the American feminist Susan Brownmiller's *Against Our Will: Men, Women and Rape*, 1975; Ringwood (Vic.), 1976, where a similar thesis is argued at greater length.

49 Juliet Mitchell, *Woman's Estate*, Harmondsworth, Eng., 1971, pp. 171-172.

50 Juliet Mitchell, *Psychoanalysis and Feminism*, Harmondsworth, Eng., 1974.

51 Beverley Kingston, *My Wife, My Daughter, and Poor Mary Ann: Women and Work in Australia*, West Melbourne, 1975, chs 2, 6.

52 *ibid.*, chs 2-3.

53 Summers, *Damned Whores*, pp. 310-311.

54 Kingston, *Poor Mary Ann*, p. 138.

55 Teresa Brennan, 'Women and work', *Journal of Aust Political Economy* I (October 1977), pp. 34-52; cf. Margaret Power, 'Cast-off jobs: women, migrants, blacks may apply', *Refractory Girl* II (June 1976), pp. 27-31.

56 Kingston, *Poor Mary Ann*, p. 28.

5 The search for laws

1 Among many studies, see esp. Perry Anderson, 'Components of the national culture', in A. Cockburn and R. Blackburn (eds), *Student Power: Problems, Diagnosis, Action*, Harmondsworth, Eng., 1969, pp. 214-284; and Geoffrey Hawthorn, *Enlightenment and Despair: A History of Sociology*, Cambridge, 1976.

2 Geoffrey Blainey, 'Scissors and paste in local history', *Historical Studies* 6, 23 (November 1954), pp. 339-344.

3 A. W. Martin, 'The Whig view of Australian history' (mimeo, n.d. [1962]), pp. 1-15.

4 Weston Bate, 'The good old *cause* in local history', *Historical Studies* 11, 41 (November 1963), pp. 120-124.

5 Ernest Nagel, 'The logic of historical analysis', repr. in Hans Meyerhoff (ed.), *The Philosophy of History in Our Time: An Anthology*, Garden City, N.Y., 1959, pp. 204-205.

6 K. S. Inglis, *The Stuart Case*, Adelaide, 1961. This book dealt with the controversial trial of Rupert Max Stuart, an Aboriginal, for the alleged murder of a white girl at Ceduna, S.A. in December 1968. Cf., e.g., K. S. Inglis, 'Catholic historiography in Australia, *Historical Studies* 8, 31 (November 1958), pp. 233-253; 'The Anzac tradition', *Meanjin* 24 (1965), pp. 25-44; 'The daily papers', in Peter Coleman (ed.), *Australian Civilization*, Melbourne, 1962, pp. 145-175.

7 Inglis, 'The daily papers', p. 152.

8 *ibid.*, pp. 174-175.

9 K. S. Inglis, *The Australian Colonists: An Exploration of Social History, 1788-1870*, Carlton (Vic.), 1974, p. xi.

10 G. C. Bolton, 'Recent trends in Australian historiography', (mimeo, 25 January 1972, University of London), p. 2.

11 Quoted in Suzanne Blake, 'Our best history books—by the experts', *National Times*, 14-19 February 1977, p. 18.

12 K. S. Inglis, 'Australia 1788-1988: A note on proposed approaches', (mimeo, April 1977, ANU), repr. in *The Push from the Bush* 1 (May 1977), p. 7.

13 Interview, 28 May 1975, Murdoch University, W.A.

14 Martin, 'Whig view'. In both this paper and in Roe's 'Challenges to Australian identity', *Quadrant* 22 (April 1978), pp. 34-40, the exact meaning of 'Whig' history is not abundantly clear, for both critics use an eclectic mixture of criteria: 'Whigs' are upbraided partly for the themes they concentrate on, partly on grounds of social theory and partly on the ideological implications of their work. I have tried to avoid this sort of 'apples and onions' approach by constructing clearer principles of criticism.

15 P. Loveday and A. W. Martin, *Parliament, Factions and Parties: The First Thirty Years of Responsible Government in New South Wales, 1856-1889*, Melbourne, 1966; their reply to critics is to be found in 'The politics of New South Wales, 1856-1889: a reply, *Historical Studies* 13, 50 (April 1968), pp. 223-232.

16 Loveday and Martin, 'A reply', p. 226, footnote 16.

17 Interview, *ibid.*

18 Interviews, 3 and 8 July 1975, University of Melbourne.

19 *ibid.*

20 Lectures, 5 and 28 June 1972, University of Melbourne.

21 Lecture, 27 July 1972, University of Melbourne.

22 Sol Encel, conversation, 30 June 1975, University of New South Wales.

23 Interview, 28 March 1974, University of Melbourne.

24 *ibid.*

25 Geoffrey Blainey, 'Scissors and paste in local history', *Historical Studies* 6, 23 (November 1954), pp. 341-342.

26 Humphrey McQueen, conversation, 11 March 1978, Fitzroy, Vic.

27 Geoffrey Blainey, *The Rush that Never Ended: A History of Australian Mining*, Carlton (Vic.), 1963; second edition, 1969; third edition, 1978; pp. 162-163.

28 *ibid.*, ch. 29 'New Age' in second edition, not first.

29 Geoffrey Blainey, *The Tyranny of Distance: How Distance Shaped Australia's History*, South Melbourne, 1966, second edition, 1975, 'Preface'.

30 Blainey, *Rush that Never Ended*, 'Preface' to first edition; repr. in second.

31 The various articles in the long-standing controversy about British motives in establishing the Port Jackson settlement have now been published in one volume: Ged Martin (ed.), *The Founding of Australia*, Sydney, 1978.

32 Blainey, *The Tyranny of Distance* (1975), p. 107.

33 *ibid.*, p. 109.

34 Geoffrey Blainey, 'If your politics are emotional that could mean you are a loser', *National Times*, 29 December 1975-3 January 1976, p. 9.

35 *Age*, 4 October 1975, p. 13.

36 Blainey's defence of the Concorde was published in *National Times*, 23-28 February 1976, pp. 11-12; for some comments on how Blainey's style differs from that of orthodox economic historians, cf. Gordon Rimmer's review of *The Tyranny of Distance, Australian Economic History Review* 7 (1967), pp. 194-196. An account of the development of economic history in Australian universities is given by C. B. Schedvin in the same issue of *AEHR*.

37 Interview, 9 July 1975, Brighton S.A.

38 *ibid.*

39 Hugh Stretton, *The Political Sciences: General Principles of Selection in Social Science and History*, London, 1969.

40 Hugh Stretton, 'Nugatory notes', *Massachusetts Review* 3 (Autumn 1961), pp. 112-118.

41 Interview, *ibid.*

42 S. Encel, 'Stretton and sociology', *Historical Studies* 14, 53 (October 1969), p. 76.

43 Stretton, *The Political Sciences*, p. 371. A general critique of this argument has been undertaken by Graham Kearns, 'Hugh Stretton's philosophy of the social sciences' (mimeo, Flinders University, 1977), p. 1-39.

44 *ibid*, p. 134.

45 Interview, *ibid.*

46 *ibid.*; this is also hinted at in a cynical passage on publishing in *The Political Sciences*, p. 70, which was 'a fairly literal record of a lunch conversation with one multinational publishing director' (interview).

47 Stretton, *The Political Sciences*, p. 148.

48 Stretton, 'Nugatory notes', pp. 115-116.

49 Hugh Street, *Capitalism, Socialism and the Environment*, Cambridge, 1976, p. 2.

50 Humphrey McQueen, 'Where Stretton fears to tread', *Nation Review*, 29 October-4 November 1976, p. 44.

51 Stretton, *Capitalism, Socialism and the Environment*, p. 203.

52 See Hugh Stretton, *Ideas for Australian Cities*, North Adelaide, 1970; 'The processes and forces to be directed by planning' in 'The Consequences of Today', supplement to *Architecture in Australia*, August 1971, pp. 706-708; I. MacKay, R. Boyd, H. Stretton and J. Mant, *Living and Partly Living*, Melbourne, 1972; 'Curb the rich or freeze the poor?', *Pelican*, 12 September 1975, p. 15 (an edited transcript of his 1974 Octagon Lecture entitled 'Inequality and environmental reform'); *Housing and Government*, Sydney, 1974, (the ABC publication of his 1974 Boyer Lectures); 'The road ahead—Australia's options', in AIPS, *Who Gets What? The Distribution of Wealth and Power in Australia*, Sydney, 1976, pp. 172-214; 'An answer to the housing crisis . . .', *National Times*, 7-12 June 1976, pp. 4-5, 14-15.

53 Stretton, 'Curb the rich', *Capitalism, Socialism and the Environment*, p. 12. Stretton has given an autobiographical account of his attempts to reform the housing industry, in 'Capital mistakes' in Colin Bell and S. Encel (eds), *Inside the Whale: Ten Personal Accounts of Social Research*, Rushcutters Bay (N.S.W.), 1978, pp. 67-92.

54 Stretton, *Ideas*, p. 163.

55 *ibid.*, pp. 158-159.

56 cf., esp., Leonie Sandercock, *Cities for Sale: Property, Politics and Urban Planning in Australia*, Melbourne, 1975. An excellent critique of this book and urban history generally may be found in Jim Gillespie, 'Theories of urbanism: from Chicago to Paris', *Intervention* 7 (October 1976), pp. 41-59.

57 Humphrey McQueen, 'Glory without power', J. Playford and D. Kirsner

(eds), *Australian Capitalism: Towards a Socialist Critique*, Ringwood (Vic.), 1972, p. 371.

58 'Humphrey McQueen', De Berg Tapes, Tape 920, 9 March 1976.

59 Humphrey McQueen, 'Convicts and rebels', *Labour History* 15 (November 1968), pp. 24-25.

60 *ibid.*, p. 25.

61 Russel Ward, 'Convicts and rebels: a reply', *Labour History* 16 (May 1969), p. 58.

62 Peter Coleman, 'Introduction: The new Australia', in Peter Coleman (ed.), *Australian Civilization*, Melbourne, 1962, p. 2.

63 Noel McLachlan, 'Tirez sur les pianistes': Humphrey McQueen's "revolutionary history" ', *Meanjin* 29, 4 (December 1970), p. 551.

64 Ian Turner rev., *A New Britannia, Historical Studies* 14, 56 (April 1971), p. 636.

65 *ibid.*, p. 637.

66 A. A. Phillips, 'The cross-eyed Clio: McQueen and the Australian tradition', *Meanjin* 30, 1 (1971), pp. 108-133.

67 Russel Ward, 'Britannia Australis', *Overland* 47 (1971), p. 47.

68 *ibid.*

69 See *Politics* 7, 1 (May 1972), pp. 53-54, for a list of thirty-one of these reviews. The two not mentioned in this list appeared in *Bulletin*, 28 November 1970, p. 60 (S. Hall) and in *Economic Record* 47 (March 1971), pp. 61-62 (unsigned).

70 Humphrey McQueen, 'Reply to Russel Ward', *Overland* 48 (1971), pp. 22-24.

71 Stuart Macintyre, 'The making of the Australian working class: an historiographical study' (mimeo, Murdoch University, November 1976), p. 6.

72 R. W. Connell, *Ruling Class, Ruling Culture: Studies of Conflict, Power and Hegemony in Australian Life*, Cambridge, 1977, p. 19.

73 Humphrey McQueen, 'Australo-Marximus: on some reactions to *A New Britannia*', *Politics* 7, 1 (May 1972), p. 51.

74 Macintyre, *loc. cit.*, p. 8.

75 *ibid.*, p. 13.

76 Connell, *op. cit.*, p. 18.

77 Humphrey McQueen, *A New Britannia: An Argument Concerning the Social Origins of Australian Radicalism and Nationalism*, pp. 141-144, 207-209; cf. Geoffrey Blainey, *The Rush that Never Ended*, pp. v, 38.

78 McQueen, 'Australo-Marximus', p. 49.

79 Humphrey McQueen, 'Living off Asia', *Arena* 26 (1971), pp. 13-37; see also, Gay Summy, 'Cairns reassessed: a critique of McQueen', *ibid.*, pp. 38-61; McQueen's paper was reprinted in a number of places, and was presented at an anti-war conference in Sydney. It met with approval in a number of places on the Left, e.g. Sean Gavin, 'Reformism—a paper tiger?', *Socialist Review* 3 (October 1971), pp. 6-10. See also, Humphrey McQueen, 'Corrected misquotations', *Arena* 28 (1972), pp. 65-67, and Gay Summy, 'The revolutionary democracy of J. F. Cairns', *Politics* 7, 1 (May 1972), pp. 55-56, esp. p. 56.

80 McQueen's further research into racism resulted in 'The sustenance of silence: racism in twentieth century Australia', *Meanjin* 30, 3 (June 1971), pp. 157-

164; 'Racism and Australian literature', in F. S. Stevens (ed.), *Racism: The Australian Experience . . . A Study of Race Prejudice in Australia,* 3 vols., vol 1: *Prejudice and Xenophobia,* Brookvale (NSW), 1971, pp. 115-122 (second edition, 1974), pp. 143-150.

81 McQueen, 'Australian literature', in F. S. Stevens, *op. cit.,* second edition, p. 149.

82 Humphrey McQueen, 'Glory without power', in J. Playford and D. Korsner, *op. cit.,* p. 345, 346.

83 *ibid.,* p. 371.

84 *ibid.,* p. 345.

85 McQueen, 'Australo-Marximus', p. 48. In early 1972 Russel Ward wrote a 'Reply to Humphrey McQueen', *Overland* 50 (Autumn 1972), pp. 79-80, which was largely a defence of *The Australian Legend,* and an exhortation to McQueen to 'do his own thing'.

86 McQueen, 'Australo-Marximus', p. 53.

87 Cf., e.g., Humphrey McQueen, 'An end to the White Australia Policy', *Australian Quarterly* 44, 1 (March 1972), pp. 92-102; 'A neglected history: Walter Hurrell and the Victorian flour millers', *Journal of Industrial Relations* 14, 12 (June 1972), pp. 184-194; 'The suckling society', *Review* 24 (30 June 1972), pp. 1020-1021, repr. in Henry Mayer and Helen Nelson, (eds), *Australian Politics: A Third Reader,* Melbourne, 1973, pp. 5-13; 'The end of equality', *Arena* 30 (1972), pp. 8-12; 'The novels of Eleanor Dark', *Hemisphere* 17, 1 (January 1973),pp. 38-41; 'Images of society in Australian criticism', *Arena* 31 (1973), pp. 44-51; 'Nationalism and the Labor vote', in Henry Mayer (ed.), *Labor to Power,* Sydney, 1973, p. 17; 'From Gallipoli to Petrov', *Historian* 25 (October 1973), pp. 27-35; 'The decline of anti-communism: the Australian case', *Quadrant* 17, 5 and 6 (September-December 1973), pp. 103-104.

88 Humphrey McQueen, 'Taking a strong stand', D. G. Dufty, et alia, (eds), *Historians at Work: Investigating and Recreating the Past,* Sydney, 1973, pp. 203-219.

89 Australian Broadcasting Commission, *Heresies,* Sydney, 1974, p. 144. This talk was reprinted in *Eco Information* 2 (October-November 1974), pp. 26-29.

90 *ibid.,* p. 149. Much of this transcript was incorporated in the following year in his *Aborigines, Race and Racism,* Ringwood (Vic.), 1974, esp. pp. 2-3.

91 *ibid.,* p. 75; cf. another McQueen display of self-scrutiny, 'Across the Mexique Ocean', *Meanjin* 34, 1 (1975), pp. 49-54.

92 Humphrey McQueen, '*Australian Cultural Elites*', *Arena* 36 (1974), pp. 40-49.

93 Humphrey McQueen, 'Victoria', in D. J. Murphy (ed.), *Labour in Politics . . .* St Lucia (Qld.), 1975, pp. 293-339.

94 'The Spanish influenza pandemic, 1919', repr. as ' "Spanish Flu" 1919: political, medical and social aspects', *Medical Journal of Australia,* 3 May 1975, pp. 565-570; and further repr. as 'The "Spanish" influenza pandemic in Australia 1918-19', in Jill Roe (ed.), *Social Policy in Australia: Some Perspectives, 1901-1975,* Melbourne, 1976, pp. 131-147.

95 Humphrey McQueen, 'Introduction' to *A New Britannia* (1975), pp. 13, 11.

96 *Nation Review,* 7-13 May 1976, p. 741.

97 Humphrey McQueen, 'Class and politics, II', *Labour History* 32 (May 1977), p. 91.

98 *ibid.*, p. 92.

99 Humphrey McQueen, *Australia's Media Monopolies*, Camberwell (Vic.), 1977.

100 Humphrey McQueen, *Social Sketches of Australia, 1888-1975*, Ringwood (Vic.), 1978, p. 196.

101 *National U*, 8 September 1975, p. 3-4, gives details of Connell's failure to get a chair at Flinders.

102 Interview, 10 July 1975, Flinders University, S.A.

103 *ibid.*

104 R. W. Connell, 'Images of Australia', *Quadrant* 12 (March-April 1968), pp. 9-19, repr. in D. E. Edgar (ed.), *Social Change in Australia: Readings in Sociology*, Melbourne, 1974, pp. 29-41; see ch. 2, above.

105 *ibid.*, p. 37.

106 Interview, *ibid.*

107 R. W. Connell, *The Child's Construction of Politics*, Carlton (Vic.), 1971. Among its reviews, see A. F. Davies in *Politics* 7, 1 (May 1972), pp. 37-39.

108 *ibid.*, pp. 106-113.

109 *ibid.*, pp. 111.

110 This is my reading of *ibid.*, pp. 113-114.

111 *ibid.*, p. 115

112 *ibid.*, pp. 234-235.

113 *ibid.*, p. 236.

114 Connell, *Ruling Class, Ruling Culture*, p. 207.

115 *ibid.*, p. 183.

116 Interview, *ibid.*

117 Connell, *Ruling Class, Ruling Culture*, ch. 1.

118 *ibid.*, p. 51.

119 *ibid.*, p. 58.

120 *ibid.*, p. 135.

121 *ibid.*, p. 187.

122 *ibid.*, pp. 188-189.

123 *ibid.*, p. 195.

124 *ibid.*, p. 211.

125 *ibid.*, p. 188.

126 For this distinction, cf. David I. Sallach, 'The meaning of hegemony', *Australian Left Review* 41 (August 1973), pp. 32-37.

127 For his early theoretical statements, see, in particular, R. W. Connell et alia, 'Class and politics in Australian Life', Henry Mayer (ed.), *Australian Politics: A Second Reader*, Melbourne, 1969, pp. 9-23.

128 An account of the experiment may be found in Ann Curthoys, 'The end of the Free U?', *Arena* 20 (1969), pp. 35-40.

129 Interview, 26 June 1975, University of Sydney.

130 For Irving's later summary of his work on New South Wales, see T. H. Irving, '1850-70', in F. K. Crowley (ed.), *A New History of Australia*, Melbourne, 1974, pp. 124-164. For Irving's attack on conventional theories of class, see

his contribution to the symposium, 'What is labour history?' *Labour History* 12 (May 1967), pp. 60-81; and Terry Irving and Baiba Berzins, 'History and the New Left: Beyond radicalism', Richard Gordon (ed.), *The Australian New Left: Critical Essays and Strategy*, Melbourne, 1970, pp. 66-94.

131 R. W. Connell and T. H. Irving, 'Yes, Virginia, there is a ruling class', in Henry Mayer and Helen Nelson (eds), *Australian Politics: A Third Reader*, Melbourne, 1973, pp. 31-47.

132 R. W. Connell and T. H. Irving, *Class Structure in Australian History* (mimeo 1974-). The final chapter of this manuscript has been published in *Intervention* II (October 1978), pp. 5-38.

133 Miriam Dixson, *The Real Matilda: Women and Identity in Australia, 1788 to 1975*, Ringwood (Vic.), 1976, pp. 121-122.

6   The manufacture of Australian history

1 Hugh Stretton, *Ideas for Australian Cities*, North Adelaide, 1970, pp. 271-284.

2 Tim Rowse, *Australian Liberalism and National Character*, Malmsbury (Vic.), 1978: the chapter on Hancock is ch. 3.

3 For specific predictions of the future see esp. C. M. H. Clark, *A Short History of Australia*, New York, revised edition, 1969, p. 268; his speech at the University of Wollongong in May 1978, as reported in the *Sydney Morning Herald*, 13 May 1978, p. 1; Anne Summers, *Damned Whores and God's Police: The Colonization of Women in Australia*, Ringwood (Vic.), 1975, 'Prospects for liberation'; L. L. Robson, 'Australia as a place to live', in Fifteen Leading Australians, *Australia 2025*, Adelaide, 1975, pp. 1-12; W. K. Hancock, *Australia*, Brisbane, 1961, e.g. pp. 102, 188, 164, 215, 271; Turner's selection of Ralph Gibson's futuristic article on socialist Melbourne, in Ian Turner (ed.), *The Australian Dream . . .*, Melbourne, 1968, pp. 334-338; Humphrey McQueen, *Australia's Media Monopolies*, Camberwell (Vic.), 1977, p. 209; Geoffrey Blainey et alia, 'Four scenarios', in Devon Mills (ed.), *Australian Management and Society: 1970-1985*, Ringwood (Vic.), 1971, pp. 339-348; Hugh Stretton, *Capitalism, Socialism and the Environment*, Cambridge, 1976, esp. p. 15.

Bibliography

INTERVIEWS AND CORRESPONDENCE

Taped interviews, discussions and correspondence were conducted with the following people between February 1974 and July 1978:

F. Alexander, M. Aveling, W. A. Bate, G. N. Blainey, G. C. Bolton, C. M. H. Clark, R. W. Connell, F. K. Crowley, G. Davison, B. K. de Garis, M. Dixson, D. G. Dufty, S. Encel, L. Evans, W. Gammage, R. A. Gollan, W. K. Hancock, T. H. Irving, F. Knopfelmacher, S. Macintyre, A. W. Martin, H. Mayer, H. D. McQueen, N. B. Nairn, P. J. O'Farrell, L. O'Neil, R. Peacock, H. Radi, R. H. W. Reece, L. L. Robson, G. Serle, A. G. L. Shaw, F. B. Smith, C. T. Stannage, H. Stretton, A. Summers, I. A. H. Turner, J. M. Ward and R. B. Ward.

Whenever a remark by one of these people is quoted or paraphrased, it has been cited in the appropriate endnote. Every effort to ensure accuracy has been made.

THEORETICAL WORKS

This list includes only those works which are directly relevant to the theoretical underpinning of the argument.

ANDERSON, PERRY. 'Components of the national culture', in A. Cockburn and R. Blackburn (ed.), *Student Power: Problems, Diagnosis, Action.* Penguin, Harmondsworth, 1969.

CONNELL, R. W. 'Images of Australia', *Quadrant* 12 (March-April 1968), pp. 9-19, repr. in Don Edgar (ed.), *Social Change in Australia: Readings in Sociology.* Cheshire, Melbourne, 1974.

GOODWIN, CRAUFURD D. W. *Economic Enquiry in Australia.* Duke University Press, Durham, N.C., 1966.

HAWTHORN, GEOFFREY. *Enlightenment and Despair: A History of Sociology.* Cambridge University Press, Cambridge, 1976.

HOARE, Q. AND SMITH, G. N. (ed.). *Selections from the Prison Notebooks of Antonio Gramsci.* New York International Pub., New York, 1978.

JAMESON, FREDERIC. 'Figural relativism, or the poetics of historiography'. *Diacritics* 7, 2 (Spring 1976), pp. 2-9.

MACINTYRE, STUART. 'Radical history and bourgeois hegemony'. *Intervention* 2 (October 1972), pp. 47-73.

MACINTYRE, STUART. 'The making of the Australian working class: an historiographical study'. (Mimeo, Murdoch University, November 1976, 45pp.)

MITCHELL, JULIET. *Psychoanalysis and Feminism.* Pantheon Book, New York, 1974.

PEPPER, STEPHEN C. *World Hypotheses: A Study of Evidence.* University of California Press, Berkley and Los Angeles, 1942.

ROWSE, TIM. *Australian Liberalism and National Character.* Kibble Books, Malmsbury (Vic.), 1978.

SALLACH, DAVID I. 'The meaning of hegemony'. *Australian Left Review* 41 (August 1973), pp. 32-37.

STEDMAN JONES, GARETH. 'History: The povery of empiricism', in Robin Blackburn, (ed.), *Ideology in Social Science: Readings in Critical Social Theory.* Fontana, London, 1972, pp. 96-115.

WHITE, HAYDEN. *Metahistory: The Historical Imagination in Nineteenth Century Europe.* John Hopkins University Press, Baltimore, 1973.

WORKS CITED IN THE TEXT

AUSTRALIAN BROADCASTING COMMISSION. *Heresies.* A.B.C. Sydney, 1974.

BATE, W. A. *A History of Brighton.* Melbourne University Press, Melbourne, 1962.

BATTYE, J. S. *Western Australia: A History from its Discovery to the Inauguration of the Commonwealth.* Oxford University Press, Oxford, 1924.

BEAN, C. E. W. *On the Wool Track.* Alston Rivers, London, 1910; rev. 1925, 1945.

BEAN, C. E. W. *The Dreadnought of the Darling.* Alston Rivers, London, 1911.

BEAN, C. E. W. *Flagships Three.* Hodder & Stoughton, London, 1913.

BEAN, C. E. W. (gen. ed.). *The Official History of Australia in the War of 1914-18.* 12 vols. Angus & Robertson, Sydney, 1921-1942.

BLAINEY, GEOFFREY. *The Rush that Never Ended: A History of Australian Mining.* Melbourne University Press, Carlton (Vic.), 1963; 2nd edn 1969, 3rd edn 1978.

BLAINEY, GEOFFREY. *The Tyranny of Distance: How Distance Shaped Australia's History.* Sun Books, Melbourne, 1966.

CANNON, MICHAEL. *Australia in the Victorian Age.* 3 vols. Thomas Nelson, West Melbourne, 1971, 1973, 1975.

CHILDE, V. G. *How Labour Governs: A Study of Workers' Representation in Australia.* Labour Publishing Co. Ltd, London, 1923.

CLARK, C. M. H. (ed.). *Select Documents in Australian History, 1788-1850.* Angus & Robertson, Sydney, 1950.

CLARK, C. M. H. (ed.). *Select Documents in Australian History, 1851-1900.* Angus & Robertson, Sydney, 1955.

CLARK, C. M. H. (ed.). *Sources of Australian History.* Oxford University Press, London, 1957.

CLARK, C. M. H. *Meeting Soviet Man.* Angus and Robertson, Sydney, 1960.

CLARK, C. M. H. *A History of Australia, II: New South Wales and Van Diemen's Land, 1822-1838.* Melbourne University Press, Carlton (Vic.), 1968.

CLARK, C. M. H. *A Short History of Australia.* New American Library, New York, 1963; revised edn 1969.

CLARK, C. M. H. *Disquiet and Other Stories.* Angus & Robertson, Sydney, 1969.

CLARK, C. M. H. *A History of Australia, III: The Beginning of an Australian Civilization, 1824-1851.* Melbourne University Press, Carlton (Vic.), 1973.

CLARK, C. M. H. *A History of Australia, IV: The Earth Abideth For Ever, 1851-1888.* Melbourne University Press, Carlton (Vic.), 1978.

CLARK, C. M. H. *In Search of Henry Lawson.* Macmillan, South Melbourne, 1978.

COGHLAN, T. A. *Labour and Industry in Australia: From the First Settlement in 1788 to the Establishment of the Commonwealth in 1901.* 4 vols. Oxford University Press, London, 1918; repr. 1969.

COLEMAN, PETER (ed.). *Australian Civilisation.* Cheshire, Melbourne, 1962.

CONNELL, R. W. *The Children's Construction of Politics.* Melbourne University Press, Carlton (Vic.), 1971.

CONNELL, R. W. *Ruling Class, Ruling Culture: Studies of Conflict, Power and Hegemony in Australian Life.* Cambridge University Press, Cambridge, 1977.

CONWAY, RONALD. *The Great Australian Stupor.* Sun Books, South Melbourne, 1971.

CRAWFORD, R. M. *The Study of History: A Synoptic View.* Presidential address to Sec. E, History, of the ANZAAS. Melbourne, 1939.

CRAWFORD, R. M. *Ourselves and The Pacific.* Melbourne University Press, Melbourne, 1952.

CRAWFORD, R. M. *Australia.* Hutchinson, London, 1952.

CRAWFORD, R. M. *A Bit of a Rebel: The Life and Work of George Arnold Wood.* Sydney University Press, Sydney, 1976.

CROWLEY, F. K. *State Election: The Fall of the Hawke Government.* The Author, Perth, 1959.

CROWLEY, F. K. AND de GARIS, B. K. *A Short History of Western Australia.* 2nd edn, Macmillan, South Melbourne, 1969.

CROWLEY, F. K. *Australia's Western Third: A History of Western Australia From the First Settlements to Modern Times.* Macmillan, London, 1960; Melbourne, 1970.

CROWLEY, FRANK AND CARTWRIGHT, LORNA. *A Citizen's Guide to Marihuana in Australia.* Angus & Robertson, London, 1977.

CROWLEY, F. K. (ed.). *Modern Australia in Documents.* 2 vols. Wren, Melbourne, 1973.

CROWLEY, F. K. (ed.). *A New History of Australia.* Heinemann, Melbourne, 1974.

DIXSON, MIRIAM. *The Real Matilda: Woman and Identity in Australia, 1788 to 1975.* Penguin, Ringwood (Vic.), 1976.

DOCKER, JOHN. *Australian Cultural Elites: Intellectual Traditions In Sydney and Melbourne.* Angus & Robertson, Sydney, 1974.

DUFTY, D., HARMAN, G. AND SWAN, K. *Historians at Work: Investigating and Recreating the Past.* Hicks Smith, Sydney, 1973.

FIFTEEN LEADING AUSTRALIANS. *Australia 2025.* Electrolux Pty Ltd, Adelaide, 1968.

FITZPATRICK, BRIAN. *A Short History of the Australian Labour Movement.* Rawson's Bookshop, Melbourne, 1940; repr. Macmillan, South Melbourne, 1968.

FITZPATRICK, BRIAN. *British Imperialism and Australia, 1783-1833: An Economic History of Australasia.* George Allen & Unwin Ltd, London, 1939.

FITZPATRICK, BRIAN. *The British Empire in Australia: An Economic History 1834-1939.* Melbourne University Press, Melbourne 1941; repr. Macmillan, South Melbourne, 1969.

FITZPATRICK, BRIAN. *The Australian People, 1788-1945.* Melbourne University Press, Carlton (Vic.), 1946.

GOLLAN, R. A. *Radical and Working Class Politics: A Study of Eastern Australia, 1850-1910.* Melbourne University Press, Melbourne, 1960.

GOLLAN, R. A. *The Coalminers of New South Wales: A History of the Union, 1860-1960.* Melbourne University Press, Melbourne, 1963.

GORDON, RICHARD (ed.). *The Australian New Left: Critical Essays and Strategy.* Heinemann, Melbourne, 1970.

GREEN, H. M. *A History of Australian Literature Pure and Applied: A Critical Review of All Forms of Literature Produced in Australia From the First Books Published after the Arrival of the First Fleet Until 1950, with Short Accounts of Later Publications up to 1960.* 2 vols. Angus & Robertson, Sydney, 1961; repr. 1962.

GREENWOOD, G. (ed.). *Australia: A Social and Political History.* Angus & Robertson, Sydney, 1955.

HANCOCK, W. K. *Australia.* Ernest Benn, London, 1930; repr. Jacaranda Press, Brisbane 1960.

HANCOCK, W. K. *Two Centuries of Change: An Elementary History for Young Australians.* Oxford University Press, Melbourne, 1934.

HANCOCK, W. K. 'Problems of Economic Policy, 1918-1939, Part 2'. *Survey of British Commonwealth Affairs,* vol. 2. London, 1940.

HANCOCK, W. K. *Politics in Pitcairn and Other Essays.* Macmillan, London, 1947.

HANCOCK, W. K. *Country and Calling.* Faber & Faber, London, 1954.

HANCOCK, W. K. *Attempting History: The University Lectures 1968.* Australian National University Press, Canberra, 1969.

HANCOCK, W. K. *Discovering Monaro: A Study of Man's Impact on his Environment.* Cambridge University Press, Cambridge, 1972.

HANCOCK, W. K. *The Battle for Black Mountain.* Australian National University, Research School of Social Sciences, Department of Economic History: Monograph 6, Canberra, 1974.

HANCOCK, W. K. *Professing History.* Sydney University Press, Sydney, 1976.

HOGAN, TERRY. *Index to Journal Articles on Australian History.* Department of History, University of New England, Armidale (N.S.W.), 1976.

INGLIS, K. S. *The Stuart Case.* Melbourne University Press, Melbourne, 1961.

INGLIS, K. S. *C. E. W. Bean: Australian Historian.* University of Queensland Press, St Lucia (Qld.), 1970.

INGLIS, K. S. *The Australian Colonists: An Exploration of Social History, 1788-1870.* Melbourne University Press, Carlton (Vic.), 1974.

JOSE, A. W. *History of Australia: With Chapters on Australian Literature and the Early History of New Zealand.* Angus & Robertson, Sydney, 1899.

JOSE, A. W. *The Royal Australian Navy, 1914-18,* vol. IX of *The Official History of Australia in the War of 1914-18.* Angus & Robertson, Sydney, 1928.

KINGSTON, BEVERLEY. *My Wife, My Daughter, and Poor Mary Ann: Women and Work in Australia.* Thomas Nelson, West Melbourne, 1975.

LOUIS, L. J. AND TURNER, I. (ed.). *The Depression of the 1930s.* Cassell, Melbourne, 1968.

LOVEDAY, P. AND MARTIN, A. W. *Parliament, Factions and Parties: The First Thirty Years of Responsible Government in New South Wales, 1856-1889.* Melbourne University Press, Melbourne, 1966.

McKAY, I., BOYD, R., STRETTON, H. AND MANT, J. *Living and Partly Living.* Nelson, Melbourne, 1971.

MANDLE, W. F. *Going It Alone: Australian National Identity in the Twentieth Century.* Allen Lane, Ringwood (Vic.), 1978.

MARTIN, GED. (ed.). *The Founding of Australia.* Hale & Iremonger, Sydney, 1978.

McQUEEN, HUMPHREY. *A New Britannia: An Argument Concerning the Social Origins of Australian Radicalism and Nationalism.* Penguin, Ringwood (Vic.), 1970; 2nd edn 1975.

McQUEEN, HUMPHREY. *Aborigines, Race and Racism.* Penguin, Ringwood (Vic.), 1974.

McQUEEN, HUMPHREY. *Australia's Media Monopolies.* Widescope International, Camberwell (Vic.), 1977.

McQUEEN, HUMPHREY. *Social Sketches of Australia, 1788-1975.* Penguin, Ringwood (Vic.), 1978.

MELBOURNE, A. C. V. *Early Constitutional Development in Australia: New*

South Wales, 1788-1856; Queensland, 1859-1922. University of Queensland Press, 2nd edn 1963.

MITCHELL, BRUCE. *The Australian Story and Its Background.* Cheshire, Melbourne, 1965.

MURPHY, D. J. (ed.). *Labor in Politics: The State Labor Parties In Australia, 1880-1920.* University of Queensland Press, St Lucia (Qld.), 1975.

NAIRN, N. B. *Civilising Capitalism: The Labour Movement in New South Wales, 1870-1890.* Australian National University Press, Canberra, 1973.

PIKE, DOUGLAS. *Australia: The Quiet Continent.* Cambridge University Press, Cambridge, 1962.

PLAYFORD, J. AND KIRSNER, D. (ed.). *Australian Capitalism: Towards a Socialist Critique.* Penguin, Ringwood (Vic.), 1972.

PORTUS, G. V. *Australia Since 1606: A History for Young Australians.* Oxford University Press, Melbourne, 1932; 2nd edn 1948.

PORTUS, G. V. *Happy Highways.* Melbourne University Press, Melbourne, 1953.

RITCHIE, JOHN. *Australia As Once We Were.* Heinemann Educational, Melbourne, 1975.

ROBSON, L. L. *The Convict Settlers of Australia: An Enquiry into the Origin and Character of the Convicts Transported to New South Wales and Van Diemen's Land 1787-1852.* Melbourne University Press, Melbourne, 1965.

ROE, MICHAEL. *Quest for Authority in Eastern Australia, 1835-1847.* Melbourne University Press, Melbourne, 1965.

SANDERCOCK, LEONIE. *Cities for Sale: Property, Politics and Urban Planning in Australia.* Melbourne University Press, Melbourne, 1975.

SCHEDVIN, G. B. AND McCARTY, J. W. (ed.). *Urbanisation in Australia: The Nineteenth Century.* Sydney University Press, Sydney, 1974.

SCOTT, ERNEST. *Australia During the War, vol. XI, The Official History of Australia in the War of 1914-18.* Angus & Robertson, Sydney, 1936.

SERLE, GEOFFREY AND GRANT, J. *The Melbourne Scene, 1803-1956.* Melbourne University Press, Melbourne, 1957.

SERLE, GEOFFREY. *The Golden Age: A History of the Colony of Victoria, 1851-1861.* Melbourne University Press, Melbourne, 1963; corr. repr. 1963.

SERLE, GEOFFREY. *The Rush to be Rich: A History of the Colony of Victoria, 1883-1889.* Melbourne University Press, Carlton (Vic.), 1971.

SERLE, GEOFFREY. *From Deserts the Prophets Come: The Creative Spirit in Australia, 1788-1972.* Heinemann Educational, Melbourne, 1973.

SHANN, E. O. G. *The Boom of 1890—and Now: a call to Australia to put her house in order lest drought and falling prices for wool and wheat overtake us again.* Cornstalk, Sydney, 1927.

SHANN, E. O. G. *An Economic History of Australia.* Cambridge University Press, Cambridge, 1930.

SHANN, E. O. G. *Bond or Free? Occasional Economic Essays.* Angus and Robertson, Sydney, 1930.

SHAW, A. G. L. *The Story of Australia.* Faber & Faber, London, 1955; 2nd edn 1962.

SHAW, A. G. L. *Convicts and the Colonies: A Study of Penal Transportation from Great Britain and Ireland to Australia and other parts of the British Empire.* Faber & Faber, London, 1966.

SHAW, A. G. L. AND NICHOLSON, H. D. *Australia in the Twentieth Century: An Introduction to Modern Society.* Angus & Robertson, Sydney, 1967.

SINCLAIR, W. A. *The Process of Economic Development in Australia.* Cheshire, Melbourne, 1976.

STEPHENSON, ROSALIE. *Women in Australian Society.* Heinemann Educational, South Yarra (Vic.), 1970.

STRETTON, HUGH. *The Political Sciences: General Principles of Selection in Social Science and History.* Routledge and Kegan Paul, London, 1969.

STRETTON, HUGH. *Ideas for Australian Cities.* The Author, North Adelaide, 1970.

STRETTON, HUGH. *Housing and Government.* Australian Broadcasting Commission, Sydney, 1974. (The Boyer Lectures, 1974.)

STRETTON, HUGH. *Capitalism, Socialism and the Environment.* Cambridge University Press, Cambridge, 1976.

SUMMERS, ANNE. *Damned Whores and God's Police: The Colonization of Women in Australia.* Penguin, Ringwood (Vic.), 1975.

TURNER, IAN. *Industrial Labour and Politics: The Dynamics of the Labour Movement in Eastern Australia, 1900-1921.* Australian National University Press, Canberra, 1965.

TURNER, IAN. *Sydney's Burning.* Heinemann, London, 1967.

TURNER, IAN. (ed.). *The Australian Dream: A Collection of Anticipations about Australia from Captain Cook to the Present Day.* Sun Books, Melbourne, 1968.

TURNER, IAN. *Cinderella Dressed in Yella.* Heinemann Educational, Melbourne, 1969; 2nd edn 1978.

TURNER, IAN AND ELLIS, RENNIE. *Australian Graffiti.* Sun Books, Melbourne, 1975.

WARD, J. M. *British Policy in the South Pacific (1786-1893).* Australasian Publishing Co., Sydney, 1948.

WARD, J. M. *Earl Grey and the Australian Colonies, 1846-1857: A Study of Self-Government and Self-Interest.* Melbourne University Press, Melbourne, 1958.

WARD, J. M. *Empire in the Antipodes, The British in Australia: 1840-1860.* Arnold, London, 1966.

WARD, J. M. *Changes in Britain, 1919-1957.* Nelson, London, 1968.

WARD, RUSSEL. *Man Makes History: World History from the Earliest Times to the Renaissance—for boys and girls in the First Year of Secondary School Courses.* Shakespeare Head, Sydney, 1952.

WARD, RUSSEL. *The Australian Legend.* Oxford University Press, Melbourne, 1958; 2nd edn. 1966.

WARD, RUSSEL. *A Nation for a Continent: The History of Australia, 1901-1975.* Heinemann Educational, Richmond (Vic.), 1977.

WHITELOCK, DEREK. *The Great Tradition: A History of Adult Education in Australia.* University of Queensland Press, St Lucia (Qld.). 1974.

WOOD, G. A. *The Discovery of Australia.* Macmillan, London, 1922.

YARWOOD, A. T. *Asian Migration to Australia.* Melbourne University Press, Melbourne, 1964.

Index